UNDER THE OLIVE TREE

Maayan Karen Raveh

UNDER THE OLIVE TREE

Palestinian Christian Theology from the 1980s to the Present

BAYLOR UNIVERSITY PRESS

Cover and book design by Elyxandra Encarnación
Cover image: George Inness (1825–1894), *Olive Trees at Tivoli*, 1873, Morris K. Jesup Fund, 1989 / The Met Museum

The Library of Congress has cataloged this book under ISBN 978-1-4813-2370-3.

Library of Congress Control Number: 2025939726

To my parents, whose lessons of curiosity, compassion,
and courage continue to shape my path.

❦

The more I climbed the nationalist mountain, the more I was conscious of my Christian identity. The more I was aware of my Christian identity, the more I became conscious of my Palestinian identity. They grew along parallel tracks, increasing to the same degree.

Munib Younan

Contents

Acknowledgments

I would like to take this opportunity to express my deepest gratitude to all those who have accompanied me along the way and helped bring this book into the world. This project is the result of many years of thought, research, and dialogue, and it could not have come to fruition without the guidance, inspiration, and support of so many individuals.

First and foremost, I would like to thank Prof. Brouria Bitton-Ashkelony, who has walked with me since my first days at the university. Her insight, sharpness, and generous spirit shaped my thinking in profound ways. I am also grateful to Prof. Peter Lodberg, whose guidance and encouragement—even from afar—meant a great deal to me throughout this process.

My heartfelt thanks go to my father, Dr. Idan Yaron, for his unwavering presence—for reading drafts, offering comments, asking challenging questions, and always believing in me. I am also deeply grateful to the many colleagues and friends who shared ideas, listened, and challenged me throughout the years: Hana Bendcowsky, Fr. Dr. David Neuhaus, Dr. Orit Ramon, Yogev Elbaz, and many more. Your voices echo throughout these pages.

I am grateful to the Center for the Study of Christianity at the Hebrew University, to the Mandel School for Advanced Studies in the

Humanities, and to the Truman Research Institute for the Advancement of Peace for their generous support of my research over the years.

Special thanks go to Prof. Uriel Simonsohn, head of the Haifa Laboratory for Religious Studies, who encouraged me to publish this book and believed in its value. His leadership and trust were pivotal in turning research into a project for broader dialogue. I also thank Uri Givan, who taught me—by example—that "impossible" is often just another word for "not yet."

To Yuval, who walked beside me through all the years this book was taking shape—thank you for your steadfast presence, your endless patience, and your belief in me even when I wasn't sure of it myself.

And last—but never least—to Lavie and Geffen, my two sons and my daily sources of wonder: thank you for your patience, your joy, and the questions that keep me grounded and alive to the world. Your presence is my greatest blessing.

Abbreviations

ICCJ	International Council of Christians and Jews
IMC	International Mission Council
IPC	Israeli-Palestinian Conflict
PCT	Palestinian Christian Theology
PLO	Palestinian Liberation Organization
WCC	World Council of Churches

Introduction

"If Jesus were to be born today, he would be born under the rubble of Gaza." These powerful words were part of the Rev. Dr. Munther Isaac's sermon on Christmas Eve, 2023. The Evangelical Lutheran theologian addressed a large crowd of Palestinian Christians in Bethlehem against the backdrop of the violent war in Gaza. "If you are not appalled by what is happening in Gaza," Rev. Isaac preached, "if you are not shaken to your core, there is something wrong with your humanism. And if we as Christians are not outraged by the genocide, by the weaponization of the Bible to justify it, there is something wrong with our Christian witness and we are compromising the credibility of our gospel message."

This poignant statement captures the essence of the present study, *Under the Olive Tree*, which delves deep into the heart of Palestinian Christian Theology (PCT). It intersects with the lived realities of occupation and struggle, vividly illustrating Palestinian Christians' physical and spiritual landscape. Isaac's powerful depiction not only highlights their mundane challenges but articulates the way theological perspectives are intertwined or entangled with a lived experience of conflict and adversity.

Growing up in Jerusalem, amid religious and political conflict, has deeply ingrained in me a preoccupation with the complex interplay between the two. My interest often arises from the tension between secular, Enlightenment ideals foundational to modern democracy—such as the separation of church and state as outlined in many European states and the U.S. Constitution—and the intertwined nature of religion and politics evident in almost every country.

This book will focus on how Palestinian Christian Theology (PCT) has contributed to the fight against Israeli occupation and the efforts to establish a nation state. Specifically, I aim to analyze the intersection between Christian theology and the Palestinian political-national discourse. I will explore how, through biblical interpretation, Palestinian theologians have attempted to construct their national-political identity in response to three groups: the Palestinian people in Palestine, Israel, or in diaspora; the global Christian community; and Western Christianity's view of Judaism. This complex identity is defined via interpretation of the Holy Scriptures (considered the Old and New Testaments) and the development of both a religious and a national-political discourse in light of Palestinian Christians' local context as both indigenous people of the Holy Land and oppressed people under what they perceive to be colonial occupation by the state of Israel.

The contribution of theologians to social groups in struggle is the ability to construct a collective identity formed through theology. Theology enables one to read the religious past and the eschatological future to interpret, shape, and reshape the national-political present. To construct a unique Palestinian narrative within the purview of global Christianity, Palestinian Christianity must challenge the Jewish-Zionist narrative that has become prominent in parts of the Christian world, particularly since the mid-twentieth century, which contends that the establishment of the modern state of Israel is linked to biblical Israel, with its legitimacy claimed through references in the Bible. In contrast, Palestinian theologians emphasize the fact that they and their congregants share with the Jewish people the biblical, mythical past of the Old Testament as an integral part of their heritage as natives of the Holy Land, and have the political right to national sovereignty in this land in the same way that Israel does. The term *Holy Land*, frequently used in Christian texts, serves as a useful reference to the region spanning approximately 18,200 square miles between the Jordan River and the Mediterranean Sea. This area encompasses the territories under the jurisdiction of both the state of Israel and the Palestinian Authority, with both entities laying claim to it as their homeland.[1]

To make this case, I will analyze theological writings published in various professional books and academic articles by theologians who define themselves as Palestinian Christians and who either live or have lived in the Holy Land. The main theologians to whom I refer hail from a range of different Protestant and Catholic denominations—Evangelical Lutheran pastor Mitri Raheb, from Bethlehem; Anglican priest Naim Ateek, from Beisan; former Latin Patriarch of Jerusalem Michel Sabbah, from Nazareth; Latin priest Rafiq Khoury, from Taybeh; Latin priest Jamal Khader, from Zababdeh; Evangelical Lutheran pastor Munther Isaac, from Bethlehem; Evangelical Baptist pastor Yohana Katanacho, from Nazareth; former bishop of the Evangelical Lutheran Church Munib Younan, from Jerusalem; and Geries Khoury, from Bethlehem.

I argue that PCT, as Palestinian clergy understand it, defines Palestinian Christian national identity and guides their understanding of both their connection to Christ and to the physical Holy Land. To go deeper into this material forces me to limit my focus to those who have acquired official clerical accreditation and who publish works of theology, minister, and operate churches in the Holy Land. Theologians who define their work as PCT but are not of Palestinian origin—for example, foreign clergy living in the Holy Land, or theologians from Arab countries such as Lebanon or Egypt—will not be considered in this study. Furthermore, while some Palestinian Christian activists and writers who are not clergy have contributed to the corpus of PCT, they will not be discussed here. While their work is compelling, the focus here is specifically on theological discourse. A prominent exception is Dr. Geries Khoury (1952–2016), who, though not a clergyman, became a pillar of Palestinian theology following his establishment of the Al-Liqa' research center in 1982 and his authorship of numerous relevant publications. Regrettably, there are no theological treatises by women available for examination. This is because the local denominations in the Holy Land generally do not ordain women (with the notable exception of Sally Azar, who was ordained in the Evangelical

1 For further reading on the delineation of the Holy Land see Robert Wilken, *The Land Called Holy: Palestine in Christian History and Thought* (Yale University Press, 1992); Dorothy Drummond, *Holy Land, Whose Land? Modern Dilemma, Ancient Roots* (Fairhurst, 2004), 7–10.

Lutheran Church in 2023). Although there are intriguing writings from laywomen, this study is constrained to ordained individuals, which at present includes only men.

Through this investigation I will argue that theology plays a unique, heretofore understudied role in constructing a collective identity in a conflictual political-national context. The foundation of my argument is the observation that theology can significantly impact social and national movements, especially in contexts where religion and politics are deeply intertwined with national identity.[2] This identity is primarily constructed through discourse, defined as the use of language within a social context to convey broad meanings and knowledge.[3] Discourse, in this context, transcends mere linguistics to incorporate three main dimensions: language, belief, and interaction.[4] It encompasses the larger contexts, practices, and social norms that both influence and are influenced by the way language is used. Discourse plays a vital role in the discussion of subjects, the formation and sharing of ideologies, and the construction and maintenance of cultural and social understandings. The concept of identity is examined here from various perspectives and within different fields of knowledge. In their seminal work, *The Social Construction of Reality* (1967), sociologists of religion Peter Berger and Thomas Luckmann refer to identity as a phenomenon arising from the dialectic between individual and society.[5] Identity, they argue, is created by social processes. Once formed, it is maintained, shaped, and reshaped by social relations.[6] The social process of identity creation and preservation is determined by social structure. At the same time, individual identities and personal awareness can affect this structure. The complex relationship between individual identities and social

[2] Elie Kedourie, *Nationalism* (Blackwell, 1993).

[3] Michael Bamberg and Anna De Fina, "Discourse and Identity Construction," in *Handbook of Identity Theory and Research*, ed. by Seth Schwartz, Koen Luyckx, and Vivian Vignoles (Springer, 2011), 177–99.

[4] Teun Van Dijk, "The Study of Discourse," in *Discourse as Structure and Process*, ed. Teun Van Dijk (Sage, 1997), 2.

[5] Peter Berger and Thomas Luckmann, *The Social Construction of Reality* (Anchor, 1967).

[6] Henri Tajfel and John Turner, "The Social Identity Theory of Intergroup Behavior," in *Psychology of Intergroup Relation*, ed. Stephen Worchel and William Austin (Chicago: Nelson-Hall, 1986), 7–24.

structure is a key aspect of the social process.[7] I will focus on the construction of a collective identity of Palestinian Christians: namely, an identity held by a significant number of people who belong to a collective that defines the members' boundaries and laws.[8]

Collective identity has been studied mostly in the context of national and social movements, examining how participants in those movements construct their social identities.[9] In periods of struggle or conflict, the construction of a collective identity is undertaken in order to promote a positive definition of the collective group, while promoting a negative identification of the opposition.[10] In alignment with sociologist Anthony Giddens's theory of structuration, which posits that individuals can act as agents who both reproduce and transform the social structure, leading to social change, we can view Palestinian Christian theologians as "agents" within a social system.[11] These theologians work to construct and shape their group's collective identity. This perspective underscores the active role that individuals and groups play in shaping social realities, highlighting the dynamic interplay between agency and structure in the context of Palestinian Christian identity formation. It is important to emphasize that these theologians do not create new systems or cultures from scratch but rather produce or transform existing ones. In essence, they are engaged in the process of remaking what has already been established.[12]

7 For a comprehensive review of recent studies on the notion of group identity, see Russell Spears, "Group Identities: The Social Identity Perspective," in Schwartz, Luyckx, and Vignoles, *Handbook of Identity Theory and Research*, 201–24.

8 Baruch Kimmerling and Dahlia Moore, "Collective Identity as Agency, and Structuration of Society: The Israeli Example," *International Review of Sociology* 7 (1997): 26.

9 George Crane, "Collective Identity, Symbolic Mobilization, and Student Protest in Nanjing, China, 1988–1989," *Comparative Politics* 26 (1994): 395. On the connection between liberation theology and social movement see Robert Mackin, "Liberation Theology and Social Movements," in *Handbook of Social Movements Across Latin America*, ed. Paul Almeida and Allen Cordero Ulate (Springer, 2015), 101–16.

10 Donatella Della Porta and Mario Diani, *Social Movements: An Introduction* (Blackwell, 1999), 98–99. On the concept of "boundaries" in identity construction see Vetra Taylor and Nancy Whittier, "Collective Identity in Social Movement Communities: Lesbian Feminist Mobilization," in *Waves of Protest: Social Movements Since the Sixties*, ed. Jo Freeman and Victoria Johnson (Rowman & Littlefield, 1992), 176–78.

11 Anthony Giddens, *Modernity and Self-Identity* (Polity, 1991), 35–36.

12 Giddens, *Modernity and Self-Identity*, 71.

It is interesting to mention in this context the observation of the American theologian David Tracy that theology has three primary publics: the church, the academy, and the people.[13] Each of them plays a vital role in religious life, and so a theology must be created that appeals not just to the church but to the public at large. Here, the term *public* has greater significance than merely *community*. The public, which shares a common language and usually a common context, is created from the space between the conflicts and tensions embedded in the group, and thus the holy and the profane in it are inseparable.[14] Following Tracy's observation I view PCT as a form of public theology. Katie Day and Sebastian Kim observed that although public theology addresses various publics, it does not refrain from criticizing any of them.[15] Public theology has a clear and stated agenda to improve the face of society and work for the "common good"—even though the "common good" is often unclear.[16] Consequently, public theology can participate in social discourse and offer answers on challenging issues. In this way, theology takes an active part in the discourse and enables the construction of different identities in society. The Palestinian Christian theologians aim to be part and parcel of a discourse that is not just intraecclesial, but transcends the notion that religion is individual on one hand, and authoritative and unreviewable on the other.[17] The purpose is to allow theology to once again be part of the public, sociocultural, and political discourse.[18]

The study of identity is understood here as structured in political and theological discourse. This approach differs from that which

13 David Tracy, "Defending the Public Character of Theology," *Christian Century* 11 (1981): 351.

14 Andrew Morton, "Duncan Forrester: A Public Theologian," in *Public Theology for the Twenty-First Century*, ed. William Storrar and Andrew Morton (T&T Clark, 2004), 25–36. One of the pioneer writings on the concept of public space is Jürgen Habermas, *The Structural Transformation of the Public Sphere: An Inquiry into a Category of Bourgeois Society*, trans. Thomas Burger (Polity, 1989).

15 Katie Day and Sebastian Kim, introduction to *A Companion to Public Theology*, ed. Tom Greggs (Brill, 2017), 5–6.

16 Day and Kim, introduction to *Companion to Public Theology*, 10.

17 Duncan Forrester, "The Scope of Public Theology," *Studies in Christian Ethics* 17 (2004): 5–19.

18 Day and Kim, introduction to *Companion to Public Theology*, 4.

presupposes essential or core features for a collective's members.[19] The basic assumption is that the definition of identity is constantly in the making, while identity agents navigate individuals or groups within the social, political, or interpersonal discourse.[20] There is a dialectical interaction between political or social events and the construction of collective identity.[21] The need to define the internal collective identity stems from external processes of change as well as continuity. Frequently, collective identity is not expressed in the hegemony of identities that make up the group.[22] Since identity is a social process, there is fluidity in the level of affiliations of people both within the group and vis-à-vis other identities.[23]

History is one of the main aspects of group identity, as it facilitates the definition of group boundaries. British historical sociologist Anthony Smith argues that in national or ethnic identities the myth of origin is one of the main definers.[24] Palestinian Christians have a myth of origin rooted in the Bible, where religion significantly contributes to stabilizing both the group and personal identities derived from this myth. This emphasizes the profound interconnection between religious narratives and the foundational stories of a community, acting as a key source of identity and a mechanism for ensuring continuity and coherence within the group. Sociologist of religion Hans Mol highlights the essential role of religion in stabilizing personal and group identity, further reinforcing the idea that

[19] See Bas ter Haar Romeny, "From Religious Association to Ethnic Community: A Research Project on Identity Formation Among the Syrian Orthodox Under Muslim Rule," *Islam and Christian-Muslim Relations* 16 (2005): 380–82; Karen Cerulo, "Identity Construction: New Issues, New Directions," *Annual Review of Sociology* 23 (1997): 387–88.

[20] Bamberg and De Fina, "Discourse and Identity Construction," 117–19.

[21] Belinda Robnett, "External Political Change, Collective Identities, and Participation in Social Movement Organizations," in *Social Movements: Identity, Culture, and the State*, ed. David Meyer, Nancy Whittier, and Belinda Robnett (Oxford: Oxford University Press, 2002), 266–69.

[22] Della Porta and Diani, *Social Movements*, 98.

[23] See, for example, Brouria Bitton-Ashkelony, "Territory, Anti-Intellectual Attitude, and Identity Formation in Late Antique Palestinian Monastic Communities," *Religion & Theology* 17 (2010): 244–67.

[24] Anthony Smith, *Myths and Memories of the Nation* (Oxford University Press, 1999), 15.

religious beliefs and practices are integral to the maintenance and development of collective identities.[25]

There is an inherent conflict within Christianity between the need of a group to define its own identity through history and religious practice, and the obligation to maintain the universal Christian message that affirms the teachings of Jesus Christ, centered on love and the availability of salvation to all humanity, irrespective of geographical location or group belonging.[26] This conflict appears through religious traditions, particularly because most recognized religions, especially monotheistic ones, are universal and, through their universality, versatile. They can be practiced simultaneously by a dominating empire or a persecuted minority group without a significant identity conflict. This versatility allows new members to convert to and join existing traditions, but it also ensures that religions are unable to advance one singular "truthful" history, given the wide range of interpretations theologians bring to the same sets of evidence.[27]

The question of the Bible's historical accuracy is pivotal within the Israeli-Palestinian conflict (IPC) framework. The Jewish people's connection to the land of Israel is rooted in a historical interpretation of biblical passages (Gen 12:1; 15:18–21; Exod 23:31–33). This connection is further intensified when the Bible is viewed as sacred Scripture or divine revelation, rendering a literal interpretation that deepens the linkage between the Jewish people and the land of Israel. However, the IPC did not unfold in isolation. The international community, including both Western and Eastern Christian factions, has consistently shown interest in this dispute. Prior to Israel's establishment, influential entities like global superpowers and the United Nations actively sought to sway the region's political landscape. This involvement significantly influenced the events that culminated in Israel's establishment. The shared biblical heritage of Judaism and Christianity, which attributes both historical and spiritual significance to the Bible, prompted many within the Christian community, both secular and religious, to

25 Hans Mol, *Identity and the Sacred: A Sketch for a New Social-Scientific Theory of Religion* (Basil Blackwell, 1976).

26 Oliver O'Donovan, "Political Theology, Tradition and Modernity," in *The Cambridge Companion to Liberation Theology*, ed. Christopher Rowland (Cambridge University Press, 2007), 265–77.

27 Jan Assmann, "Monotheism and Its Political Consequences," in *Religion and Politics: Culture Perspective*, ed. Bernhard Giesen and Daniel Suber (Brill, 2005), 141.

contemplate the establishment of a Jewish state in the land of Israel's theological and historical implications. Hence, the connection between the state of Israel and the Bible could affect the IPC in several ways, all of which require consideration by Palestinian theologians.

First, *theological meaning*. The specific issue here is Jewish-Christian relations. Many of the basic premises on which the Christian-Zionist theology stands, viewing Israel as the fulfillment of the divine promise, are critical cornerstones of Christianity that will be considered herein. First and foremost is the question of God's attitude toward Judaism today. While in the Western Christian discourse of the post–World War II (WWII) era, many changes have been made in the theological understandings surrounding this question, there is no implied consensus on the meaning and political implication of the notion of divine election, and certainly not on the issues that accompany it. Do the Jewish people, for example, have a special status in God's eyes? And if so, what does that mean? Another important question concerns the literal meaning of the Scripture. Should the text be understood in a literal, allegorical, or spiritual way?

Second, *historical meaning*. In political conflicts over territory, each side asserts its affinity and connection to that territory based on claims of nativity, antiquity, and authenticity. This means that each side may try to prove that it has a greater claim to the territory based on factors such as its longstanding presence in the area, its historical and cultural ties to the land, or its authenticity as a representative of the local population. Since the biblical narrative is read by the Jews not only as a religious story but also as a historical document, it becomes a tool for proving the historical affiliation of the Jewish people with the land of Israel. Moreover, the historical affiliation not only gives a political advantage in the competition to show "who was here first," but also strengthens the identity of that group. Thus it creates a profound connection between the religious symbolic-spiritual level and the political reality of the land in dispute.

Third, *sociocultural and moral meaning*. Since the question of divine election lies at the heart of the divine promise, the notion of chosenness has a direct impact on a group's self-definition.[28] The existence of a myth that endows a particular group of people with religious significance and legitimation is an essential tool in constructing that

[28] Anthony Smith, *Chosen People* (Oxford University Press, 2003), 48.

group's identity and sustaining its solidarity. Therefore, the Bible's interpretation and understanding of the divine promise affects not only the political aspects but also the sociocultural and moral ones. It gives rise to the question of whether the election of one group of people drives away the others from the bosom of the almighty God.

My research is centered on contemporary Christian theology, particularly focusing on the theological developments in Western Christianity and its effects on global Christianity from the second half of the twentieth century to the present. This timeframe allows for an in-depth exploration of how Christian theologians have engaged with political and social discourse during a period marked by significant paradigmatic changes. This era, shadowed by the devastation of WWII, is characterized by vigorous efforts to address and make sense of its aftermath.[29] Two critical changes in the development of Christian theology in the West occurred during this period. The first is the reconciliation with the transition from Christendom to a post-Christendom era (which some scholars date to as early as the end of the nineteenth century): the acknowledgment by the Western Churches that their political power had been undermined by secularism and other prominent ideologies.[30] The second is the dramatic demographic change in the Christian world, as the majority of believers are no longer in Europe and the United States but in the global South.[31] These changes, combined with the acceptance of poststructural and postcolonial theories that questioned the rule and the mission of the church, opened the way for the development of a political public theological discourse in diverse social movements in various parts of the world. Poststructuralism, with its skepticism toward fixed structures and universal truths, challenged the traditional, hierarchical interpretations of scripture and doctrine.[32] It emphasized the fluidity of meaning and the importance of context, encouraging a more pluralistic and democratic approach to theological discourse. This shift allowed for diverse voices within the church to be heard, promoting a theology that is more responsive

29 See Tony Judt, *Postwar: A History of Europe Since 1945* (Penguin, 2005).

30 Elaine Graham, *Between a Rock and a Hard Place: Public Theology in a Post-Secular Age* (SCM, 2013), 12–13.

31 See Philip Jenkins, "The Christian Revolution," in *The Next Christendom: The Coming of Global Christianity* (Oxford University Press, 2002), 1–14.

32 Derek Attridge, Geoff Bennington, and Robert Young, *Post-Structuralism and the Question of History* (Cambridge University Press, 1987).

to the needs and perspectives of different communities. Postcolonial theory, on the other hand, critically examined the legacy of colonialism within Christianity, questioning the Eurocentric perspectives that have often dominated Christian theology and practice.[33] It highlighted how the church's mission had been complicit in colonial projects, urging a reevaluation of its role in perpetuating inequality and injustice. By advocating for the decolonization of theology, postcolonial theory sought to recover and elevate the voices and experiences of marginalized communities within the global church.

My goal in this book is to explore the construction of identity in Palestinian Christian theology as it relates to Western Christianity. However, PCT has developed concurrently in English and Arabic. In many cases, these are not translations of the same works, but rather distinct types of writings created by the same theologians: one set is intended for a Western Christian audience, while the other is aimed at the Arab community. In this study, I shall refer to the theology written in Arabic only in chapter 1. The analysis of biblical hermeneutic in Arabic is unfortunately beyond the limits of this work. Hence, it is important to clarify that the construction of identity I deal with is not an internal one, but is focused on the way Palestinian theology is formed within the Western Christian discourse. In future research, I hope to critically examine Palestinian theology written in Arabic. It is important to bear in mind that Palestinian Christians exist at the intersection of two major civilizations: Western Christianity and Eastern Arab culture. When Palestinian Christian theologians write in English, they often conform to the universalist Western Christian premises established in the aftermath of WWII and the Holocaust. When they write in Arabic, they adjust to the universal Eastern Arab or Muslim premises shaped by internal and external trends within this civilization, such as Islamization and the Arab Spring—a wave of antigovernment demonstrations and uprisings that swept through much of the Arab world in the early 2010s. As a result, Palestinian Christian theologians are simultaneously engaged in two distinct universalist discourses. When referring to Palestinian theology, I refer in this study especially to Western Christian traditions—such as Anglican, Catholic, and Lutheran. In these practices I of course do not ignore the

33 Robert Young, *Postcolonialism: An Historical Introduction* (John Wiley & Sons, 2016).

role played by Eastern Christianity, and particularly that of the Greek Orthodox Church. Most of the local Christian communities in the Holy Land are of Eastern origin. However, as the Palestinian theologians that I am concerned with in this study adhere to the Western tradition, my focus is on that realm.

The primary research method of this study is discourse analysis, which I use to comprehend the context of theological discourse. The term *discourse* carries different meanings to different scholars in different fields of study. For many it is defined as anything "beyond the sentence," and seen as part of linguistic study.[34] However, with the rise of critical theorists and their followers, discourse can be understood as a broad conglomeration of linguistic and nonlinguistic social practices and ideological assumptions, considered in the social sciences as well as in the humanities. The linguist Norman Fairclough characterized it as a method of representing a specific domain of social practice from a distinct viewpoint.[35] He understands discourse analysis as the exploration of relationships between causality and determination, between discursive practices and wider social and cultural structures, and the investigating of the modes in which such practices are shaped by relations of power and struggles over power.[36] The baseline of this approach is that the social setting influences and even shapes the discourse, while the discourse itself influences and shapes social and political processes.[37]

Given that this study's starting point is the transformation of theological discourse in recent years, the "discourse-historical approach," as outlined by Ruth Wodak, proves particularly useful.[38] This approach aims to integrate a wide range of knowledge about the historical sources and the backdrop of the social and political fields that support discursive "events." Moreover, it investigates the historical dimension of discursive actions by examining the ways specific genres of discourse

[34] Deborah Schiffrin, Deborah Tannen, and Heidi E. Hamilton, introduction to *The Handbook of Discourse Analysis*, ed. Deborah Tannen, Heidi E. Hamilton, and Deborah Schiffrin (Blackwell, 2001), 1–10.

[35] Norman Fairclough, *Critical Discourse Analysis: The Critical Study of Language* (Longman, 1995), 14.

[36] Fairclough, *Critical Discourse Analysis*, 132.

[37] Martin Reisigl and Ruth Wodak, "The Discourse Historical Approach," in *Methods of Critical Discourse Analysis*, ed. Ruth Wodak and Michael Meyer (Sage, 2001), 66.

[38] Reisigl and Wodak, "Discourse Historical Approach," 64.

undergo change over time. The approach considers four levels of context relevant to discourse analysis: (1) the immediate language, or text-internal context; (2) the intertextual and interdiscursive relationships among utterances, texts, genres, and discourses; (3) the extralinguistic social variables and institutional frameworks of a specific situational context; and (4) the wider sociopolitical and historical context in which discursive practices are situated and to which they are related.[39] Hence I conduct this study from the perspective of intellectual history, that is, the study of human thoughts and ideas.[40] Accordingly, while I discuss theology, I assume that it always develops within a historical, cultural, and social context. This approach allows me to study the evolution of ideas over time and the development of different elements of identity, such as religion and politics.[41] It also recognizes that theological writings or religious ideas are part of a general system of social thought.[42] Nevertheless, theological discourse, even if influenced or shaped by its social and political setting, is still practiced within the close bounds of theology and religious beliefs.[43]

This study is conducted from a discursive approach to theology rather than a normative one.[44] A discursive approach examines the ways theological narratives are produced, the rhetorical strategies employed, and the implications of these narratives for individuals and communities. By situating theological discussions within broader discourses, this approach seeks to uncover the underlying assumptions, values, and interests that shape religious thought and practice. A normative approach, on the other hand, typically involves evaluating

[39] Ruth Wodak, "Critical Discourse Analysis, Discourse-Historical Approach," in *The International Encyclopedia of Language and Social Interaction*, ed. Karen Tracy (Wiley-Blackwell, 2015), 1–14.

[40] See, for example, Felix Gilbert, "Intellectual History: Its Aims and Methods," *Historical Studies Today* 100 (1971): 80–97; Russell Jacoby, "A New Intellectual History," *The American Historical Review* 97 (1992): 405–24; Dominick Lacapra, "Rethinking Intellectual History and Reading Texts," *History and Theory* 19 (1980): 245–76.

[41] Lloyd Kramer, "Martin Jay and the Dialectical of Intellectual History," in *The Modernist Imagination: Intellectual History and Critical Theory*, ed. Peter Gordon et al. (Berghahn Books, 2009), xi–xii.

[42] Lilian Calles Barger, *The World Come of Age: An Intellectual History of Liberation Theology* (Oxford University Press, 2018), 8–9.

[43] Wesley Kort, *Bound to Differ: Dynamics of Theological Discourses* (Pennsylvania State University Press, 1992), 23.

[44] Donald Dworkin, *Justice for Hedgehogs* (Harvard University Press, 2011).

theological concepts against a standard or set of principles considered to be universally valid or superior. This evaluative stance aims to determine the correctness of beliefs and practices, often with the intention of guiding behavior or reforming tradition. By using a discursive approach, this study steers clear of making value judgments about theological positions. Instead, it aims to provide a nuanced understanding of how theological discourse operates within and impacts the wider sociocultural landscape, acknowledging the complexity and diversity of religious expression and thought.

Expanding on the existing scholarly groundwork, my research sets itself apart by examining PCT as an overarching category, with a particular focus on its discursive construction. By delving into the ways theological narratives are crafted, debated, and interacted with both within the Palestinian Christian community and beyond, this study aims to provide an in-depth understanding of theology's role within the wider sociopolitical framework of the IPC. In undertaking this analysis, my work introduces a distinctive viewpoint to scholarly conversation, underscoring the vibrant and complex character of PCT amid the backdrop of contemporary social and political challenges.

The state of the art in the study of the Promised Land and its theological significance within the IPC reveals a rich tapestry of normative theology. Influential works by scholars such as William Davies,[45] Walter Brueggemann,[46] Peter Walker,[47] and Gary Burge[48] have laid foundational understandings of the theological significance of the land in both the Old and New Testaments, offering perspectives that range from the land as central to biblical thinking to interpretations of its significance in Christian thought. Recent contributions have aimed to relate theological understandings of the land to contemporary realities, with scholars like Robert Wilken,[49] Andrew Jacobs,[50] Alain Marchadour

[45] William Davies, *Gospel and the Land: Early Christianity and Jewish Territorial Doctrine* (University of California Press, 1974).

[46] Walter Brueggemann, *The Land: Place as Gift, Promise and Challenge in Biblical Faith* (Fortress, 1977).

[47] Peter Walker, *Jesus and the Holy City: New Testament Perspectives on Jerusalem* (Eerdmans, 1996).

[48] Gary Burge, *Jesus and the Land* (Baker Academic, 2010).

[49] Wilken, *Land Called Holy*.

[50] Andrew S. Jacobs, *Remains of the Jews: The Holy Land and Christian Empire in Late Antiquity* (Stanford University Press, 2004).

and David Neuhaus,[51] and Munther Isaac[52] providing insights into the historical development and contemporary theological interpretations of the Holy Land.

Furthermore, studies by Adam Gregerman,[53] Edward Kessler,[54] and John Pawlikowski,[55] have explored the complex interrelations between theological interpretations, political ideologies, and the IPC, offering critical analyses of Christian attitudes toward the state of Israel and its implications for Jewish-Christian relations. Works such as *The Wrath of Jonah* by Rosemary Radford Ruether and Herman J. Ruether,[56] *Christian Attitudes Towards the State of Israel, 1948–2000* by Paul Charles Merkley,[57] and *Zionism and the Quest for Justice in the Holy Land*, edited by Donald Wagner and Walter Davis[58] have expanded the discussion to include the ideological foundations of Zionism and the political ramifications of theological positions.

Notably, a few seminal studies have specifically addressed PCT. Lance Laird's analysis of the writings of Naim Ateek and Mitri Raheb before 2000 highlights how Palestinian theology serves as a tool for liberating Palestinian Christians from the perception of a battle against the "chosen people."[59] Leonard Marsh's work on the response of Palestinian Christians to the establishment of the state of Israel and its actions sheds light on the active participation of Church members

51 Alain Marchadour and David Neuhaus, *The Land, the Bible and History: Toward the Land That I Will Show You* (Fordham University Press, 2007).

52 Munther Isaac, *From Land to Lands, from Eden to the Renewed Earth* (Langham, 2015).

53 Adam Gregerman, "Comparative Christian Hermeneutical Approaches to the Land Promised to Abraham," *CrossCurrents* 64 (2014): 409–24.

54 Edward Kessler, *An Introduction to Jewish-Christian Relations* (Cambridge University Press, 2010), 147–69.

55 John Pawlikowski, "Land as an Issue in Christian-Jewish Dialogue," *CrossCurrents* 59 (2009): 197–209.

56 Rosemary Ruether and Herman J. Ruether, *The Wrath of Jonah: The Crisis of Religious Nationalism in the Israeli-Palestinian Conflict* (Harper & Row, 1989).

57 Paul Charles Merkley, *Christian Attitudes Towards the State of Israel, 1948–2000* (McGill-Queen's University Press, 2001).

58 Donald Wagner and Walter Davis, *Zionism and the Quest for Justice in the Holy Land* (Lutterworth, 2014).

59 Lance Laird, "Meeting Jesus Again in the First Place: Palestinian Christians and the Bible," *Interpretation* 55 (2001): 401–10.

in the Palestinian political struggle.[60] Samuel Kuruvilla's comparative study of the theologies of Ateek and Raheb emphasizes the distinction between liberation theology and contextual theology, underscoring the diversity within PCT.[61]

Contributions from Palestinian theologians and scholars themselves, such as Mitri Raheb's collective volume on Palestinian liberation theology,[62] Nur Masalha and Lisa Isherwood's volume on the theology of liberation,[63] and the anthology edited by Rafiq Khoury and Rainer Zimmer-Winkel[64] provide critical insights into the evolving theological discourse from a local Palestinian perspective. These works present a new biblical interpretation of the IPC and explore the role of theology in promoting peace.

As we navigate the chapters in this book, it will become clear that the examination of PCT transcends mere academic inquiry. This exploration delves into the essence of a community engaged in a profound struggle with intricate issues of identity, belonging, and faith, all against the backdrop of ongoing geopolitical conflict. The book begins with a historical survey of Christianity in the Holy Land, laying a foundational context for understanding the intricate position of Arab Christians within this region. This section is crafted to highlight the unique experiences of local Christians, a community that straddles the complex interplay between their ethnic (Arab) heritage and their religious (Christian) beliefs. It delves into the historical trajectory of Christianity from its early inception in the region, through the Byzantine and Ottoman eras, and into the modern challenges posed by the IPC. This exploration is not merely a chronological recounting of

60 Leonard Marsh, "Palestinian Christians: Theology and Politics in the Holy Land," in *Christianity in the Middle East: Studies in Modern History, Theology, and Politics*, ed. Anthony O'Mahony (Melisende, 2008), 205–18.

61 Samuel Jacob Kuruvilla, *Radical Christianity in the Holy Land: A Comparative Study of Liberation and Contextual Theology in Palestine-Israel* (University of Exeter, 2009); Samuel Kuruvilla, "Theologies of Liberation in Latin America and Palestine-Israel in Comparative Perspective: Contextual Differences and Practical Similarities," *Holy Land Studies* 9 (2010): 51–69.

62 Mitri Raheb, *The Biblical Text in the Context of Occupation: Towards a New Hermeneutics of Liberation* (Diyar, 2012).

63 Nur Masalha and Lisa Isherwood, *Theologies of Liberation in Palestine-Israel: Indigenous, Contextual, and Postcolonial Perspectives* (Lutterworth Press, 2014).

64 Rafiq Khoury and Rainer Zimmer-Winkel, *Christian Theology in the Palestinian Context* (AphorismA, 2019).

events but a deep dive into the cultural, social, and political currents that have shaped the identity of Arab Christians. It examines how historical developments, such as the Crusades, the fall of the Ottoman Empire, the mandate period, and the establishment of the state of Israel, have had profound impacts on this community.

Chapter 1 delves into the emergence of PCT during the 1980s, a period marked by significant sociopolitical upheavals in Palestinian society. It begins with an exploration of the rise of Palestinian resistance movements and the growth of a Palestinian identity, setting the stage for understanding the broader nationalistic fervor that enveloped the Palestinian people. This context is crucial for comprehending the emergence of PCT not just as a theological response to external stimuli but as an intrinsic component of the Palestinian struggle for identity and self-determination.

As the narrative unfolds, the chapter examines Muslim-Christian relations in Palestinian society, revealing how the interfaith dynamics, especially the rising prominence of Islamic identity, played a critical role in shaping the theological discourse of the Palestinian Christian community. This section delves into the complexities of navigating a shared nationalistic goal amid differing religious narratives, highlighting the challenges Palestinian Christians faced in asserting their place within the broader national identity. The segment on The First Intifada (1987–91) provides a vivid account of this grassroots uprising against Israeli occupation, underscoring a period of intensified Palestinian national consciousness. It examines how the Intifada served as a catalyst for Palestinian Christians to articulate their theological and political stances, fostering a unique theological perspective deeply intertwined with the national liberation struggle. The chapter argues that the evolution of PCT was significantly influenced by an identity and nationality crisis within the Palestinian Christian community. This crisis was not solely a reaction to the theological implications of the Bible being used to legitimize the state of Israel but was rooted in the internal dynamics of Palestinian society itself. The chapter posits that the early formation of PCT in the 1990s can be attributed to these internal dynamics, occurring concurrently with the evolution of political theology in global Christian conversations.

By examining these foundational themes, the chapter sets the stage for understanding PCT as both a product of and a response to the unique historical, social, and political contexts of Palestinian society. It reveals that PCT is not just a theological discourse but an integral part of the Palestinian narrative of resistance, identity formation, and quest for self-determination.

Chapter 2 charts the profound transformation in Western Christianity's perception of Judaism following the Holocaust and the emergence of post-Holocaust theology. This period marks a critical reevaluation of theological stances, prompting a reconsideration of long-held beliefs and the development of new theological frameworks that seek to address the atrocities and the theological complicity observed during the Holocaust. The chapter further delves into the rise of diverse contextual theologies and postcolonial critiques that challenge the previously unchallenged dominance of Western theological perspectives. It portrays a theological landscape in flux, where non-Western voices strive for recognition and legitimacy within a global discourse still heavily skewed toward Western norms and expectations. This quest for acknowledgment often necessitates a delicate balancing act—asserting unique theological insights while engaging with Western theological norms to gain visibility and influence.

Furthermore, the chapter examines the seismic impact of postmodern thought on Western collective consciousness, particularly its skepticism toward the notion of objective historical truths and universal narratives. This epistemological shift has profound implications for theology, questioning foundational assumptions about history, truth, and the nature of religious belief. For PCT, these developments offer both challenges and opportunities. The postmodern critique of universal narratives resonates with Palestinian Christian efforts to articulate their unique theological perspectives against the backdrop of political conflict and cultural displacement. The chapter illuminates how PCT interacts with, and is influenced by, the broader trends of post-Holocaust and postcolonial theologies, navigating the complexities of identity, memory, and resistance. Through this exploration, readers gain insights into the dynamic interplay between PCT and these predominant theological movements, highlighting the unique contributions and challenges of Palestinian Christian voices within the global theological discourse.

Chapter 3 embarks on an in-depth exploration of the hermeneutics of PCT, positioning it at the critical intersection of post-Holocaust and postcolonial theological perspectives. This exploration is committed to unraveling the intricate tensions between the specific historical narratives of the IPC and the quest for universal theological truths. Employing the "hermeneutical circle," a framework popularized by Uruguayan liberation theologian Juan Luis Segundo, the chapter meticulously analyzes and interprets Palestinian Christian theological discourse. This methodological approach serves as a pivotal tool for understanding how PCT theologians engage with biblical texts, framing them within a broader dialogue that spans historical realities, cultural identities, and political aspirations. It recognizes the cyclical process of interpretation, asserting that an understanding of specific biblical passages or theological positions is intertwined with the overarching narrative of the IPC and global theological discussions.

The chapter investigates the dual approach of PCT theologians to scripture, which involves honoring the spiritual depth of biblical narratives while also acknowledging their historical implications and the realities of contemporary geopolitical struggles. This involves a critical engagement with biblical texts, reevaluating stories traditionally interpreted in purely spiritual terms through the lens of their historical significance and contemporary relevance. Through this lens, the chapter highlights how PCT theologians articulate a theology that is rooted in Christian faith and responsive to the calls for justice, peace, and self-determination. By integrating faith and history, spirituality and politics, these theologians navigate the challenges of interpreting scripture in a way that speaks to the Palestinian experience. Furthermore, this chapter illuminates the broader theological and ethical questions that arise when biblical texts are engaged as both sacred scripture and historical narrative. It offers valuable insights into the distinctive contributions of PCT to theological discourse, demonstrating the theologians' adept navigation of the complex interplay between faith and history, identity and resistance, in their quest to articulate a theology that resonates with the heart of the Palestinian experience.

Chapter 4 argues that Palestinian theologians articulate their national-political identity through the pivotal concept of "witness." This framework allows Palestinian Christian theologians to position the Palestinian struggle not merely as a regional or ethnic conflict but as part of a broader, universal quest for justice and equality. By doing so, they imbue the Palestinian national identity with profound theological significance, underlining a narrative that transcends the immediate political discourse to touch upon timeless themes of justice, suffering, and redemption. This chapter outlines the ways Palestinian Christian theologians leverage the concept of witness to interpret and engage with the realities of their context. Witness here is multifaceted, encompassing witness to historical truths, to enduring faith amid suffering, and to a steadfast commitment to peace and justice. It is through this lens of witness that the theologians frame the Palestinian experience, drawing parallels between biblical narratives of suffering and perseverance and the contemporary Palestinian struggle for self-determination and dignity.

This narrative of witness serves to highlight the unique connection of the Palestinian people to their land. It is not merely a territorial claim but a profound bond that is spiritual, historical, and cultural, deeply rooted in the Palestinian Christian theological understanding. This connection is articulated as part of God's creation, entrusted to the Palestinian people who bear witness to their faith, history, and rights in the face of adversity. Through the concept of witness, Palestinian Christian theologians thus offer a powerful theological articulation of national identity, one that frames the Palestinian struggle within the larger Christian narrative of suffering, hope, and resurrection. This approach not only provides meaning and depth to the Palestinian national identity but also positions the Palestinian struggle within a global conversation on justice, human rights, and the Christian call to stand with the oppressed. In doing so, the chapter argues, PCT contributes a unique voice to the discourse on national identity and political struggle, one that challenges both the international community and the broader Christian world to reconsider the Palestinian issue through a theological lens that champions universal justice and equality.

Historical Survey

Christians native to the Holy Land have long grappled with the tension between their deep-seated connection to their land—a connection both personal and communal—and the land's status as a universally venerated site, sacred not just to the broader Christian community but also to Judaism and Islam. This widespread reverence for the Holy Land has spurred pilgrimages, conquests, and ongoing involvement from global powers, merging the land's religious importance with intricate geopolitical dynamics. As a result, the identity of local Christians has been molded by external influences, particularly from the Muslim world and the Western-Christian sphere. This dynamic has created a complex interplay between their direct sociopolitical environment and the extensive religious landscapes that surround them, shaping their identity in unique ways.

In *Justice and Only Justice* (1989), Naim Ateek embarks on a narrative journey to dismantle stereotypes, beginning with a self-introduction that illuminates the complexity of identity within the Holy Land. Ateek describes himself through a prism of identities: Christian, Palestinian, Arab, Israeli, and Anglican Episcopalian. He articulates how each label is burdened with myths and stereotypes, and their convergence within a single individual can lead to confusion for outsiders. This personal narrative sets a precedent for understanding the layered identities of Christians in the Holy Land, highlighting the intricate relationship between personal and communal identity, religious affiliation, and national belonging.

This study delves into the intricate issues of identity within the theological realm, grounded in the premise that identity and history are intrinsically linked. It begins with a concise historical survey of Christianity in the Holy Land, providing a backdrop essential for understanding the subsequent theological exploration. It sketches a general trajectory of the development of Christian communities and their theology, which stands at the heart of this study. It posits that the history and identity of these communities are fundamentally woven into their theological fabric.

The investigation addresses critical questions of ethnic or national identity and ecclesiastical identity, examining how these facets of identity are expressed and negotiated across different epochs and settings. Through this analysis, the study offers insights into the dynamic interrelation between community identity, historical context, and theological expression, contributing to a deeper understanding of the complex tapestry of Christian life in this sacred, contested space.

CHRISTIAN COMMUNITIES IN LATE ANTIQUITY

From its inception, the Church of Jerusalem strove for recognition of its historical relevance and importance to Christianity and advocated for special status.[1] The significance of the Holy Land and of Jerusalem, with its glorious holy places, was first recognized in the time of Constantine.[2] During the fourth and fifth centuries, a significant transformation occurred in the status of Jerusalem within the Christian world, largely due to the concerted efforts of the bishops of Jerusalem, ranging

1 Robert Wilken, *The Land Called Holy: Palestine in Christian History and Thought* (Yale University Press, 1992); Jacob Ashkenazi, *The Mother of All Churches: The Church of Palestine from Its Foundation to the Arab Conquest* (Yad Izhak Ben-Zvi, 2009).

2 Lorenzo Perrone, "'Rejoice Sion, Mother of All Churches': Christianity in the Holy Land During the Byzantine Era," in *Christians and Christianity in the Holy Land: From the Origins to the Latin Kingdoms*, ed. Ora Limor and Guy Stroumsa (Yad Izhak Ben-Zvi, 2006), 147–48. The legend about the discovery of the Holy Cross in Jerusalem played a significant part in promoting Jerusalem and its holy sites. See Stephan Borgehammar, *How the Holy Cross Was Found: From Event to Medieval Legend* (Almquist & Wiksell, 1991).

from Cyril (AD 313–86) to Juvenal (d. AD 358).[3] Juvenal's tenure in particular (AD 422–58) marked a turning point as he later became the first patriarch of Jerusalem, elevating the city's ecclesiastical standing to a new height. The campaign to elevate Jerusalem to a patriarchate was driven by more than just ecclesiastical ambition. It was rooted in profound theological struggles concerning the sanctity of the city and its significance for Christianity at large. Through their efforts, these bishops sought to underscore Jerusalem's unique role in Christian salvation history, emphasizing its connection to the life, death, and resurrection of Jesus Christ. Behind the efforts to turn the city into a patriarchate were theological struggles regarding the city's sanctity and its meaning for Christianity. The main debate was between Cyril, the bishop of Jerusalem (AD 313–86), and Eusebius, the bishop of Caesarea (AD 260/5–339).[4]

By the fourth century, such was the prominence of Jerusalem that the church there began referring to itself as the "mother of all churches."[5] This title reflected not only the city's foundational role in Christian history but also its enduring spiritual and theological significance.

The unique position of the Patriarchate in Jerusalem, the many pilgrims that visited the city, and the establishment of monasteries in the surrounding Judean desert, created a diverse and exceptional demography in the Jerusalem area.[6] The Judean desert monasteries were, first and foremost, a uniquely cosmopolitan community whose clerics came from all over the Byzantine Empire.[7] The Christian population consisted of indigenous communities and of pilgrims, espe-

3 Saul Colbi, *A History of the Christian Presence in the Holy Land* (University Press of America, 1988), 9–26.

4 See Peter Walker, *Holy City, Holy Places?* (Clarendon, 1990); Ze'ev Rubin, "The Church of the Holy Sepulcher and the Conflict Between the Sees of Caesarea and Jerusalem," *Jerusalem Cathedra* 2 (1982): 79–105.

5 Eusebius, *Life of Constantine* 3.25–53, trans. Ernest Cushing Richardson, in *Nicene and Post-Nicene Fathers*, ed. Philip Schaff and Henry Wace (Christian Literature, 1890); Wilken, *Land Called Holy*, 171.

6 On pilgrimage to Jerusalem in late antiquity see Ora Limor, "Jewish and Christian Pilgrims to Jerusalem in Late Antiquity," in *Jerusalem II: Jerusalem in Roman-Byzantine Times*, ed. Katharina Hayden and Maria Lissek (Mohr Siebeck, 2021), 311–24. On the history of the Judean desert in late antiquity see Yizhar Hirschfeld, *The Judean Desert Monasteries in the Byzantine Period* (Yale University Press, 1992); Joseph Patrich, *Sabas, Leader of Palestinian Monasticism: A Comparative Study in Eastern Monasticism, Fourth to Seventh Centuries* (Dumbarton Oaks, 1995).

7 Ashkenazi, *Mother of All Churches*, 233.

cially monks and clerics who had settled in the land.[8] Most inhabitants of the area were bilingual, speaking both their language of origin and Greek. In the monasteries, whose population consisted of pilgrims from across the empire, and in the Jerusalem patriarchate, the language of the official liturgy was Greek.[9] Syriac was the language of the native Christians in Jerusalem. This language was a brother dialect of Galilean and Samaritan.[10] Among the evidence we have for the existence of Syriac speakers in the land of Israel, and their position in the church, is Egeria's description of the Anastasis ceremony at the Patriarchate in Jerusalem.[11] In this passage, Egeria, a Hispano-Roman Christian who embarked on a pilgrimage to the Holy Land around AD 381/2–84, describes how the bishop spoke in Greek and was translated simultaneously into Syriac. The same procedure was followed when reading from the New Testament.[12] The Syriac speakers in the land of Israel, probably the majority of the population, lived mainly in the suburbs, far from the main cities where Greek was dominant. However, it is likely that most residents of the big cities spoke Syriac in addition to Greek.[13] The division between the Greek-speaking communities and the Syriac ones was not the only thing that divided the Christian communities. From the fifth century onwards, Christian communities in the region were embroiled in numerous Christological controversies concerning the nature, identity, and understanding of Jesus Christ. On the eve of the Islamic conquest, following the Council of Chalcedon, which addressed these debates, two primary Christian factions were present in the Holy Land: the Non-Chalcedonian Churches, which did not accept the council's decisions, and the Greek Byzantine Ortho-

[8] See Leah Di Segni and Yoram Tsafrir, "The Ethnic Composition of Jerusalem's Population in the Byzantine Period (312–638 CE)," *Liber Annuus* 62 (2012): 405–54.

[9] Patrich, *Sabas, Leader of Palestinian Monasticism*, 249–52; Sidney Griffith, "From Aramaic to Arabic: The Language of the Monasteries of Palestine in the Byzantine and Early Islamic Period," *Dumbarton Oaks* 51 (1997): 12–13.

[10] On Christian Palestinian Aramaic see Christa Muller-Kessler, "Christian Palestinian Aramaic and Its Significance to the Western Aramaic Dialect Group," *Journal of the American Oriental Society* 19 (1999): 631–36.

[11] Egeria, *Egeria's Travels to the Holy Land*, trans. John Wilkinson (Ariel, 1981), 146.

[12] Griffith, "From Aramaic to Arabic," 17.

[13] Griffith, "From Aramaic to Arabic," 17.

dox, who were in agreement with the council's findings.[14] The invading Arabs found a heterogeneous and divided Christian society, and the differences would only grow wider under Islamic rule.

CHRISTIANITY IN THE HOLY LAND UNDER THE ISLAMIC CONQUEST

For the Christian population in the Holy Land, the Muslim conquest (AD 636–37) brought about radical change.[15] The Jerusalem Church and its believers had thrived in Late Antiquity. The Church held great power, and its influence extended to all domains of Christian life. With the conquest, Christians were demoted from the ruling power to protected *dhimmi* of inferior status.[16]

In the immediate aftermath of the Muslim conquest, Christians were persecuted. The Greek-speaking Christian population, which had enjoyed a relatively high status, fled. The Syrian-speaking population, which did not have the means to leave, remained under Muslim rule, and had to find ways to cope with the decrees of the new regime.[17] Despite the challenges, Christian pilgrimage to Jerusalem and the holy places continued, albeit in smaller numbers, and some of the pilgrims remained on as residents of the city.[18]

Under Islamic rule, the Christian communities of the Holy Land underwent both Arabization and Islamization.[19] The impact of Arab

[14] See Christine Chaillot, *The Dialogue Between the Eastern Orthodox and Oriental Orthodox Churches* (Volos Academy, 2016); Anthony O'Mahony, ed., *The Christian Communities of Jerusalem and the Holy Land* (University of Wales Press, 2003).

[15] On Christianity under Islamic rule see Sidney Griffith, *The Church in the Shadow of the Mosque: Christians and Muslims in the World of Islam* (Princeton University Press, 2007).

[16] Colbi, *History of the Christian Presence*, 29–36. On the surrender agreement of Jerusalem and its implications on the Christian communities see Milka Levy-Rubin, *Non-Muslims in the Early Islamic Empire: From Surrender to Coexistence* (Cambridge University Press, 2011); Boaz Shoshan, "The Islamic Conquest: Continuity and Change," in *Jerusalem II: Jerusalem in Roman-Byzantine Times*, ed. Katharina Heyden and Maria Lissek (Mohr Siebeck, 2021), 459–74.

[17] Amnon Linder, "The Christian Communities in the City," in *The History of Jerusalem: The Early Muslim Period 638–1099*, ed. Yehoshua Prawer (Yad Izhak Ben Zvi, 1987), 115–16.

[18] Linder, "Christian Communities in the City," 117.

[19] See Milka Levy-Rubin, "Arabization Versus Islamization," in *Sharing the Sacred: Religion Contacts and Conflicts in the Holy Land*, ed. Aryeh Kofsky and Guy Stroumsa (Yad Izhak Ben Zvi, 1998), 149–61.

culture manifested in three main ways: a shift to Arabic names, a shift to dating according to the Hijra, and the adoption of the Arabic language.[20] As early as the eighth century, we see the first writings of the Christian community in Arabic. More than sixty Christian manuscripts written in Arabic—transcribed between the eighth and eleventh centuries and belonging to the community—have survived.[21] Scholars have noted the unique characteristics of Arabic in writings from the Holy Land. The Arabic used by the Christian community has its own grammatical, morphological, and syntactic features.[22] From the ninth century, the Arabic language began to occupy a prominent place in the Jerusalem Patriarchate. Arabic penetrated the monasteries and churches and became the spoken language of the population at large.

Another result of the Muslim conquest, no less dramatic for the Christian population in the region, was the separation from the Greek Byzantine Church based in Constantinople. Scholars debate whether monks in Jerusalem and the Judean Desert in the ninth century maintained their ties with the Byzantine Empire.[23] According to historian Sidney Griffith, by the time of the reunification with Constantinople in the eleventh century, two separate groups had already formed within the Byzantine Orthodox Church in the area: the Greek Orthodox and the Melchites (or Arab Orthodox).[24]

The Muslim conquest introduced new opportunities for the Syriac-speaking population, opportunities that were largely unavailable during the Byzantine period. This group had previously occupied a less favorable position compared to their Christian Greek-speaking counterparts, primarily because Syriac was neither used as an official

[20] Linder, "Christian Communities in the City," 119.

[21] Levy-Rubin, "Arabization Versus Islamization," 153.

[22] Sidney Griffith, "The Monks of Palestine and the Growth of Christian Literature in Arabic," *The Muslim World* 78 (1988): 6–7. The uniqueness of the Christian Arabic that developed in the Holy Land in the early Muslim period and its grammatical characteristics are comprehensively reviewed by Yehoshua Blau, *A Grammar of Christian Arabic: Based Mainly on South-Palestinian Texts from the First Millennium* (Secrétariat du Corpus SCO, 1967).

[23] Linder, "Christian Communities in the City," 119–20.

[24] Sidney Griffith, "The Church of Jerusalem and the 'Melkites': The Making of an 'Arab Orthodox' Christian Identity in the World of Islam," in Limor and Stroumsa, *Christians and Christianity in the Holy Land*, 186–90. One should not confuse the Melkites in the Islamic period, i.e., Arab Orthodox, with the Melkite communities from the eighteenth century that are Rome-Greek Catholics.

language nor as an exclusive liturgical language, with all significant political and administrative affairs being conducted in Greek.[25] However, the linguistic closeness between Aramaic, from which Syriac derives, and Arabic facilitated a relatively smooth transition for the Syriac-Christian population to adopt Arabic.

The Syriac-speaking Christians' marginal status under Byzantine rule likely accelerated the Arabization process of the Christian population within the Patriarchate of Jerusalem, compared to the slower pace in the neighboring patriarchates of Alexandria and Antioch.[26] Consequently, the Syriac population in the Holy Land gradually embraced Arabic. In contrast, in Antioch and Alexandria, where the Oriental churches had a more pronounced influence, local languages like Coptic and Syriac were revered in the church's liturgical practices, leading local Christians to resist the shift to Arabic and strive to preserve their native languages.[27]

THE CHRISTIANS OF THE HOLY LAND AND THE CRUSADER CONQUEST

The Christian community in the Holy Land maintained its majority status until the ascendance of the Mamluk Empire toward the end of the eleventh century.[28] Throughout the period of Muslim dominion the experiences of Christians fluctuated significantly, with periods of persecution often linked to the broader Muslim world's responses to perceived threats from both Latin and Greek Christianity. An important historical moment in this narrative is the Crusader conquest, which ushered in a century of Christian rule over the Holy Land.[29]

25 Levy-Rubin, "Arabization Versus Islamization," 153.

26 Linder, "Christian Communities in the City," 120; Blau, *Grammar of Christian Arabic*, 22–30.

27 Levy-Rubin, "Arabization Versus Islamization," 149–61.

28 On the reasons for the demographical changes, see Nimrod Luz, "Aspects of Islamization of Space and Society in Mamluk Jerusalem and Its Hinterland," *Mamluk Studies Review* 6 (2002): 133–54.

29 On Jerusalem in the time of the crusades, see Joshua Prawer, "Political History of Crusader and Ayyubid Jerusalem," in *The History of Jerusalem: Crusaders and Ayyubids (1099–1250)*, ed. Joshua Prawer and Haggai Ben-Shammai (Yad Izhak Ben-Zvi, 1991), 1–67; Adrian Boas, *Jerusalem in the Time of the Crusades: Society, Landscape and Art in the Holy City Under Frankish Rule* (Routledge, 2001). Almost all the local communities belonged at that time to the Orthodox or Oriental churches. See Johannes Pablitzsch and Daniel Baraz, "Christian Communities in the Latin Kingdom

Contrary to expectations, the Crusader era, marked by Catholic Christian governance and its attendant upheavals, did not significantly alter the character or identity of the indigenous Christian community. This contrasts with the impact of European involvement in the Holy Land during Ottoman rule, which had more profound implications for the local Christian population.

One of the reasons for the relatively unchanged status of the local Christian community during the Crusades can be attributed to the perception and treatment of the Orthodox Church by the Latin Crusaders. The Orthodox Church was regarded by the Latins as a part of the universal church, in stark contrast to their view of the non-Chalcedonian churches—among them the Syrian, Coptic and Armenian churches—which were deemed heretical.[30] Consequently, the Latin rulers sought to integrate the Orthodox ecclesiastical hierarchy into the newly established Latin Patriarchate rather than supplant it.[31] This approach helped preserve the continuity of the Orthodox community's religious practices and structures, mitigating the potential disruptive effects of Latin rule on the local Christian identity.

Thus, following the Mamluk reconquest in AD 1260, the majority of the Christian community remained Orthodox and regained the Orders of the Orthodox Patriarch.[32] Moreover, one of the main consequences of the Crusader conquest was the renewed connection of the Church of Jerusalem with Constantinople, leading to a process of Byzantization.[33] The Christian communities once again became a heterogeneous society that included Greek and Arabic speakers, and the Patriarchate of Jerusalem became subordinate to Constantinople, both politically and liturgically.[34]

---

of Jerusalem," in Limor and Stroumsa, *Christians and Christianity in the Holy Land*, 234. See also Richard Rose, "Communities of Eastern Christians in Crusader Jerusalem," in Prawer and Ben-Shammai, *History of Jerusalem*, 176–93.

30 See Jonathan Harris, *Byzantium and the Crusades* (Bloomsbury, 2014), 52–58.

31 Pablitzsch and Baraz, "Christian Communities in the Latin Kingdom of Jerusalem," 206.

32 Pablitzsch and Baraz, "Christian Communities in the Latin Kingdom of Jerusalem," 206.

33 Johannes Pablitzsch, "Latins in Byzantium and Orthodox Christians," in *A Companion to Byzantium and the West, 900–1204*, ed. Nicolas Drocourt and Sebastian Kolditz (Brill, 2022), 402. On the concept of Byzantinization see Daniel Galadza, *Liturgy and Byzantinization in Jerusalem* (Oxford University Press, 2018).

34 Pablitzsch, "Latins in Byzantium and Orthodox Christians," 402.

CHRISTIANITY IN THE OTTOMAN PERIOD

The Ottoman period was a watershed in the history of Christian communities in the Holy Land. Until the eighteenth century, almost all Christians in the Holy Land belonged to Eastern Christianity, which included Orthodox Christianity and the Oriental, or non-Chalcedonian, churches. Throughout most of the Ottoman period, control of the city was exercised by the Orthodox patriarchate and the Greek-speaking communities, as the Greek patriarch in Constantinople was appointed as the representative—political as well as religious—of all the Orthodox Christians in the Empire. The Armenian patriarch was representative of all the other Christian communities: the Armenians, the Oriental churches, and the Latins.[35] In the eighteenth century, various groups within the Orthodox Church withdrew from their mother churches and united with the Catholic Church and became Roman or Greek Catholic (also known as Melkite)—albeit without giving up their Eastern traditions, customs, and forms of prayer.[36]

Throughout the nineteenth century the Holy Land witnessed a considerable expansion of European influence, characterized by a surge of Christian organizations that established a wide array of missionary institutions, including schools, orphanages, hospitals, and various welfare centers.[37] This growing interest in the region was not solely due to the attraction of its holy sites. It was also driven, especially within Protestant circles, by a fervent missionary zeal aimed at the Jewish population.[38] This zeal was inspired by the desire to fulfill the biblical

[35] Anthony O'Mahony, "The Christian Communities of Jerusalem and the Holy Land: A Historical and Political Survey," in O'Mahony, *Christian Communities of Jerusalem and the Holy Land*, 6–7. On the Armenian Church in Jerusalem see Michael E. Stone, Roberta R. Ervine, and Nira Stone, eds., *The Armenians in Jerusalem and the Holy Land* (Peeters, 2002).

[36] Peter Galadza, "Eastern Catholic Christianity," in *The Blackwell Companion to Eastern Christianity*, ed. Ken Parry (Blackwell, 2007), 291–318.

[37] See Alex Carmel, "Activities of the European Powers in Palestine," *Asian and African Studies* 19 (1985): 43–91; Alan Dowty, "Prelude to the Arab-Israel Conflict: European Penetration of Nineteenth Century Ottoman Palestine," *Contemporary Review of the Middle East* 1 (2014): 3–24; Konstantinos Papastathis, "Missionary Politics in Late Ottoman Palestine: The Stance of the Orthodox Patriarchate of Jerusalem," *Social Sciences and Missions* 32 (2019): 342–60.

[38] Thomas Hummel, "Between Eastern and Western Christendom: The Anglican Presence in Jerusalem," in *The Christian Communities of Jerusalem and the Holy Land*, ed. Anthony O'Mahony (University of Wales Press, 2003), 148.

prophecy to Abraham (Gen 12:1–3) regarding the restoration of the Jews to the Promised Land. Nonetheless, the involvement of European powers in the Holy Land was motivated by factors that extended beyond the religious sphere.

The decline of the Ottoman Empire, which foreshadowed its eventual collapse, coupled with the Holy Land's strategic importance—further amplified by the construction of the Suez Canal in 1869, which created a direct maritime link between South Asia and the Middle East—captured the attention of numerous European superpowers eager to establish their influence in the area. The Tanzimat reforms, initiated in the Ottoman Empire during this era, altered the region's sociopolitical landscape.[39] These reforms recognized the non-Muslim population with equal status within the Empire and permitted foreigners to take up residence, sparking a revival of pilgrimage and a renewed religious interest in the Holy Land and its esteemed sites.

A significant outcome of the Tanzimat reforms was the implementation of the capitulation system. This arrangement allowed European nations to offer protection to their citizens living in the Ottoman Empire by establishing embassies. Such a legal structure not only enhanced the safety and rights of foreigners in the region but also impacted the Holy Land's social fabric, promoting a surge of religious tourism and settlement.[40] The influx of European missionary efforts and the founding of educational, healthcare, and social welfare institutions led to a significant transformation of the local environment, both materially and spiritually. When their attempts to convert Jews and Muslims failed, Catholic mission officials, as well as Protestants (mainly Anglicans and Lutherans), turned to serving the local

39 On the history of the nineteenth-century reforms in Jerusalem under the Ottoman Empire see Bashir Abu-Manneh, "Jerusalem in the Tanzimat Period," *Die Welt des Islam* 30 (1990): 1–44; Haim Gerber, "A New Look at the Tanzimat: The Case of the Province of Jerusalem," in *Palestine in the Late Ottoman Period: Political, Social, and Economic Transformation*, ed. David Kushner (Yad Izhak Ben-Zvi, 1986), 30–45.

40 O'Mahony, "Christian Communities of Jerusalem," 7. See also Yoram Shalit, *The European Powers' Plans Regarding Jerusalem Towards the Middle of the Nineteenth Century* (Klaus-Schwarz-Verlag, 2004); Haim Goren, "Nineteenth Century Jerusalem as a Test Case of European Involvement in the Near East: A Reappraisal," in *The History of Jerusalem: The Late Ottoman Period (1800–1917)*, ed. Israel Bartal and Haim Goren (Yad Izhak Ben-Zvi, 2010), 19–32.

Christian communities and to increasing attempts to convert them.[41] The desire to create a local community led to the establishment of the joint Anglican-Lutheran bishopric in the year 1841. In response, the Latin Patriarchate—which until then had only a Franciscan representation in the region—was reestablished in 1849.[42] Thus the local Christian population became divided between the different communions. Russian involvement in the area also influenced the Orthodox Church. By establishing local education systems, the Russian Orthodox supported the Arab Orthodox efforts to create a national church which was not under Greek control.[43]

Thus, while the Ottoman period could be considered a time when the Jerusalem community was at least primarily united under the Orthodox Patriarch, in the mid-twentieth century the Orthodox community was struggling with internal tensions and contradictions between the Arab local community and the Greek leadership, and—at the same time—lost its majority among the local Christian population. A prominent example of this trend is the case of the Latin Catholic Church. In the middle of the nineteenth century, the community numbered only a few thousand souls, but at the beginning of the twentieth century it had grown to over twenty thousand.[44] As a result, the Christian communities in the Holy Land are divided today between more than fifteen different churches. The largest are the Orthodox Church, Roman-Greek Catholic, and Latin Catholic. Other communities, such as the Coptic or Syrian, number only a few dozen or hundreds of believers.[45]

41 On Catholic Church efforts to convert the local Christian communities see Daphne Tsimhoni, "The Latin Patriarchate of Jerusalem, from the Middle of the Nineteenth Century to the Present Day—Institutional and Social Aspects," *The New East* 24 (1992): 114; Pierre Medebielle, *The Diocese of the Latin Patriarchate* (Jerusalem, 1963), 33–34. On the Protestant Churches see Julius Richter, *A History of Protestant Missions in the Near East* (AMS, 1910).

42 Colbi, *History of the Christian Presence*, 94; Medebielle, *Diocese of the Latin Patriarchate*, 33–34.

43 Sotiris Rousso, "The Greek Orthodox Patriarchate and Community of Jerusalem: Church, State, and Identity," in O'Mahony, *Christian Communities of Jerusalem*, 41–42.

44 Medebielle, *Diocese of the Latin Patriarchate*, 33–34.

45 See Daniel Rossing, "Microcosm and Multiple Minorities: The Christian Communities in Israel," *Israel Yearbook & Almanac* 53 (1999): 28–43.

One of the most important implications of the Ottoman period was the protected person (*dhimmi*) and millet-structure of the Ottoman-society. This structure used religious association to determine membership in the core of the state, causing sectarianism within society.[46] During the British Mandate period, sectarianism was a significant aspect of the political landscape. The British rulers encouraged the Christian communities, which comprised about 10 percent of the population, to form political representation as a religious minority.[47] The sectarianism that arose during this time has had a lasting impact on the national and political identity of Palestinian Christians, placing them in contrast to Muslims.

CHRISTIANS IN THE STATE OF ISRAEL AND THE PALESTINIAN AUTHORITY TODAY

The Christian community in Israel today is a minority group: according to official data, Christian Arabs living in the state of Israel currently number about 139,000, less than two percent of the general population.[48] Even in the territories of the Palestinian Authority, Christians make up a minor portion of the total population, and their number is estimated at 40,000—1.5 percent of the total Palestinian population.[49]

Apart from the Arab-Christian communities whose members were natives of the land, the fact that the Holy Land is a constant magnet for pilgrims from abroad results in a relatively large group of clergy

[46] See Bruce Masters, *Christians and Jews in the Ottoman Arab World* (Cambridge University Press, 2001); Michelle Campos, "From the 'Ottoman Nation' to 'Hyphenated Ottomans': Reflections on the Multicultural Imperial Citizenship at the End of Empire," *Ab Imperio* 1 (2017): 163–81.

[47] See Laura Robson, *Colonialism and Christianity in Mandate Palestine* (University of Texas Press, 2011); Daphne Tsimhoni, "The Status of the Arab Christians Under the British Mandate in Palestine," *Middle Eastern Studies* 20 (1984): 166–92.

[48] "Christmas 2021—Christians in Israel," Israeli Central Bureau of Statistics, December 2021, https://www.cbs.gov.il; Bernard Sabella, "Comparing Palestinian Christians on Society and Politics: Context and Religion in Israel and Palestine" (paper presented at the meeting of the Middle East Studies Association, San Francisco, November 2001), 2.

[49] David Neuhaus, *Je vous écris de la Terre Sainte* (Bayard Presse, 2017), 87–89; "Migration of Palestinian Christians: Drivers and Means of Combating It," Palestinian Center for Policy and Survey Research, 2020, https://www.arabbarometer.org/2020/06/migration-of-palestinian-christians-drivers-and-means-of-combating-it/.

from around the world who serve in the Holy Land.[50] These church members—clergy and members of religious orders—live in monasteries and churches scattered throughout the land, carry out religious activities in the local churches and holy sites, serve the pilgrims, or engage in religious and spiritual activities of prayer and study.

In recent years, new members have joined the local Christian body: migrant workers and asylum seekers, as well as a few thousand new immigrants from the Soviet Union who immigrated to Israel under the Law of Return. They have helped fill churches and houses of prayer in the heart of Jewish cities, and especially in greater Tel Aviv-Jaffa. These Christians are integrated in Jewish society and work with and for Jews; some even send their children to schools that are part of the Jewish education system.

The complicated political situation in the region has sparked a great deal of tension in the broader Christian community in the Holy Land, which feels the need to define its position regarding the IPC. Most local Christians see themselves as Palestinian-Arabs, and some of them even take an active part in the national Palestinian struggle.[51] At the beginning of the twentieth century, the Arab national movement was headed by Christian Arabs, mostly Orthodox, who saw their national identity as being shared with their Muslim brothers.[52] The Palestinian Christian communities have undergone frequent changes in the definition of their identity in recent decades, arising from their sensitive position vis-à-vis the Jewish majority on the one hand and the Muslim on the other.

The ideologies promoted by the Zionist movement, gaining momentum since the late nineteenth century and culminating in the establishment of the state of Israel, have brought to the forefront the issue of self-determination for Christian Arabs in the region (to be elaborated in the next chapter). This development introduced a new layer of complexity to their status, particularly as the sociopolitical landscape shifted dramatically with the emergence of Israel. The transformation of Jewish communities into the controlling majority and the relegation of the Palestinian population, including Christian Arabs, to

50 Palestinian Center for Policy and Survey Research, "Migration of Palestinian Christians."

51 O'Mahony, "Christian Communities of Jerusalem," 17–18.

52 See Albert Hourani, *Arabic Thought in the Liberal Age, 1798–1939* (Cambridge University Press, 1962), 260–324.

minority status, has deeply impacted the dynamics of identity, governance, and rights within the region. Since the establishment of the state of Israel, Christian Arabs have tended to define themselves as a "minority within a minority"—an Arab minority within Jewish society and a Christian minority within Muslim-Arab society.[53] According to the sociologist Lewis Wirth, a "minority group" is a community distinguished by physical or cultural traits from the broader society in which they reside, experiencing differential or unequal treatment, and thus perceiving themselves as a collective subject to discrimination.[54] In the state of Israel, the separation between the groups is even greater due to its unique nature—first, as an essentially Jewish state where the Arab minority is a nonnational minority; second, as an ethnic state that gives constitutional validity to every group, when every person in Israel is obliged to belong to a religious community that has constitutional authority regarding their status (concerning marriage, divorce, wills, etc.).[55] While Christians share with the Muslims their language, culture, and the fact of being a non-Jewish minority in a Jewish state, they are closer to the Jewish majority in terms of education and adaptation to modernity. In a survey conducted by the sociologist Sammy Smooha in 2004, it was found that 50 percent of Christians in Israel defined their identity according to their citizenship (Israeli), 35.6 percent according to nationality (Arab), and only 15 percent according to religion (Christian). These data provide another perspective on the difficulty in self-definition of a group that needs to define itself via two majority groups that differ not only in national factors but also in religious ones. The Palestinian Christian communities are also grappling with the challenge of defining their identity, as they struggle to balance their strong connections to the Western world and Christianity with their place within the Palestinian Arab culture and society.[56]

[53] Elias Chacour, *Blood Brothers* (Chosen Books, 1984), ix; Gabriel Horenczyk and Salim Munayer, "Acculturation Orientations Toward Two Majority Groups: The Case of Palestinian Arab Christian Adolescents in Israel," *Journal of Cross-Cultural Psychology* 38 (2007): 83.

[54] Louis Wirth, "The Problem of Minority Groups," in *The Science of Man in the World Crisis*, ed. Ralph Linton (Columbia University Press, 1945), 347.

[55] See David Sassoon, "The Israel Legal System," *American Journal of Comparative Law* 16 (1968): 405–15.

[56] George Sabra, "Two Ways of Being a Christian in the Muslim Context of the Middle East," *Islam and Christian-Muslim Relations* 17 (2006): 44.

The distinction created between the Palestinian citizens within the borders of the Palestinian Authority and the Palestinian citizens of Israel has forced the Palestinian Christian community to deal with another element of identity: civil affiliation. This distinction led, on the one hand, to tensions between the two groups that were separated from each other, and on the other hand, to the strengthening of the Palestinian identity of Christian citizens of Israel, who sought to maintain their connection to the Palestinian nation and culture.[57]

Not all Christians in Israel embraced the consolidation of Palestinian national identity. A minority of Israeli Christians chose to identify as Israeli, distancing themselves from Arab Palestinian identity. They oppose the definition of Christians in Israel as Arabs or Palestinians and claim that they belong to the Armenian ethnicity.[58] This group is known for its support of the state of Israel and provoked many reactions when it proposed the recruitment of Arabic-speaking Christians to the Israeli Defense Force, something perceived by many Christians as a real threat, if not treason. An example of this can be found in a letter issued by the Latin Patriarchate in 2014, which calls on Christians to retract support for these concepts.[59] In the letter the Patriarchate calls the few Christian Palestinian Arabs in Israel who support this idea to "come back to your senses. Do not harm your people, because of idle promises and personal egoistic gain." The letter states that what Israel really requires is Christians who embrace the teachings of Jesus, particularly the call to be peacemakers.

The discourse that the Christians brought to the nationalist movements in the early and mid–twentieth century was primarily secular in nature, emphasizing ideas of pan-Arabism and the blurring of religious differences. It can be argued that this was a reflection of the local Orthodox tendency, which was predominantly influenced by Russian

57 Adi Mana et al., "On Both Sides of the Fence: Perceptions of Collective Narratives and Identity Strategies Among Palestinians in Israel and in the West Bank," *Mind & Society* 14 (2015): 73.

58 See Rima Farah, "The Rise of a Christian Aramaic Nationality in Modern Israel," *Israel Studies* 26 (2021): 1–28.

59 "Recognition of the 'Arameans': An Attempt to Divide Palestinian Christians?" *The Justice and Peace Commission, Assembly of the Catholic Ordinaries of the Holy Land*, September 2014, https://aocts.org/justice-and-peace-commission/recognition-of-the-arameans-an-attempt-to-divide-palestinian.

ideology in the late nineteenth and early twentieth centuries.[60] It was only during the First Intifada, at the end of the 1980s, that Christian theologians began to take an active part in the conflict and confronted the traditional claim that the state of Israel is the fulfillment of the divine promise anchored in the Holy Scriptures.

Throughout the ages, Christians in the Holy Land have often found themselves caught between majority and minority groups, and between peripheral and central interests. The centrality of Jerusalem and the importance of the holy places only emphasized the peripherality of the local communities, at the mercy of regional superpowers. Time and again local Christian communities were shaken by forces invading the Holy Land. The history of Christians in the Holy Land reveals vast interreligious and intracultural tensions and contradictions: between East and West, between contesting monotheistic religions—Christian, Jewish, and Muslim—and between various Christian denominations. This entanglement of identities has been the catalyst for an emerging Palestinian theology.

Palestinian Christian theologians strive to construct their identity in the face of the majority groups that surround them, both Jewish and Muslim, and they seek to establish their particularized identity in a universal, Western church. Likewise, each Christian community in the Holy Land aims to tell its own story and maintain its culture. These are formidable tasks indeed.

60 See Hanna Kildani, *Modern Christianity in the Holy Land* (Authorhouse, 2010), 146–54.

1
Political Conflict and the Development of PCT

INTRODUCTION

This chapter examines the emergence of PCT in the 1980s and traces the circumstances that contributed to PCT's transformation of Christian theology as it pertains to the Holy Land, thereby sharpening our understanding of the motivations that lay behind PCT and the methods of discourse it employs. The genesis of PCT was not solely rooted in a theological crisis, contrary to the common narrative presented by Palestinian theologians. Rather, it emerged significantly from an identity crisis within the community. While shifts in Christian theological thought certainly provided a fertile ground for the development of PCT, its inception in the late 1980s was primarily driven by internal processes and changes within Palestinian society. This perspective does not overlook the intrinsic dynamics of theological evolution but aims to highlight a particular trajectory of influence: the movement from social reality to ideology and theology, while also acknowledging the reciprocal influence of theological and ideological developments on social reality. This approach underscores the complex interplay between societal changes and theological responses, positioning the emergence of PCT as a multifaceted phenomenon deeply intertwined with the broader sociopolitical and identity-based challenges facing the Palestinian community. For this reason, I treat PCT as a "contextual theology," that is, a theology based on a local context that considers the social, historical, and cultural milieu.[1]

In a paper written in Arabic, Evangelical Lutheran Palestinian Pastor Mitri Raheb (b. 1962) posits that the roots of Palestinian theology can be traced back to the 1930s.[2] This period marked a critical juncture for local Christians as they first faced the political ramifications and theological challenges posed by the burgeoning Zionist movement. Central to this theological crisis was the Balfour declaration in 1917, a political statement issued by British Foreign Secretary Arthur Balfour with profound theological undertones, which introduced a novel Christian interpretation of biblical promises casting the Holy Land as the exclusive homeland of the Jewish people. Raheb emphasizes that these challenges intensified after 1948, following the establishment of the state of Israel. This event propelled local Palestinian Christians into a deeper theological dilemma, as they were forced to navigate the complexities of their faith in light of the new geopolitical realities that redefined their historical claims and spiritual connection to the land. The Anglican Palestinian pastor, Naim Ateek (b. 1937), also emphasized this point: "The establishment of the state of Israel was a seismic tremor of enormous magnitude that has shaken the very foundation of their beliefs."[3]

At the heart of the profound upheaval experienced by the Palestinian Christian community is a hermeneutical dilemma, or perhaps more accurately a contested narrative stemming from the fact that both Christians and Jews draw upon the same biblical texts to ground their historical identities and interpret their collective destinies. This shared reliance on the Bible for spiritual and historical validation has led to conflicting interpretations and claims, particularly poignant in the context of the IPC. Raheb explained that the tragedy of the Palestinians is not only that they lost their *land* but that they also lost their *narrative*. This loss of narrative has precipitated the need among Palestinian Christians to develop a theology that weaves biblical history into the fabric of their own people's history, asserting that the spiritual

1 Stephen Bevans, *Models of Contextual Theology* (Orbis, 1992), 1.

2 Mitri Raheb, *The Arab Christians and the Matter of the Nation: The Variables of the Context and the Periods* (Diyar, 2013), 28.

3 Naim Ateek, *Justice and Only Justice: A Palestinian Theology of Liberation* (Orbis, 1989), 77.

patriarchs—Abraham and his descendants—are not just figures of religious significance but are also their ancestral forefathers. This theological endeavor is not merely an academic exercise but a profound reclamation of identity. It represents an attempt to affirm their historical presence in the land and to reinterpret biblical narratives in a way that resonates with their experiences and aspirations.[4]

The theological crisis presented by the Establishment of the state of Israel, upheld by Christians' support of the gathering of the Jews in Israel, based on their claim to the land of Palestine, had two important repercussions for Palestinian Christians.[5] The first (and perhaps the most dramatic) was the distancing of both Palestinian clergy and laity from the Old Testament.[6] Mitri Raheb himself, in his description of the theological crisis he experienced during his theological studies in Germany, clearly points to this phenomenon: "The God that I know since my childhood as love had suddenly become a God who confiscated land, waged 'holy wars', and destroyed whole people."[7]

The second repercussion of the theological crisis was that Palestinian Christians started to distance themselves from European Christian theology. This alienation derived mainly from their disdain toward European theologians, who, far from condemning the Zionist reading of the Bible, largely approved it—either out of guilt related to their churches' antisemitic pasts that culminated in the Holocaust, or out of a genuine belief in such a reading. The significance of this distancing became apparent with the recognition that a new theological approach, one that would meet the theological challenges that the new political circumstances posed for Palestinian Christians, was required to replace the no-longer-useful European version. Hence Mitri Raheb, for example, declares in his later writings that he is abandoning European theological writing for a Palestinian theology or, as he phrased

4 Mitri Raheb, "Towards a New Hermeneutics of Liberation: A Palestinian Christian Perspective," in *The Biblical Text in the Context of Occupation: Towards a New Hermeneutics of Liberation*, ed. Mitri Raheb (Diyar, 2012), 26.

5 See, for example, Naim Ateek, introduction to *Challenging Christian Zionism: Theology, Politics and the Israel-Palestine Conflict*, ed. Naim Ateek, Ceder Duaybis, and Maurin Tobin (Melisende, 2005), 13; Yohanna Katanacho, *The Land of Christ: A Palestinian Cry* (Pickwick, 2013), 11–13; Mitri Raheb, *Faith in the Face of Empire: The Bible Through Palestinian Eyes* (Orbis, 2014), 30–33.

6 Ateek, *Justice and Only Justice*, 77.

7 Raheb, *I Am a Palestinian Christian* (Fortress, 1994), 56.

it: "It is time that we put the organs aside and take out our drums."[8] Naim Ateek as well, even if his style is less declarative, refers to this issue at the beginning of his book. Ateek describes the need to create a Palestinian theology in response to European theology and dedicates several chapters to the problems of European theology, and particularly Christian Zionist theology.[9]

I contend that PCT emerged only in the late 1980s and early 1990s. This period marked a significant juncture for Palestinian Christians as they navigated the complexities of defining their identity amid the expanding influence of Islamic ideologies. The development of PCT during this time can be seen as an attempt to articulate a distinct Christian Palestinian identity that engages with and differentiates itself from the dominant Islamic narrative, seeking to carve out a space for Christian voices and perspectives within the broader tapestry of Palestinian national identity.

In the late 1980s, theological writings from a distinctively Palestinian perspective began to flourish. In this period, a growing number of Palestinian theologians began to refer to the IPC from a Christian Palestinian perspective. They did so in conferences, in books, and in articles, and notably via the establishment of three new research centers devoted to the subject: the Al-Liqa' Center, the Sabbel Center, and the Diyar Center. I will elaborate on this shortly.

For the first time, PCT confronted the new challenges raised by Zionist ideologies, especially Christian Zionism. To be sure, in earlier periods there were church leaders in the Holy Land who referenced the political situation, the implications of the establishment of the state of Israel, or the relationship between biblical Israel and modern Israel and its impact on the Palestinians. However, these church leaders were not Palestinians, having originated from various countries in the Arab world or from western countries.[10] Furthermore, their writings maintained a clear distinction between political and religious stances. In his PhD dissertation, David Neuhaus analyzed the political role of the Christian cleric in Palestinian Christian society in Israel from 1948 until the 1990s. Neuhaus's study shows that there are several cases in which Christian clerics intervened in political matters (something that

8 Raheb, "Towards a New Hermeneutics of Liberation," 27.

9 Ateek, *Justice and Only Justice*, 60–71.

10 In chapter 2 I elaborate on various theological responses to the establishment of the State of Israel in Europe and in Arab Christianity.

has become more common over the years). However, he claims that their political involvement reflected the fact that their roles as religious leaders sometimes put them in a position of serving as community representatives and was not motivated by their religious roles as such.[11]

In arguing that PCT began only in the late 1980s and early 1990s, I draw on the observation of the Latin Palestinian theologian Rafiq Khoury (b. 1943). While Khoury is aware of the theological difficulty for Palestinian Christians, described by Raheb and Ateek, in common readings of the Bible, he does not view this as a crisis for Palestinian Christian society in general, and certainly not as one that began before the establishment of the state of Israel. According to Khoury, this religious crisis began only when several Palestinian clerics from various churches, such as Raheb and Ateek, acquired their theological education in the West, where they encountered biblical interpretation that was used to justify Israeli policy.[12] As a result, some felt compelled to develop a theology that would respond to the approaches to which they were exposed in the West.[13] Thus, Khoury believes, the push to develop a new interpretation of the biblical narrative was more a response to Western theology than a solution to a theological crisis that challenged the Palestinian community. Indeed, Khoury's explanation matches Raheb's own personal case, on which Raheb expands in his first book, where he describes his personal crisis of faith in meeting with German readings of the Bible at a seminary in Germany. He explains how the theologian's astonishment at the Holocaust, alongside the victories of the modern state of Israel over Arab nations, leads to an uncritical and ahistorical conflation of contemporary Israel with biblical Israel by some Westerners.[14]

It seems that in Khoury's view, the issue of biblical interpretation is secondary to the larger issue of the identity crisis of Palestinian Christians that began in the early 1970s. Khoury posits that the growth of

[11] David Neuhaus, "Between Quiescence and Arousal: The Political Functions of Religion—A Case Study of the Arab Minority in Israel; 1948–1990" (PhD diss., Hebrew University of Jerusalem, 1991).

[12] Rafiq Khoury, "Palestinian Contextual Theology: A General Survey," in *Christian Theology in the Palestinian Context*, ed. Rafiq Khoury and Rainer Zimmer-Winkel (AphorismA, 2019), 18.

[13] See Edward Norman, *Christianity and the World Order* (Oxford University Press, 1979), 43–53.

[14] Raheb, *I Am a Palestinian Christian*, 58.

the Palestinian resistance movement prompted Palestinian Christians to explore their place within both the broader Palestinian community and the resistance itself. He narrates their journey of self-discovery, initiated by introspective questions: "Who are we? What is the meaning of our presence in the Holy Land? What is our identity? . . . What does it mean to be an Arab Christian here and now? Where do we come from? What are our roots?"[15]

Is it important to consider the distinction between the two ways of understanding the Palestinian Christian theological crisis, so that we can better appreciate the end goals that result from the two approaches (characterizing the crisis as an issue of national identity versus one of biblical narrative). On the one hand, PCT may be seen as an intracommunal quest to shape a Palestinian Christian identity within the greater Palestinian national struggle; on the other, PCT may be seen as an outward-facing effort to create a Palestinian narrative to counteract certain pro-Zionist interpretations that exist in the Western world.

THE DEVELOPMENT OF A PALESTINIAN CONTEXTUAL THEOLOGY

In the late 1980s, increasing numbers of theologians who defined themselves as Palestinians began to formulate a theology that refers to the realities of Palestinian Christian life. One of the documents that demarcates the appearance of this phenomenon was published by the heads of the churches in Jerusalem on June 22, 1989. In this document, for the first time, the heads of the local churches united to issue an official response to the political events in the Holy Land, following the first Intifada, and notes the suffering of their people in the West Bank and the Gaza Strip: "We, the Heads of the Christian Communities in Jerusalem, would like to express in all honesty and clarity that we take our stand with truth and justice against all forms of injustice and oppression."[16] The document continues with a statement of solidarity with the suffering, the oppressed, the refugees, and the victims of injustice.

The release of this document marks a pivotal and paradigmatic moment in the evolution of Palestinian Christian theologi-

15 Khoury, "Palestinian Contextual Theology," 18.

16 Statement by the Heads of Christian Communities in Jerusalem, Jerusalem, January 22, 1988; quoted in Melanie May, *Jerusalem Testament: Palestinian Christians Speak, 1988–2008* (Eerdmans, 2010), 20–22.

cal discourse concerning the Holy Land and the state of Israel. This significance is underscored by the fact that no previous document of this nature—endorsed by the heads of the churches in Jerusalem and directly engaging in the political reality—has ever been published before. There are several factors and circumstances that led to the writing of this historical document and the development of PCT in parallel. For simplicity, I divide these factors into internal processes concerning Palestinian society and the IPC on one side, and broader processes related to global Western Christianity on the other (to be elaborated in the next chapter).

In the following discussion, I provide an overview of the various internal factors that led to the development of PCT in the late 1980s and early 1990s.

The Rise of Palestinian Resistance Movements and the Growth of a Palestinian Identity

Following the 1948 war and the subsequent establishment of the state of Israel, the fabric of Palestinian society underwent a significant and enduring transformation. The result was a bifurcation of the Palestinian community into two distinct groups: those who came under the governance of the newly formed state of Israel, and were subsequently granted Israeli citizenship, and those who became refugees, living under the jurisdiction and often in the refugee camps of neighboring Arab states. This division marked the beginning of a complex and multifaceted struggle for identity and sovereignty that continues to influence the Palestinian narrative.

In the 1950s and into the early 1960s, the movement for pan-Arabization gained momentum among Palestinians, as well as across the broader Arab world.[17] This movement, which advocated for Arab unity as a strategic and ideological means to counter Israel and its Western allies, attracted many Palestinians to its cause. Pan-Arab organizations and parties, espousing the ideal of a unified Arab front, became a significant force in the political landscape of the Middle East, promising a collective effort to reclaim Palestinian land and rights through the solidarity of Arab nations. The rise of pan-Arabism had a profound impact on Palestinian identity. As the Palestinian cause was increasingly framed

[17] Helga Baumgarten, "The Three Faces/Phases of Palestinian Nationalism, 1948–2005," *Journal of Palestine Studies* 34 (2005): 28–29.

within the context of pan-Arab unity and struggle, the distinctiveness of Palestinian identity began to blur.[18] The Arabization of the Palestinian issue meant that the struggle for Palestinian self-determination was often subsumed under the broader agenda of Arab nationalism. This shift had far-reaching implications for how Palestinians perceived their own identity and struggle, as well as how they were viewed by the international community and within the Arab world itself.

Among the Palestinian pan-Arab groups that emerged in response to the geopolitical shifts in the Middle East was the Movement of Arab Nationalists (*harakat al-qaumiyyin al-'arab*), founded by George Habash (1926–2008), a Palestinian Christian from Lydda (Lod). Habash became a prominent figure in the pan-Arab movement, advocating for the unity and modernization of Arab nations as crucial strategies to counter and ultimately defeat Israel.[19] This group was deeply influenced by the ideology of the Syrian Christian intellectual Constantin Zurayk (1909–2000), who emphasized the necessity of modernization and unity among Arab nations for their empowerment and success against external adversaries, particularly Israel. Most of the leaders of this group were intellectual Christians. There are two main reasons for that. First, their ideas of modernization and nationalism were directly influenced by European thinking, to which Christians were more exposed. Second, the emphasis on a secular state allowed the creation of an inclusive society in which Christians, as members of a religious minority, could partake equally.[20]

This period also witnessed significant political and sociological developments, such as the formulation of the Palestinian National Charter (*al-Mithaq al-Qawmi al-Filastini*) in 1964.[21] This document is noteworthy for its almost complete omission of references to Palestinian and Muslim identities, focusing instead on the broader Arab identity. The phrase "We the Palestinian Arabs" is recurrent throughout the document, underscoring the pan-Arab perspective that characterized

[18] Manuel Hassassian, "Historical Dynamics Shaping Palestinian National Identity," *Palestine-Israel Journal* 8 (2001): 50–60.

[19] Baumgarten, "Three Faces/Phases of Palestinian Nationalism," 27–28.

[20] Helga Baumgarten, "The Politicization of Muslim-Christian Relations in the Palestinian National Movement," in *Islam, Judaism, and the Political Role of Religions in the Middle East*, ed. John Bunzl (University Press of Florida, 2004), 87.

[21] The full document can be found online at https://www.pac-usa.org/the_palestinian_charter.htm.

the movement. Furthermore, the first paragraph explicitly states, "Palestine is an Arab homeland bound by strong Arab national ties to the rest of the Arab Countries and which together form the great Arab homeland," highlighting the emphasis on Arab nationalism and unity.

Since the mid-1960s and, more dramatically, following the 1967 war, there has been a clear shift in Palestinian self-determination.[22] In the wake of the defeat that the pan-Arab forces suffered, the pan-Arab ideology was subjected to serious questioning for its failure to deliver a win for the Palestinians. Eventually, pan-Arab identity was replaced by a Palestinian national identity that significantly crystallized after the war.[23] The most salient result of this shift was the Fatah movement's takeover of the Palestinian Liberation Organization (PLO) following the war.

Yasser Arafat (1929–2004) had established Fatah in Kuwait almost a decade earlier, in 1958–59. Its main emphasis was on what Arafat called "The Armed Struggle" (*al-Kifah al-Musalah*): the notion that occupied Palestine could be liberated only by force.[24] The PLO, headed by the Fatah movement, dictated a new Palestinian national ideology that called for the Palestinian people to participate in the Palestinian struggle for the liberation of their occupied land.[25] In the decade that followed the 1967 war, under the leadership of the PLO, almost all Palestinians adopted a Palestinian identity and a sense of national affiliation.[26] Embracing the concept of the armed struggle in the occupied

[22] For studies on Palestinian citizens of Israel see, for example, Eli Rekhes, "The Arabs of Israel After 1967: The Worsening of the Orientation Problem," *Skirot* 45 (1976): 9–56; Eli Rekhes, *The Arab Village in Israel: A Renewed Political-National Center* (Markaz Dayan, 1985); Mahmoud Mi'ari, "Traditionalism and Political Identity of Arabs in Israel," *Journal of Asian and African Studies* 22 (1987): 33–44; Sammy Smooha, "The Arab Minority in Israel: Radicalization or Politicization?" *Studies in Contemporary Jewry* 5 (1989): 59–88. For studies on Palestinians in the Palestinian territories see Mahmoud Mi'ari, "Political Behavior of University Students in Palestine," *Dirasat: 'Olum Insaniyya* 23 (1996): 278–98 and Mahmoud Mi'ari, "Transformation of Collective Identity in Palestine," *Journal of Asian and African Studies* 44 (2009): 579–98.

[23] Baumgarten, "Three Faces/Phases of Palestinian Nationalism," 30–31.

[24] Anat Kurz, *Fatah and the Politics of Violence: The Institutionalization of a Popular Struggle* (Sussex Academic Press, 2005), 6–31; Yezid Sayigh, *Armed Struggle and the Search for State: The Palestinian National Movement, 1949–1993* (Clarendon & Institute for Palestine Studies, 1997), 92–80.

[25] Mi'ari, "Transformation of Collective Identity," 582.

[26] Mahmoud Mi'ari, "Development of Political Identity of Palestinians in Israel," *Majallat al-Ólum al-Ijtimaéyya* 14 (1986): 215–33.

territories under the auspices of Fatah, various guerrilla groups began operations.[27] The Palestinians living in Israel also joined the national struggle to a large extent, either via political parties or through popular demonstrations and demands for recognition of their right to a sovereign Palestinian state.[28] The PLO was accepted throughout the world as the sole legitimate representative of the Palestinian people, allowing the Palestinians—for the first time—to represent themselves in official international organizations such as the United Nations, and to mobilize international public opinion to promote their cause.[29]

Palestinian Christians were important partners in the Fatah movement, albeit no longer in leadership positions.[30] Although Fatah had more prominent Islamic characteristics than previous Palestinian movements—some of its founders were members of the Muslim Brotherhood—the official political aspiration was still to establish a secular Palestinian state.[31] Notably, even as secular nationalism played a major role in the Middle East in the mid-twentieth century, and especially within the pan-Arab movement, Islam was central at the grassroots level. After the Arab defeat in the 1967 war, the voices critical of the modernist approach—Western and secular in character—became louder. Consequently, the idea of secular nationalism lost its appeal, as it was perceived as an attempt to introduce Western ideas alien to Arab culture. Instead, many in the Arab world called for a return to Islam, as both a religious and political organizing force.[32]

Beginning in the late 1970s, Islam steadily gained power in the West Bank and Gaza Strip. The establishment of the Hamas movement in 1987 was a result of this trend.[33] The return to religion among Arabs in Israel was also a broad phenomenon.[34] The encounter with the Arabs of the West Bank and the Gaza Strip—which was facilitated by Israeli occupation—opened a window to a variety of religious lifestyles that

27 Sayigh, *Armed Struggle*, 195–202.

28 Smooha, "Arab Minority in Israel," 62–80.

29 Baumgarten, "Three Faces/Phases of Palestinian Nationalism," 36.

30 Baumgarten, "Politicization of Muslim-Christian Relations," 88.

31 Baumgarten, "Politicization of Muslim-Christian Relations," 88–91.

32 Neuhaus, *Between Quiescence and Arousal*, 144–46.

33 Lisa Taraki, "The Islamic Resistance Movement in the Palestinian Uprising," *Middle East Report* 156 (1989): 30–32.

34 Eli Rekhes, "The Islamic Movement in Israel and Its Relation to Political Islam," in *The Jewish Arab Split in Israel*, ed. Rut Gavizon and Dafnah Haker (Israel Democracy Institute, 2000), 272.

had been unfamiliar to many Israeli Arab Muslims. In addition, the renewed access of Israeli Jews and Arabs to their joint holy sites in Hebron and Jerusalem, and the struggles that arose between Jews and Muslims over these places, also served to bolster the religious faith of many Israeli Arabs.[35] Social studies described a dramatic return to religion among Israeli Muslims in the first half of the 1980s.[36] This return to religion resulted in the fading and eventual disappearance of the idea of a secular state. In the Palestinian Declaration of Independence, proclaimed by the Palestine National Council in Algiers in November 1988, there was no longer any mention of a secular state.[37]

The abandonment of secularism, along with the development of the Palestinian national movement in the spirit of Islam, had a crucial impact on the Christian community. Muslim movements gradually became more and more central to the national struggle and in the formation of Palestinian identity. Henceforth, Palestinian nationalism was expressed in active participation in the political struggle, which, in turn, gradually took on the characteristics of a religious, Islamic war. The Christian concern was not whether Christians are part of the Palestinian people, but how they might rise to the expectations of the Palestinian people at large by doing their part for the national cause.[38] This concern paralleled that of the Muslims. The Islamic Movement (and especially Hamas) emphasized that the Christians in Palestine are part of the Palestinian people. As Hamas declared, "Hamas undertakes advocacy for the cause of the Palestinian people without discrimination between religious, ethnic groups or sects."[39]

The escalating influence of Islam within Palestinian society marked a significant turning point for Palestinian Christians eager to partake in the national struggle. It became increasingly clear that political factions previously advocating for the creation of a secular Palestinian state were losing traction, as their ideological stance no longer resonated with the prevailing sentiments of Palestinian society. This shift posed a dilemma for Palestinian Christians. If they wished to contribute to the national cause while distancing themselves from a liberal secular approach—often criticized as a foreign, Western imposition—they

35 Rekhes, "Islamic Movement in Israel," 272.
36 Smooha, "Arab Minority in Israel," 68.
37 Baumgarten, "Politicization of Muslim-Christian Relations," 91.
38 Baumgarten, "Three Faces/Phases of Palestinian Nationalism," 43.
39 As cited in Baumgarten, "Politicization of Muslim-Christian Relations," 95.

needed to explore alternative avenues of engagement. The emergence of PCT presented a novel solution to this challenge. By articulating a theological perspective that emphasized the Christian community's rootedness in the land and history of Palestine, PCT provided a framework through which Palestinian Christians could assert their commitment to the national struggle. This theological approach allowed for a dialogue that was pro-Palestinian, fostering understanding and solidarity with Western audiences, while also ensuring that the religious dimensions of the Palestinian identity were respected and preserved.[40] PCT hoped to prevent two outcomes of the development of Palestinian identity, succinctly summarized by Raheb: "It is an alternative both to escaping into religious fundamentalism and to discarding religion for secularism."[41]

Muslim-Christian Relations in Palestinian Society

In order to understand the implications of the development of Palestinian identity in the 1980s and onward on Christian society, and the subsequent growth of PCT, we must first review the relations between Christians and Muslims in Palestinian society, the changes that Palestinian society has undergone in general, and the rise of the Islamic movements that increased the tension between those two groups in particular. The Palestinian theologian Geries Khoury, the founder of the Al-Liqa' Center in Bethlehem in 1982, addressed these issues in an article on the importance of Christian-Muslim dialogue. He argued that the rise of Islamic movements in the Holy Land has significantly underscored the importance of fostering dialogue between Christians and Muslims. Such dialogue is crucial for cooperation, mutual understanding, reinforcing national unity, and addressing the challenges and concerns of the nation and its people.[42]

Its importance notwithstanding, the sensitive issue of Muslim-Christian relations is not easily examined. If we rely only on the writings of Palestinian Christian theologians, it seems as if Muslims

40 Peter Lodberg, "Palestinian Theology Between Construction and Identification: A Comparative Analysis of the Theology of Naim Stifan Ateek and Mitri Raheb," in *The Biblical Text in the Context of Occupation: Towards a New Hermeneutics of Liberation*, ed. Mitri Raheb (Diyar, 2012), 81–83.

41 Raheb, *I Am a Palestinian Christian*, 43.

42 Geries Khoury, "Christian-Muslim Dialogue in the Holy Land," in Khoury and Zimmer-Winkel, *Christian Theology in the Palestinian Context*, 197–98.

and Christians in Palestine live in harmony or, at worst, the issue of Muslim-Christian relations is not as pressing as the political reality, the urgency of which demands immediate attention.[43]

Historian Noah Haiduc-Dale presents a compelling argument regarding the influential role of local Christian leadership in shaping Christian-Muslim relations in Palestine.[44] Haiduc-Dale's analysis suggests that the emphasis on a shared national identity over religious differences has been a crucial factor in fostering a sense of unity and solidarity among Palestinians, regardless of their faith. By prioritizing their Palestinian Arab identity, local Christian leaders have effectively navigated the complex dynamics of interreligious relations, highlighting the common ground and shared experiences that bind the Christian and Muslim communities together.

Further supporting this perspective, Rafiq Khoury elucidates the nature of these good relations by pointing to the shared experiences of "suffering, struggle, and aspiration" that unite Palestinian Christians and Muslims.[45] Khoury's observation underscores the idea that the challenges faced by Palestinians as a whole, including occupation, displacement, and the quest for self-determination, transcend religious divides and serve as a unifying force for the community. In the same way, the former Latin Patriarch of Jerusalem Michel Sabbah (b. 1933) opined in a letter to his community that there are other matters more essential to Palestinians than Muslim-Christian tensions. These challenges must be surmounted to attain the shared national goal: "The Muslim faithful is your fellow citizen. You are bound together by the same future, the same country, and the same heritage."[46] Sabbah calls on his community not to allow everyday conflicts to weaken their sense of togetherness or obscure their shared connection to their homeland, heritage, and culture.

Relations between Christians and Muslims in Palestine are better than in other places in the Middle East. But we must analyze this relation critically and take into account the political and social tensions between the groups, and the political importance of creating

43 Baumgarten, "Politicization of Muslim-Christian Relations," 83.

44 Noah Haiduc-Dale, "Rejecting Sectarianism: Palestinian Christians' Role in Muslim-Christian Relations," *Islam and Christian-Muslim Relations* 26 (2015): 75–88.

45 Rafiq Khoury, "Palestinian Contextual Theology," 14.

46 Michel Sabbah, *The Second Pastoral Letter: Pray for Peace in Jerusalem* (Latin Patriarchate of Jerusalem, 1990), sec. 58.

an apparently unified society. Thus, despite the efforts of the Palestinian leadership to create a united Christian-Muslim society, tensions and distrust have persisted between the two groups, and have only increased in light of attempts to define Palestinian nationalism in Islamic terms.[47] The very efforts that have been made by Christian theologians and religious leaders to promote Muslim-Christian dialogue attest to its less-than-ideal state. As the main issue in this section is the background for the development of PCT in the early 1990s, I am only addressing the state of relations between Palestinian Christians and Muslims at that time. The nature of the relationship has changed since then, as Islamic movements have become more powerful—and more so, after the rise of ISIS and the persecution of Christians in the Middle East under its rule. While this type of persecution has not been the lot of Palestinian Christians, at least not directly, they have undoubtedly clouded the relationship.

One of the major, often contentious, sticking points in Christian-Muslim relations in the Arab world is the belief that Christianity, despite its roots in the Middle East, is a Western religion, and that being a believing Christian is equivalent to harboring an affinity for foreign colonial Western powers.[48] Indeed, various religious institutions promote ties between Christianity in the West and Christianity in the Middle East. Thus, for example, in the modern period, many Middle Eastern clerics completed their theological education in the West. Since the nineteenth century, Western Christians have established many missionary organizations in the Middle East that aim to provide religious and welfare services to locals.[49]

The connection between Christians in the Middle East and those in the West—and the tensions which arise from them—are nothing new. They have existed since the beginning of Islam. At that time,

[47] Daphne Tsimhoni, *Christian Communities in Jerusalem and the West Bank Since 1948: An Historical, Social and Political Study* (Praeger, 1993), 182.

[48] Paul Rowe, "The Middle Eastern Christian as Agent," *International Journal of Middle East Studies* 42 (2010): 472–74.

[49] Anthony O'Mahony, "The Christian Communities of Jerusalem and the Holy Land: A Historical and Political Survey," in *The Christian Communities of Jerusalem and the Holy Land*, ed. Anthony O'Mahony (University of Wales Press, 2003), 6–10. On the positive effects that the operation of church institutions had on Christian-Muslim relations see Baumgarten, "Politicization of Muslim-Christian Relations," 84.

the Christians were identified with the Byzantine Empire.[50] Although Christians in the Arab world had undergone a process of Arabization, and later even Islamization, both Muslims and Western Christians often viewed Christians as Western agents.[51] The involvement of the Western world in the Middle East—whether by the Byzantine Empire in late antiquity, the Crusaders in medieval times, or Western countries in modern times—created enormous tensions between Christians and Muslims, with local Christians often caught in the middle.[52]

Mitri Raheb elucidates that Arab Christians inhabit both the Arab Islamic and Christian worlds, often finding themselves in a precarious position, caught between two stools. This unique stance frequently leads to them being misunderstood and, at times, feeling betrayed by both sides.[53]

The rise of the Islamic Movement in Israel, Hamas, and the strengthening of religion in Palestinian society increased the tension between the two identities of Palestinian Christians—religious and ethnic. Additionally, any hostile action by Western countries against the Arab world was perceived as nothing less than a Christian act against Islam.[54] Geries Khoury, for example, lists the main issues to which Christians should pay attention to before calling upon Muslims to dialogue.[55] The list consists of nine different categories of actions that are attributed to the West and seen as being taken against the Arab world or Islam. Among the themes that he mentions are missionary movements, colonial oppression, Western attitudes toward the

[50] George Sabra, "Two Ways of Being a Christian in the Muslim Context of the Middle East," *Islam and Christian-Muslim Relations* 17 (2006): 45. For more on the local Christian communities under Islamic rule see Sidney Griffith, *The Church in the Shadow of the Mosque: Christians and Muslims in the World of Islam* (Princeton University Press, 2007).

[51] Laura Robson, "Recent Perspectives on Christianity in the Modern Arab World," *History Compass* 9 (2011): 312; Rowe, "Middle Eastern Christian as Agent," 472–74.

[52] Rafiq Khoury, "Christian-Muslim Relations: Past, Present and Future," in *Holy Land, Hollow Jubilee: God, Justice and the Palestinians*, ed. Naim Ateek and Michael Prior (Melisende, 1999), 220–21, 223–24; George Sabra, "Two Ways of Being a Christian," 45.

[53] Raheb, *I Am a Palestinian Christian*, 11.

[54] Robson, "Recent Perspectives on Christianity," 312.

[55] Khoury, "Christian-Muslim Dialogue in the Holy Land," 185–89.

Palestinian problem, the war in Iraq, and the status of Muslims in the West after the September 11 attacks on the United States.

Jonny Mansur, a Palestinian Christian historian, discusses the impact of the conflict initiated by radical Islamic movements against the United States on local Christian communities. He notes that Islamic fundamentalism often casts Christians in the Middle East as adversaries of Islam, presumed to be allies of America and the West, thereby justifying their harassment and persecution as a Muslim duty.[56] This perspective leads to the sidelining of the longstanding national unity between Muslims and Christians in the Middle East, as well as the shared history and coexistence. Consequently, Muslim fundamentalists transform their battle against the United States and the West into a direct conflict with Arab Christianity in the region. While many Middle Eastern Christians maintained close ties with the West, mostly through Christian schools in the region in which the language of instruction was a European one, this was not generally an issue until political tensions between the Arab world and the Christian West accentuated the differences between Middle Eastern Christians and Muslims. Because Christians were never fully integrated into Arab society as equals, and those under Islamic rule were even classified by Islam as *Dhimmi*, the rise of Islamic movements and the intensification of the religious affiliation of Palestinian society widened preexisting gaps between these groups and amplified accusations against the Christians as allies of the West.

The involvement of Arab Christian intellectuals in national movements that called for the modernization of the Arab world also contributed to widening the gap. Some Islamic groups perceived these calls in the late 1970s as an attempt by the Western world to subjugate Arab culture and Islam.[57] After clarifying the close ties of Arab Christians to the Arab world and its culture, Rafiq Khoury explains that Palestinian Christian intellectuals supported nationalist ideas and modernization because they were fascinated by the West, and therefore adopted

[56] Johnny Mansour, "International Political Changes and Their Influence on Christian Arabs in the Middle East," *Al-Liqa' Journal* 24 (2005): 93. Although this article was written a decade after the period discussed in this section, I believe it sheds light on the growing tension in Muslim-Christian relations in the Middle East as part of the struggle of some Islamic movements against the West.

[57] Dafna Tsimhoni, "The Problem of the National Identity of the Christian Arabs in Jerusalem and the West Bank," *Studies in the History of Israel* 3 (1993): 469.

concepts such as secularism and democracy. He opens his article on Christian involvement in national movements with, "Christianity is not alien to the East. The East, particularly Palestine, is the cradle of Christianity and its launching point for the rest of the world."[58] However, he also says that the inclination of Arab Christians toward this mindset cannot be faulted, as the Christian education they received within their churches lacked a historical perspective that incorporates the social, cultural, and political contexts of Arab societies. Consequently, when Arab Christian intellectuals sought to engage with the cultural life of their communities, they found the Christian teachings from their churches inadequate. Thus they turned to the ideologies of the West, even when these ideologies were peripheral to, in opposition to, or significantly distanced from their faith.[59] Khoury sees the desire of Arab Christian intellectuals to bring Western ideologies to the Arab world as a kind of "stumble" that stems from religious difficulty. In the first half of the nineteenth century, various local churches, Western and Eastern alike, did not give Christians the space to take an active part in politics or national struggles, so they had to look elsewhere. Thus, according to Khoury, the purpose of Palestinian Christian theology was to bridge this gap in Christian life and thought. Khoury describes Palestinian Christian theology as a contextual theology that serves two purposes. First, it allows for the development of a theology that represents Arab culture and values. Second, it is a means of countering the influence of Western thought on Arab Christians and the broader Arab world.[60]

Another issue that affects Christian-Muslim relations in Palestinian society, both in Israel and in the Palestinian Authority, is the attitude of Christianity toward Judaism and the Bible. At the sociopolitical level, the Second World War and the horrors of the Holocaust led many in Europe to initially support the establishment of the state of Israel. At the religious level, the choice of the land of Israel for the establishment of the Jewish state derives from a reliance on the text shared by both religions: the Bible (as we will explore in the next chapter). Therefore, Christian relations and dialogue with Judaism directly affect Christianity's as well as the world's support for the state of Israel, and so affect

[58] Rafiq Khoury, "The Role of the Arab Christian in the Arab National Movements," *Al-Liqa' Journal* 35 (2010): 29.

[59] Khoury, "Role of the Arab Christian," 54–55.

[60] Khoury, "Role of the Arab Christian," 54–55.

the relationship between Christians and Muslims in Palestinian society. As Ateek states, numerous Muslims, failing to distinguish between various forms of Christianity, conflate Christian Zionism with the central doctrines of mainstream churches.[61] Although local Palestinian Christians are not usually accused of supporting Zionist ideas, the issue nonetheless casts a shadow on Muslim-Christian relations. In addition, the Christian world's great effort to strengthen its ties with Judaism and its publication of statements that condemn antisemitism, mainly in the immediate aftermath of the Holocaust, had negative repercussions in the Muslim world because similar attempts were not made to denounce anti-Islamic attitudes within Christianity.[62] Palestinian Christian theologians devote considerable energy to breaking the automatic connection that Zionism proposes between the Bible and the state of Israel—not only in order to challenge pro-Zionist perceptions in Western Christian thinking, but also to signal to the Muslim world that the Christian religion is not necessarily an ally of the state of Israel.[63]

The tension between Muslims and Christians combines two aspects: identity or self-definition, on the one hand, and politics on the other. Palestinian Christian communities must find a way to be part of the Palestinian people, even when many of the latter equate Palestinian identity with Muslim identity. This delicate situation echoes throughout the Christian reality of the entire Middle East. In some respects, Palestinian Christian theologians are not only looking for a definition of their national identity but also of their ethnic one. Their search reverberates in the difficulty other Arab Christians have in finding their place in their respective local societies, and even in the difficulty of the general Arab world to define its place in a changing, modern world.[64]

The establishment of the state of Israel brought these feelings into sharper relief, as it forced Christians to deal with often-latent doubts and aspersions as to their loyalty: Are you with us or with them? The rise of Islamic movements also had a significant impact on the development of PCT because it pushed Christians to firmly assert their

61 Ateek, *Justice and Only Justice*, 66.

62 Geries Khoury, "Olive Tree Theology: Rooted in the Palestinian Soul," *Al-Liqa' Journal* 26 (2006): 87.

63 Raheb, *I Am a Palestinian Christian*, 61.

64 See, for example, *Theology and the Local Church in the Holy Land*, Al-Liqa' Center, 1988, https://al-liqacenter.org.ps/?p=1528.

identity as Palestinians.[65] The development of PCT, which is in essence a political theology, was a Christian response to Muslim claims against Christians. Such theology allows Christians not only to take an active part in the national struggle and prove their loyalty, but also to turn to their advantage that same dual identity for which they were held in suspicion. As Geries Khoury opines, the Arab Christians "are the only ones capable of being a true bridge for understanding, dialogue, friendship, and true cooperation between the East and West."[66]

The Indignation of the Local Church

Local churches in the Holy Land had not felt the need to take an active role in the political struggle before the 1980s, primarily because their ecclesiastical leadership was not Palestinian but foreign, with limited commitment to the local Arab communities.[67] The only significant religious hierarchies to be Arabized were those of the Greek Catholic and Maronite sects, but those churches also refrained from making political statements, and often declared their loyalty to the state.[68] This meant that the spiritual leadership within Palestinian Christian communities often did not mirror the identities or political sentiments of their congregations. Instead of vocalizing political stances, the leaders of churches in the Holy Land were primarily focused on safeguarding the interests of the international church, prioritizing these global concerns over the specific needs and aspirations of their local communities.

The theologian and historiographer David Neuhaus presents three main reasons why foreign Christian leaders refrained from interfering in political matters during the first decades after the establishment of the state: Church leaders had to tread a delicate political line so as to avoid alienating Israel or the Arab countries; the creation of pro-Jewish lobbies within local Christian institutions; and the schism and distress in the Orthodox Church between Greek bishops and Palestinian Arab laity and clergy.[69] For the churches in the Holy Land, the complexity

65 Leonard Marsh, "Palestinian Christianity—A Study in Religion and Politics," *International Journal for the Study of the Christian Church* 5 (2005): 152.

66 Khoury, "Christian-Muslim Dialogue in the Holy Land," 214.

67 Jamal Khader, "The Role of the Palestinian Church in the Palestinian Problem in the Aftermath of the June 1967 War: Repercussions of the War on Christian-Muslim Relations," *Al-Liqa' Journal* 28 (2007): 41.

68 Neuhaus, *Between Quiescence and Arousal*, 54–74.

69 Neuhaus, *Between Quiescence and Arousal*, 54–74.

of the Palestinian question derived not only from diplomatic relations, but also from Jerusalem's special status in Christianity, as well as the centrality of the holy sites. The churches in Jerusalem had never served only the local population, but also (and sometimes solely) the pilgrims and clerics who visited the Holy Land. Thus the commitment of the churches in Jerusalem was often first and foremost to the leadership of their main Church and not to the local community.

This situation was valid for almost all churches in the Holy Land until the late 1970s. During the late 1970s and throughout the 1980s, many Holy Land churches underwent a strong process of indignation, that is, an increased identification with the local community.[70] That was taken as part of the strengthening of Palestinian identity in Christian communities, and parallel to various processes that took place in Christianity worldwide (as we will see in the next chapter). This process began with voices, inside the churches and among Christian communities in the Holy Land, calling on the churches to take an active part in the Palestinian political struggle.[71] These calls increased the tension between church leadership and Palestinian Christian communities, especially in the Orthodox Church, and led to a renewal of the demands from the communities to replace the foreign leadership of the churches with a local one.[72]

The Orthodox Church historically showed resistance to the appointment of indigenous leaders in the Holy Land. This stance persisted until a significant turning point in 2005, the appointment of Archbishop Theodosius (Atalla Hanna). In contrast, most of the other churches in the Holy Land had started to appoint Palestinian Christians to leadership positions decades earlier. The first such appointment was that of Bishop Daud Haddad in the Lutheran Church in 1979.[73] In 1987 the Catholic Church took a significant step in appointing, for the first time, a Palestinian Patriarch of Jerusalem, Michel Sabbah (b. 1933). From his early days in this influential position, Sabbah took it upon himself to be actively involved in politics, express a firm stand on the Palestinian question, and support the PLO.[74]

70 Neuhaus, *Between Quiescence and Arousal*, 194.

71 Khoury, "Palestinian Contextual Theology," 18.

72 Neuhaus, *Between Quiescence and Arousal*, 192–97.

73 Khoury, "Palestinian Contextual Theology," 18.

74 Anthony O'Mahony, "The Latin of the East: Jerusalem and the Palestinian Christians," in O'Mahony, *Christian Communities of Jerusalem and the Holy Land*, 108.

The First Intifada (1987–91)

Many Palestinian theologians, as well as members of Palestinian society in general, viewed the first *Intifada* (uprising) as a significant turning point in the Palestinian struggle against Israel. For the first time, Palestinians took their national struggle into their own hands and understood that they were capable of promoting their own cause. According to Palestinian sociologist Bernard Sabella (b. 1945), from the perspective of Palestinians and their leaders, the Intifada was seen as a call for peace with Israel, based on the principle of mutual recognition and coexistence of two peoples within the same territory.[75] It symbolized their resolve to confront Israelis on equal terms and emerged as a profound source of national pride for the Palestinian community. The Palestinian Christians were part of the political awakening that spread among the Palestinian people at this time.[76] An important part of the Intifada was civil disobedience. Due to their economic power, the main action of the Palestinian Uprising was general trade strikes.[77] This form of nonviolent resistance allowed the Christians, who largely refrained from participation in violent struggle, to join and take an active part in the national awakening. As the Palestinian identity became more dominant than the Muslim one during the Intifada, the joint struggle created unity on the Palestinian street and gave the Christians hope of alleviating the tensions between Muslims and Christians.[78]

The Intifada also demonstrated to the Palestinians that they could influence world public opinion and tilt it in their favor. Raheb pointed out that this was one of the main goals of the Intifada, and that it had succeeded in large measure.[79] The Palestinians managed to attract the attention of the world, as news channels all around the world were filled with live broadcasts from the Intifada. This was the main impact of the Palestinian Christians on the Intifada; they took upon themselves the mission of communication with the West.[80] As Palestinian Christians sought to take an active part in the Intifada, without participating in violence, raising public opinion in favor of the Palestinians

[75] Marsh, "Palestinian Christianity," 151.

[76] Baumgarten, "Politicization of Muslim-Christian Relations," 78–79.

[77] Moshe Shemesh, "The PLO Road to Oslo: 1988 as a Turning Point in the History of the Palestinian National Movement," *Iyunim* 9 (1999): 186–245.

[78] Mi'ari, "Transformation of Collective Identity," 588.

[79] Raheb, *I Am a Palestinian Christian*, 33.

[80] Tsimhoni, "Problem of the National Identity of the Christian Arabs," 470.

became their main strategy. In this respect, they had a built-in advantage because of their ties to the West and their shared religion. Their choice to preserve a nonviolent struggle further helped them to justify the Intifada to the West.[81] The Intifada was an opportunity for Palestinian Christians to raise awareness of the Palestinian situation, as western media attention was already directed toward the uprising. Senior Christians in the PLO took a leading role in promoting the Palestinian cause, among them Hanna Siniora (b. 1937) and Hanan Ashrawi (b. 1946). The mayor of Bethlehem, Elias Freij (1918–98), was also active in the Western media, and his decision to cancel the traditional Christmas Mass in 1987 stirred up a lot of attention.[82] With the eyes of the West pointed to the IPC, the new crop of Palestinian church leaders were empowered by the Intifada to issue the historical document of the heads of the churches in the Holy Land on June 22, 1989. After this event, local church leaders published many more official statements, which invited international intervention in the conflict.[83]

A significant event that underscored the involvement of Christians in the Intifada and highlighted the influence of local church leaders took place on April 11, 1990. On that day, Israeli settlers made their way into St. John's Hospice, a property owned by the Greek Orthodox Patriarchate, situated near the Church of the Holy Sepulcher. The reaction from the Christian community was profound, with notable support coming from high-ranking church figures such as Catholic Patriarch Michel Sabbah and Orthodox Patriarch Diodorus (1923–2000). Their involvement exemplified the unity and resolve within the Christian leadership in response to the encroachments.

The event reached its peak when all Christian houses of worship in the area closed for one day in protest, a move paralleled by the Muslim Wakf's decision to close the al-Haram al-Sharif (Temple Mount) compound.[84] This act of solidarity between Christian and Muslim communities highlighted the shared struggle against the infringements on their religious sites and rights. The closures sparked widespread protests both within the region and internationally, drawing attention to

[81] Laura Robson, "Palestinian Liberation Theology, Muslim-Christian Relations, and the Arab-Israeli Conflict," *Islam and Christian-Muslim Relations* 21 (2010): 45.

[82] Tsimhoni, "Problem of the National Identity of the Christian Arabs," 470.

[83] Most of these documents can be found in May, *Jerusalem Testament*.

[84] Dafna Tsimhoni describes this event in detail in "Problem of the National Identity of the Christian Arabs," 476–78.

the religious dimensions of the conflict and the collective resistance of the faithful in the Holy Land. This moment was emblematic of the broader involvement of religious communities in the Intifada, showcasing a unified stance against violations of sacred spaces and the rights of religious minorities.[85] This incident not only underscored the active participation of the Christian community in the broader Palestinian resistance but also showcased the significant role those religious leaders played in defending their communities' rights and properties amid the ongoing conflict.

For Palestinian Christian theologians, the possibility of stimulating global public opinion and recruiting it for their struggle had become a key component of their strategy. The more the world media dealt with the situation in the region and with the coverage of the Intifada, the more the discourse expanded to other topics, including theological questions raised by the very establishment of the state of Israel. The years following the Intifada saw the first peak in PCT activism. In an attempt to keep the Palestinian issue at the forefront of global public consciousness and to theologically engage with the political reality, Palestinian theologians have authored an unprecedented quantity of books and articles.

While the Intifada had succeeded in winning attention for the Palestinian cause, various worldwide factors led to the speedy evaporation of that global gaze. As Raheb attests, "The eyes of the world were suddenly turned in their direction. The Intifada continued, but it no longer attracted the attention it had previously. The world got used to the Intifada once again."[86] Christian Palestinian theologians published books and articles in European languages to arrest or even reverse that trend. For example, Raheb's book *I Am a Palestinian Christian*, published in 1994, was translated into no fewer than forty languages.

THE MAIN THEMES AND FEATURES OF PALESTINIAN CONTEXTUAL THEOLOGY

The beginning of Palestinian contextual theology can be traced to the establishment of three theological centers in the Holy Land in the mid-1980s: the Al-Liqa' Center in Bethlehem, the Sabeel Center in Jerusalem, and the Diyar Center in Bethlehem. Each of these centers,

85 Tsimhoni, "Problem of the National Identity of the Christian Arabs," 476–78.

86 Raheb, *I Am a Palestinian Christian*, 60–61.

established by people who eventually became the leaders of PCT, focused on a slightly different theological approach, yet they all had a common goal: the creation of a PCT that would directly relate to the context of the IPC.

The first was the Al-Liqa' Center (اللقاء, the "encounter"), established in 1982 by Geries Khoury. Its full name is Al-Liqa' Center for Religious and Heritage Studies in the Holy Land in Bethlehem. Its goal was the promotion of Muslim-Christian relations within Palestinian society.[87] In 1987, a new branch of the center, under the name, "Theology and the Local Church in the Holy Land," was founded. In this branch, an effort was made to create and develop a Palestinian contextual theology.[88] In a seminal document prepared for a conference on contextual theology in 1987, which precipitated the establishment of the second branch of the Al Liqa' Center, a collective of theologians presented their interpretation of contextual theology. They argued that this approach empowers believers to delve into their extensive heritage, thereby enhancing their understanding of faith, its articulation, and practice within the contours of a distinct historical period. This period is characterized by its own set of demands, challenges, questions, hopes, difficulties, and aspirations. Through contextual theology, the theologians posited, faith becomes a living, breathing entity that interacts dynamically with the temporal conditions and societal context of the believers, enabling a more meaningful and relevant expression of religious belief and practice.[89]

This description is a good indication of the theology that the Al-Liqa' Center was seeking to develop as a theological basis for understanding Palestinian reality: a theology that focuses on the history and heritage of local Christianity. Considering the center's concomitant goal of promoting Muslim-Christian relations, an emphasis was placed on dialogue with Islam and the creation of a united Palestinian society. This is evident in the writings of Geries Khoury and Rafiq Khoury—both leading theologians of the center.[90] Unlike the other centers, which more fre-

[87] See the Al-Liqa' Center website, http://www.al-liqacenter.org.ps.

[88] Al-Liqa' Center website, http://www.al-liqacenter.org.ps.

[89] Al-Liqa' Center, *Theology and the Local Church in the Holy Land*, 1987. The latest edition of this document is from 2015 and is available on the Al-Liqa' center website: https://al-liqacenter.org.ps/?p=1547.

[90] See, for example, Rafiq Khoury, "Christian-Muslim Relations"; Rafiq Khoury, "Religious Discourse Between Christians and Muslims," *Al-Liqa' Journal* 16 (2001): 1–28; Rafiq Khoury, "The Role of Religious Thought in Building Trust Between the

quently address the Western world, the Al-Liqa' Center issues mostly Arabic-language publications aimed at the local Christian community and the Muslim community. Thus, for example, Geries Khoury's book *The Intifada of Heaven and Earth* (1989) is a very unusual book in Palestinian theology. The book is devoted to the theological analysis of the Intifada, with reference to the interpretation of the Holy Bible, but unlike the other books dedicated to the subject it is written in Arabic with only a brief introduction in English.[91] The center organizes annual conferences for its two branches and, since 1985, has published a quarterly journal in Arabic and an annual journal in English, both under the center's name.[92] The *Al-Liqa' Journal*, published in Bethlehem, has become a significant source for the publication and analysis of PCT.

The Anglican Pastor Naim Ateek founded the Sabeel Center (سبيل, the "way") in 1990 as an "Ecumenical Liberation Theology Center." The center was established a year after the publication of Ateek's book *Justice and Only Justice: A Palestinian Theology of Liberation*, in which Ateek explains the need for what he views as a Palestinian liberation theology and a recommended methodology for achieving it.[93] Sabeel's statement of purpose articulates its foundation as an ecumenical, grassroots movement within liberation theology, embedded in the teachings and life of Jesus Christ and aimed at Palestinian Christians. Its mission is to enhance the faith of Palestinian Christians, promoting unity for active social participation.[94] As evident in its purpose statement, Sabeel emphasizes a spirituality that values love, justice, peace, nonviolence, freedom, and reconciliation among various national and religious communities. It also strives to elevate global awareness of the identity, presence, and contributions of Palestinian Christians, while addressing their present-day challenges. Sabeel encourages individuals and groups worldwide to advocate for a just, comprehensive, and lasting peace, based on truth and fueled by both prayer and active engagement.[95]

Arab and Muslim World and the West," *Al-Liqa' Journal* 39 (2012): 58–73; and Geries Khoury, "Christian-Muslim Dialogue in the Holy Land."

91 Geries Khoury, *The Intifada of Heaven and Earth* (Al-Hakim, 1989).

92 See the journals section of the Al-Liqa' Center website, https://al-liqacenter.org.ps/?cat=41.

93 Ateek, *Justice and Only Justice*.

94 See the Sabeel website, https://sabeel.org.

95 While no longer on the Sabeel website, the Sabeel purpose statement in full is available at https://bigbulkyanglican.typepad.com/bigbulkyanglican/2006/03/palestine_and_s.html.

The Sabeel center, as a liberation theology center extensively influenced by South African theological movements, focuses mainly on confronting Zionist ideology, aiding the politically abused, and correcting perceived errors in biblical hermeneutics.[96] To facilitate its efforts, it created an international network of supporters, the "Friends of Sabeel," who work in partnership with Sabeel.[97] Sabeel also organizes international conferences and publishes books in English on liberation theology, most often with cotheologians and academics from different parts of the world.[98]

Lutheran pastor Dr. Mitri Raheb founded the Diyar Center (ديار, the "homelands") or the International Center of Bethlehem (ICB) in 1995. The center objective is centered on the creation of a civil society and the promotion of sustainable economic development, with a keen emphasis on respecting and incorporating Palestinian cultural heritage. This cultural center offers various programs in several areas and acts as a forum for dialogue between the Christian faith and Arab cultures. However, its main emphasis is on the development of a Palestinian contextual theology.[99] The center organizes international conferences, and in 2011 it founded a publishing house under the name Diyar.[100] Raheb was also a member of the Al-Liqa' Center at its inception, and he has frequently collaborated with Sabeel. He later chose to focus on his own center. Samuel Kuruvilla references Raheb's distinction between the methodologies of Sabeel and Diyar (ICB). He notes that Sabeel, under Naim Ateek, is wholly devoted to advocacy efforts, both within the local context and internationally, encompassing outreach to both clerical and lay communities. Conversely, the primary objective of the International Center of Bethlehem (ICB) and its affiliated organizations is to establish a foundation of physical, material, technological, and spiritual resources. This foundation aims to assist the Palestinian people in self-reconstruction and in the rebuilding of their "nation."[101]

In addition to those centers, and often in collaboration with them, several prominent theologians from various churches have published

96 Naim Ateek, *A Palestinian Christian Cry for Reconciliation* (Orbis, 2008), 3–14.

97 Naim Ateek, *A Palestinian Theology of Liberation* (Orbis, 2017), 131–38.

98 See https://sabeel.org/books/.

99 See https://sabeel.org/books/.

100 See https://www.facebook.com/diyarconsortium/.

101 Samuel Kuruvilla, *Radical Christianity in the Holy Land: A Comparative Study of Liberation and Contextual Theology in Palestine-Israel* (University of Exeter, 2009), 167.

theological books and articles on PCT. The most prominent among them are Michel Sabbah, Munib Younan, Elias Chacour, Jamal Khader, Rafiq Khoury, Yohanna Katanacho, and Munther Isaac.

Palestinian contextual theology also finds expression in theological statements published by the patriarchs and heads of local churches in Jerusalem. The first group statement was published in 1988 in light of the first Intifada, and it has been followed by more than seventy such statements.[102] These statements of the patriarchs and heads of local churches in Jerusalem are mostly intended for their local communities and relate to the daily life of Christians in the Holy Land, and to the difficulties that they face in light of the conflict. However, they are frequently directed to heads of state and address the worldwide Christian and international communities.[103] Although these statements often do not contain theology per se, they nevertheless reflect the political position of the heads of the various churches on the IPC, refer to the need for justice and peace, and often contain a call for action. For example, in their statement from 2006, we find the following appeal: "The churches in Jerusalem and the Holy Land need you to speak with the moral authority of the church from the ethical perspective of the Christian faith."[104] In this statement they advocate for individuals to inform lawmakers and politicians in their countries that the churches are acutely conscious of the continuous suffering resulting from the Occupation, leading to further insecurity. Moreover, they emphasize that the churches are increasingly engaging in proactive efforts to pursue a just and peaceful resolution.

One of the most significant manifestations of PCT was the publication of the Palestinian *Kairos Document* (2009). This document was written with the cooperation of various Palestinian thinkers and theologians, including scholars from the three centers mentioned above. The document, based on the South African *Kairos Document*, was circulated widely and garnered support from different churches around the world, and from various church organizations. The document called on Christians around the world to partake in nonviolent

[102] May, *Jerusalem Testament*, 1.

[103] May, *Jerusalem Testament*, 1.

[104] "Church Leaders in Jerusalem Urge World Churches and All Christians to Advocate for Peace," 2006. The full statement can be found on the World Council of Churches website at https://www.oikoumene.org/en/resources/documents/other-ecumenical-bodies/church-leaders-in-jerusalem-urge-world-churches-and-all-christians-to-advocate-for-peace.

resistance to the Israeli occupation and suggested doing so by engaging in "divestment and in an economic and commercial boycott of everything produced by the occupation."[105] Following the document, a Global Kairos Network was founded in 2011. The network, whose members are Christian centers in the United States, Europe, and countries in the Southern Hemisphere such as Brazil, India, and South Africa, seeks to bring together people who believe in the Kairos concept and its prophetical obligation for a nonviolent resistance.[106]

These three centers, and the various theologians and church leaders who chose to take an active role in the creation of a Palestinian contextual theology, created a new and innovative world of scholarship. In the last thirty years, these theologians succeeded in mobilizing supporters—clergy, theologians, and lay people—around the world, who joined them in developing a novel theological discourse that takes into account the religious and political implications that the IPC has on the Palestinian people.

Although PCT is complex and there are several variants, it is possible to discern several common themes and characteristics. Rafiq Khoury presents three fundamental features of PCT.[107] The first is theology in context—a theology that is written from "the fruit of direct confrontation and painful suffering" that dominates for Christian entities in the Arab world in general and in Palestine in particular. For Khoury, the context of Palestinian theology is not just the IPC but also Christian life as a minority in the Arab world.

The second core characteristic of PCT is its commitment to ecumenical theology. This approach signifies a nondenominational initiative, aimed at fostering unity among diverse Christian traditions and denominations. The desire for ecumenism has characterized Palestinian theology from the beginning and can be seen clearly in the joint statements of the heads of the churches. The need for ecumenism derives from two main causes: the diversity of churches in the Holy Land, and the lofty status of Jerusalem and the Holy Land for the world's churches. Despite the tendency toward ecumenism, Palestinian contextual theologians come almost exclusively from the

105 *Kairos Document* (Palestine), para. 4.2.6, https://www.kairospalestine.ps/index.php/about-kairos/kairos-palestine-document.

106 See https://www.kairospalestine.ps/index.php/about-kairos/global-kairos.

107 Rafiq Khoury, "Theology in Palestine: Meaning and Structure," *Al-Liqa' Journal* 29 (2007): 14–17.

Protestant or Catholic Churches, both Latin and Eastern alike. The Orthodox Church and the Oriental Churches have almost no representation in the creation of this new theology. The Greek Orthodox Patriarch, as well as the Patriarchs of the Oriental Churches, take part in the joint statements that are published by the churches, but they do not write theology or relate to the theological questions that may arise from the context of political conflict. Their lack of participation may be explained by the non-Western affiliation of these churches and their consequent isolation from the changes that the Western world underwent in the wake of WWII. Hence, the ideas of contextual theology or the writings of political theology were less prominent in Orthodox theology.[108] Another perspective, while rooted in the same underlying factors, suggests that Oriental theologians possess a distinct approach to the issue of the divine promise due to their differing engagement with Western theological discourse, particularly in relation to Judaism post-Holocaust. These theologians were not directly involved in the Western discussions that led to a rejection of supersessionism—the belief that the Christian Church has replaced Israel in God's plan. As a result, Orthodox Christianity, as represented by these theologians, does not accept the religious claims of Zionism regarding the Holy Land.[109]

The third pillar of PCT is practical theology. According to the traditions of liberation theology, from which PCT developed, theology should lead to action. As Rafiq Khoury put it: "Palestinian Theology does not only describe reality but also seeks to change it."[110] PCT emerged from the Palestinian context of the IPC in order to influence political reality. Thus, this theology deliberately focuses on several main issues: theology of the land, biblical interpretation, Jewish-Christian relations, Muslim-Christian relations, and the relationship between faith and politics in contemporary Christianity.[111] PCT does not primarily identify with a particular historical group, but with a

[108] See Vasilios Makrides, "Why Does the Orthodox Church Lack Systematic Social Teaching?" *Skepsis: A Journal of Philosophy and Interdisciplinary Research* 23 (2013): 281–312.

[109] See Harold Smith, "Supersession and Continuance: The Orthodox Church's Perspective on Supersessionism," *Journal of Ecumenical Studies* 49 (2014): 247–73.

[110] Khoury, "Theology in Palestine," 15.

[111] Rafiq Khoury, "Palestinian Context and Contextual Theology," *Al-Liqa' Journal* 40 (2013): 27–28.

distinct geographical group known as the "people of the land" who have inhabited the region for an extended period.[112]

As it will become clear, PCT has two different target audiences: the internal community, comprising both Christians and Muslims, and the Western Christian world. This distinction, sometimes made by PCT writers themselves, is critical for understanding the type of discourse that the theologians use and cultivate. As the goal of PCT is to change political reality, it has to convince its audiences of its righteousness. The choice of language and the mode of discourse are decisive to the success of its mission.

For the primary target audience, which is the Palestinian Christian community, it is essential that the theology be articulated in Arabic. PCT is committed to a deep exploration of the Palestinian Christian identity, concentrating on theological discussions that are pertinent to this community and affirm its distinct identity. Another internal target audience of this theology, even though it is usually not the official audience of these writings, is the rest of the Palestinian people—namely, Palestinian Muslims and the Arab Muslim world. The discourse is tailored to the ears of this target audience as well. Even if the Palestinian Christians see themselves as an inseparable part of the Palestinian people and the Arab world, they are nevertheless a minority religious group within a society that is becoming increasingly religious. Palestinian Christians are seeking to define their place in a Palestinian society that has intensified the pressure upon them to prove their loyalty. Thus, for instance, in the adoption of Arab notions such as Resistance (مقاومة), translated into Christian theological concepts, Palestinian Christians attempt to take an active part in the Palestinian national struggle and prove that they still have an important place in it.

The topics Palestinian theologians engage when they are dealing with Arab audiences differ from those they engage in when they address a Western audience. Arab-facing topics are less concerned with biblical interpretations and with Judaism. Instead, they give more prominence to the place of Christianity in Arab culture, and of Christians in Arab society and in the Middle East. A cursory glance at the articles published in the *Al-Liqa' Journal* in Arabic provides a good illustration of the main themes that preoccupy theology written in Arabic: Muslim-Christian relations, the involvement of churches in political reality, the contribution of Christians to the national struggle,

112 See, for example, Raheb, "Towards a New Hermeneutics of Liberation," 16.

etc. Although this theological approach is important and requires thorough examination, due to the scope of this current study, an in-depth analysis of this theology, particularly the elaboration on Arabic texts, will not be the central focus of this book. Such an examination demands further scholarly inquiry and analysis to fully understand and appreciate the theological nuances and contributions of PCT as expressed in the Arabic language.

The Western Christian world, in Europe and North America, serves as the second primary audience for PCT. Aimed at an international readership, PCT is frequently articulated in English or other European languages with the strategic goal of reshaping Western perceptions of the IPC. This external branch of Palestinian theology seeks to challenge the foundational beliefs and narratives upheld by Christian Zionist theologians and their adherents. The selection of discourse and its presentation are significantly influenced by the target audience, tailored to engage Western readers effectively. Despite facing criticism from some quarters that label Palestinian theology as a whole as antisemitic, writings in English or European languages are careful to navigate these sensitivities. Specifically, they generally steer clear of any rhetoric that might be interpreted as negating the divine election of the Jewish people. The discourse adapts to the prevalent styles and sensitivities of the Western world, particularly those dominant in the late twentieth and early twenty-first centuries.

Influential movements such as liberation theology and South African theology have played a pivotal role in inspiring a new form of discourse within PCT, one deeply rooted in postcolonial thought and contemporary Christian engagement. This approach not only resonates with the broader trends in Western theology but also aligns with the global call for justice, equity, and liberation. Palestinian theologians leverage this discourse to appeal to the Christian world, advocating for support and solidarity with the Palestinian cause. This strategic use of language and thematic focus underscores the dynamic interplay between theology and geopolitics, illustrating how PCT engages with and contributes to the global theological conversation, all while advocating for the Palestinian people's rights and recognition on the international stage.

Rafiq Khoury delves into the complexities of the dichotomy present in theological discourse, noting that much of this theology is penned in languages not native to its primary subjects, such as

French, English, or German.[113] He questions the intended audience of this theology—whether it is aimed at foreign or local readers. While acknowledging the value of exposing foreign audiences to these theological discussions due to the deep relevance of the issues at hand, Khoury argues that this should not detract from engaging with the local audience. He emphasizes the need for attention and research to achieve a balance between catering to both local and foreign audiences, particularly given that the local community is the one most directly impacted by the theological issues being discussed.

Although the stated goal of PCT that is calibrated to the Western world is to obtain Western support for the Palestinian cause, this does not mean that the identity questions of Palestinian Christians do not occupy a central role in that theology or that it ignores its home audience. Even when writing to Europeans and Western audiences, Palestinian theologians may construct and shape their own identity, including their particular Palestinian identity, along with their religious identity as part of the Christian world. This identity formation may be fostered by comparison to, and distinction from, those they perceive as their rivals: Israeli Jews.

We have analyzed the historical factors and circumstances that led to the development of Palestinian contextual theology. The analysis should be understood against the backdrop of the evolution of Palestinian identity after the 1967 war, the strengthening of religiosity in Palestinian Muslim society, and the rise of political Islamic movements such as the Muslim Brotherhood and Hamas. Taken together, these factors have all strongly influenced the identity crisis experienced by Palestinian Christians, which some argue they are still experiencing today. PCT emerged as a response to that identity crisis, and as a way for Palestinian Christians to partake in the national struggle for their land without having to give up their Christian identity. Furthermore, it enabled them to act as intermediaries, turning their religious connections with the West into an advantage instead of a threat. Palestinian Christians have been able to use their dual identity to promote the Palestinian cause abroad and thus promote their social status at home.

113 Khoury, "Theology in Palestine," 15.

2
Between and Betwixt
PCT in Light of Post-Holocaust and Postcolonial Theologies

INTRODUCTION

The origins of PCT can be found in the Israeli-Palestinian conflict and in the conflicting loyalties of Palestinian Christians. But its development has been facilitated by shifts that have taken place in the Christian world since the founding of the state of Israel. Notably, PCT did not develop in a theological vacuum; rather, it is an integral part of broader theological discourses. PCT can be understood as emerging from the complex and often unaddressed tension between two significant theological movements within the Christian world: post-Holocaust theology and postcolonial theology. While the terminology used to describe these movements may be subject to debate and considered problematic by some, the concept of "post" remains essential for grasping the essence of this theological framework.[1] It

[1] Post-Holocaust theology is often referred to as "holocaust theology." See, for example, Stephen Haynes, "Christian Holocaust Theology: A Critical Reassessment," *Journal of the American Academy of Religion* 62 (1994): 553–85. Postcolonial theology as defined here could also be categorized as global South theology, or third world theology. See John Parratt, "Introduction," in *An Introduction to Third World Theologies*, ed. John Parratt (Cambridge University Press, 2004).

underscores the necessity of reevaluating and realigning Christian theology in response to monumental historical events.

The post-Holocaust theological movement primarily involves the Western Christian reengagement with Judaism, sparked by the profound moral and ethical questions raised in the aftermath of the Holocaust. This movement seeks to address Christian complicity and to redefine Christian-Jewish relations. Conversely, postcolonial theology emerges predominantly from the southern hemisphere, focusing on deconstructing the legacy of colonialism in Christian thought and practice, and advocating for a theology that resonates with the experiences of formerly colonized peoples. Both movements share a fundamental concern with reexamining Christian theology's exclusivist tendencies and its implications for interfaith and intercultural relations. They represent pivotal shifts in theological thought, challenging traditional narratives and seeking more inclusive understandings of faith in light of historical atrocities and injustices.

For Palestinian Christians, however, the intersection of these two movements presents a unique challenge, resulting in what can be described as a dramatic clash. This encounter reflects the particular historical and geopolitical realities faced by Palestinian Christians, who must navigate the theological implications of both the Holocaust's legacy and the ongoing realities of colonialism and occupation in their land. The tension between these global theological currents and the local Palestinian context gives rise to a distinctive theological discourse that seeks to articulate a Christian identity and faith that is both aware of and responsive to the complex realities of Palestinian existence.

The devastation of WWII, and especially the Holocaust, brought a discourse on Judaism to the fore in many Western Christian theological circles, and specifically on the anti-Jewish views in Christian theology that contributed to the mass annihilation of millions of Jews. In the decades following WWII, a number of Christian theologians marked the war, and especially the Holocaust, as a turning point, or even a rupture, after which Christian theology—in relation to Judaism in particular, or to humanity in general—could not remain the same.[2] The American theologian Alice Eckardt claimed that the Holocaust "must become a turning point in Christian history—in its understand-

2 See Haynes, "Christian Holocaust Theology," 554.

ing of the nature of God and God's actions."[3] Eckardt stressed that the Holocaust should influence the way Christianity understands and interprets history, both divine and human, and its relation to other peoples and faiths, but most importantly "its relation to and theology about Judaism and the Jewish people."[4] Putting the matter differently, the Catholic theologian Johann-Baptist Metz stated that the impact of the Holocaust on Christian thinking "is not really a matter of revising Christian theology with regard to Judaism, but a matter of revising Christian theology altogether."[5]

In this chapter, I will present the evolving discourse concerning Christianity's conception of Judaism after the Holocaust, and the development of various theological currents that have been influenced by the political theology of Jürgen Moltmann and Johannes Metz, which form the basis on which PCT developed. This will allow me to analyze the challenges that PCT faces in its encounter with post-Holocaust theology and postcolonial theologies.

THE CHRISTIAN PERCEPTION OF JUDAISM: A POST-HOLOCAUST THEOLOGY

Changes in the Christian perception of Judaism following the Holocaust took time to emerge. In the first decades after the war, only a handful of writings were dedicated to questions or challenges that Christianity might face in light of the Holocaust.[6] The book *Jesus and Israel*, written by the Jewish French historian Jules Isaac and published in 1948, was perhaps the first to offer an analysis of antisemitism and its roots in Christian theology after WWII.[7] Isaac concluded his book by suggesting eighteen points for rectification in Christian teaching, which later became the *Ten Points of Seelisberg*, a document written jointly by a group of Christians and Jews from the International Council of Christians and Jews (ICCJ). This document contains ten guidelines for the Christian Church that aimed to "prevent any animosity towards the Jews which might arise from false, inadequate or mistaken

[3] Alice Eckardt, "Post-Holocaust Theology: A Journey Out of the Kingdom of Night," *Holocaust and Genocide Studies* 1 (1986): 229.

[4] Eckardt, "Post-Holocaust Theology," 229.

[5] Johann-Baptist Metz, "Christians and Jews After Auschwitz," in *The Baptist Emergent Church: The Future of Christianity in a Postbourgeois World*, trans. Peter Mann (Crossroad, 1981), 22.

[6] Stephen Haynes, *Prospects for Post-Holocaust Theology* (Scholars, 1991), 3–5.

[7] Jules Isaac, *Jésus et Israël*, trans. Sally Gran (Holt, Rinehart and Winston, 1971).

presentations or conceptions of the teaching and preaching of the Christian doctrine."[8]

Another significant document was the *Report on the Christian Approach to the Jews*, published in 1948, at the first meeting of the World Council of Churches (WCC), a worldwide Christian inter-church organization founded following WWII.[9] The report opens with a reference to the events of the Holocaust and declares that "no people in this one world have suffered more bitterly from the disorder of man than the Jewish people." Following this declaration, the report emphasizes the special meaning of the Jewish people for the Christian faith and the need to fight antisemitism, as it is "a sin against God and man." Yet these two important documents were not immediately followed by any significant theological discussion of the relevant issues.

Serious theological discussion regarding the church's response to the Holocaust and the need to examine church doctrine vis-à-vis Judaism began with the Second Vatican Council and the *Nostra Aetate* declaration, published in 1965.[10] It is noteworthy to underscore that the theological underpinnings of *Nostra Aetate* are not exclusively derived from a reactive stance toward the Holocaust. Rather, they are informed by a constellation of enduring processes within the Catholic Church throughout the 20th century, encompassing the influence of Protestant exegesis of scriptural texts, most notably Romans 9–11.[11] Following the council, many Catholic and Protestant theologians consecrated their theological work to a reassessment and critical examination of Christian history and doctrine in the light of the Holocaust. Throughout the 1970s, theologians like Roy and Alice Eckardt,[12] Rosemary Ruether,[13]

8 International Council of Christians and Jews, *An Address to the Churches (The Ten Points of Seelisberg)* (1947).

9 World Council of Churches, *Concerns of the Churches—The Christian Approach to the Jews* (World Council of Churches, 1948), https://www.oikoumene.org/en/resources/documents/assembly/1948-amsterdam/concerns-of-the-churches-the-christian-approach-to-the-jews.

10 Vatican Council II, *Nostra Aetate*, 1965, https://www.vatican.va/archive/hist_councils/ii_vatican_council/documents/vat-ii_decl_19651028_nostra-aetate_en.html.

11 John Connelly, *From Enemy to Brother: The Revolution in Catholic Teaching on the Jews, 1933–1965* (Harvard University Press, 2012).

12 See, among others, Roy Eckardt and Alice Eckardt, *Your People, My People* (Quadrangle, 1974).

13 Rosemary Ruether, *Faith and Fratricide: The Theological Roots of Anti-Semitism* (Seabury, 1974).

and Gregory Baum[14] dedicated themselves to uncovering antisemitic thinking in Christian theology. These theologians, among others, felt that Christian antisemitism is rooted in the attitude of the New Testament toward Jews.[15] This attitude includes not only the culpability of the Jewish people for the killing of Jesus by the Roman governor Pontius Pilate and their rejection of Jesus's gospel, but other accusations and stereotypes that describe "the Jews" in general as hypocrites and Judaism as a legalistic doctrine. This group of theologians argued that when the text is read in its proper historical context, it is clear that the statements and attitudes against Judaism therein represent hostility between competing groups and should not be read as anything more than that.[16] Despite this, the anti-Judaic approach apparent in the New Testament had permeated Christian theology. Ruether, for example, argued that anti-Judaic myth is "neither superficial nor a secondary element in Christian thought."[17] In her view, the roots of anti-Judaic ideas can be traced back to the New Testament itself. These ideas were subsequently elaborated upon during the classical era of Christian theology, laying the groundwork for attitudes and behaviors that perpetuated harmful consequences throughout history. For Ruether, Christianity's self-understanding is shaped by a dualistic structure wherein Judaism is seen as the antithesis of Christianity.[18] Since anti-Judaism is an expression of Christian self-affirmation, "possibly, anti-Judaism is too deeply embedded in the foundation of Christianity to be rooted out entirely without destroying the whole structure."[19]

Covenant and Election

One of the most fraught issues in Christianity's understanding of Judaism is the idea of the divine election of the people of Israel and the covenant that follows it, as laid out in the Old Testament. This issue is particularly delicate, as acknowledging God's covenant with the Jewish people challenges Christianity's understanding of its own covenant with God. Since divine election is a central issue in the Old Testament,

14 Gregory Baum, *Theology After Auschwitz* (Council of Christian and Jews, 1976).

15 See Eckardt and Eckardt, *Your People, My People*, 8–14.

16 See Christiaan Beker, "The New Testament View of Judaism," in *Jews and Christians: Exploring the Past, Present, and Future*, ed. James Charlesworth (Crossroad, 1990), 64–65.

17 Ruether, *Faith and Fratricide*, 226.

18 Ruether, *Faith and Fratricide*, 229.

19 Ruether, *Faith and Fratricide*, 228.

any reference to this topic contains within it the question of how Christians should read and understand the Old Testament. Until the mid-twentieth century, and in fact until the Second Vatican Council, the conception that Christians had replaced or superseded the Jews as the people of God dominated Christian thinking in the West, in the Catholic Church as well as in mainline Protestant churches. In this classic Christian understanding, once Jesus arrived on the stage of history, divine election was transferred from Israel to the church, either because of Jewish sins against God, or because of the Jews' rejection of Christ.[20] Accordingly, the church became the new Israel, and the Jewish people lost their place in God's salvific history, as salvation could only be achieved through association with Christ or his church.[21] The roots of this theological notion, generally referred to as "replacement theology" or "supersessionism,"[22] go back to the second century CE, and some argue that it can even be found in the New Testament.[23] In the decades after the Holocaust, this theological conception was seen to be at the heart of Christian antisemitism. Consequently, various churches attempted to expunge this thinking from ecclesiastical theology.

Notably, the terms *supersessionism* and *replacement theology* were themselves first coined in the 1970s.[24] Theologian Michael Azar critiques the use of the term *supersessionism* as an anachronistic label when applied to the attitudes of early church fathers toward Judaism. He argues that such a categorization retroactively imposes a modern

[20] Michael Vlach, "Rejection Then Hope: The Church's Doctrine of Israel in the Patristic Era," *The Master's Seminary Journal* 19 (2008): 54–55.

[21] See Marianne Moyaert and Didier Pollefeyt, "Israel and the Church: Fulfillment Beyond Supersessionism," in *Never Revoked: "Nostra Aetate" as Ongoing Challenge for Jewish-Christian Dialogue*, ed. Marianne Moyaert and Didier Pollefeyt (Eerdmans, 2010), 159–60.

[22] See Michael Vlach, "Various Forms of Replacement Theology," *The Master's Seminary Journal* 20 (2009): 57–69, where Vlach presents the theological difference between replacement theology and fulfillment theology. On the reception of the term *supersessionism*, see Terence Donaldson, "Supersessionism and Early Christian Self-Definition," *Journal of the Jesus Movement in Its Jewish Setting* 3 (2016): 1–32.

[23] For example, in Paul: "And if you belong to Christ, then you are Abraham's offspring, heirs according to the promise" (Gal 3:29). See Michael Vlach, "The Church as a Replacement of Israel: An Analysis of Supersessionism" (PhD diss., Southeastern Baptist Theological Seminary, 2004), 29–30. Michael Azar, "Origen, Scripture, and the Imprecision of 'Supersessionism,'" *Journal of Theological Interpretation* 10 (2016): 157–72.

[24] Donaldson, "Supersessionism and Early Christian Self-Definition," 3.

theological concept onto the patristic period, potentially oversimplifying or misrepresenting the complex and varied theological views on Judaism held by early Christian theologians.[25]

The American systematic theologian Kendall Soulen has distinguished between three types of supersessionism: punitive, economic, and structural.[26] According to Soulen, in punitive supersessionism, God invalidates his covenant with Israel because Christ was rejected by the Jewish people.[27] This is the most common notion of supersessionism and it was prevalent in the patristic literature in late antiquity. Consider, for example, the following excerpt from Irenaeus in the second century CE: "As the former [the Jews] have rejected the Son of God and cast Him out of the vineyard when they slew Him, God has justly rejected them, and given to the Gentiles outside the vineyard the fruits of its cultivation."[28] Other early church fathers also expressed this notion.[29] The destruction of Jerusalem was especially accentuated in this regard, because it was seen as evidence of God's punishment of the Jewish people.[30]

Economic supersessionism, unlike punitive supersessionism, does not perceive the replacement of Israel as a response to its disobedience or as a form of punishment, but rather as part of a greater divine plan. In this interpretation, God planned from the beginning that with the coming of Christ, Israel's exclusive role as his people would end and the universal church would become his new people. This notion is based in the distinction, initially made by Paul (Rom 7:5–6), between carnal Israel (i.e., the Jews) and spiritual Israel (i.e., believing Christians). With the coming of Christ, all the promises regarding Israel would be fulfilled—but not for the Jews. Instead, all the followers of Christ would become the new Israel and merit salvation.[31] In this way, the national or particular Jewish quality of the Old Testament becomes universal. Thus, the church in its role as the

25 Michael Azar, "Origen, Scripture, and the Imprecision of 'Supersessionism.'"

26 Kendall Soulen, *The God of Israel and Christian Theology* (Fortress, 1996), 30–33.

27 Soulen, *God of Israel and Christian Theology*, 30.

28 Irenaeus, *Against Heresies* 36.2, trans. Dominic Unger (Paulist, 1992).

29 Clement of Alexandria, *The Instructor* 2.8, trans. William Wilson, in *Ante-Nicene Fathers*, ed. Alexander Roberts, James Donaldson, and A. Cleveland Coxe (Christian Literature, 1885); Tertullian, *An Answer to the Jews* 1, trans. S. Thelwall, in *Ante-Nicene Fathers*. See Vlach, "Church as a Replacement of Israel," 41–42.

30 Vlach, "Rejection then Hope," 55.

31 Vlach, "Various Forms of Replacement Theology," 62.

new spiritual Israel also entails the "ontological, historical, and moral obsolescence" of historic Israel.[32]

The final form of supersessionism is structural. As Soulen explains: "The problem of supersessionism coincides with the way in which Christians have traditionally understood the theological and narrative unity of the Christian canon as a whole."[33] According to Soulen, the standard canonical narrative (for example, in the writings of Justin Martyr and Irenaeus) begins with the creation of Adam and his fall, after which it skips over thousands of years to Christ's incarnation and the establishment of the church, and ends with the final consummation.[34] In this reframing of the Christian narrative, Soulen has argued, not only is God's engagement with humanity seen purely in universal terms, but most of the Hebrew Bible is omitted and thus the covenant of God with Israel, or indeed any affiliation between God and the Jewish people, is elided.[35]

Michael Vlach has suggested another distinction, namely, one between "strong supersessionism," which denies both Israel's salvation and restoration, and "moderate supersessionism," which only denies Israel's restoration.[36] Nonsupersessionists, according to Vlach, "believe Israel as a nation will be saved and they also believe Israel will be restored to a place of prominence among the nations."[37]

While many Christian churches agree in principle that supersessionism is linked to antisemitism and should therefore be condemned, there is no consensus as to exactly which theological conceptions fall within this category. Furthermore, the degree to which Christianity should give up its own self-image in order to prevent supersessionist views and their attendant antisemitism is up for debate. The different forms and definitions of supersessionism described above reflect the various attempts of Christian theologians to propose an alternative theology to replace this problematic doctrine. A good example of such contestation can be found in a WCC document from 1967 on the

32 Soulen, *God of Israel and Christian Theology*, 30.

33 Soulen, *God of Israel and Christian Theology*, 33.

34 Soulen, *God of Israel and Christian Theology*, 31.

35 Soulen, *God of Israel and Christian Theology*, 31.

36 See Vlach, "Various Forms of Replacement Theology," 65. David Novak talks about "mild supersessionism" in a similar way in Novak, *Talking with Christians: Musings of a Jewish Theologian* (Eerdmans, 2005), 164.

37 Novak, *Talking with Christians*, 164.

relationship between the church and the Jewish people. The document clarifies that "God in faithfulness will not abandon the Jewish people."[38] But it also stresses that while they can collectively acknowledge this point, it's crucial to recognize that when it comes to the theological identity of Israel in relation to the contemporary Jewish people, there is a division among them. Some firmly believe that, despite certain elements of continuity between today's Jews and historical Israel, it is unacceptable to assert the ongoing election of the Jewish people alongside the church. On the other hand, some argue that it is not sufficient to merely affirm some form of continuity between present-day Jews, whether religious or not, and ancient Israel. They contend that contemporary Jews are, in fact, still Israel, meaning that they continue to be God's chosen people.

In order to understand the process that various Western churches have undergone in the past forty years with regard to supersessionism, a brief overview of the official statements of the Catholic Church and the mainline Protestant churches on the subject may be helpful. As I have noted above, the Catholic Church was the first to declare its detachment from this kind of belief—the term supersessionism was not yet in use—in the *Nostra Aetate*, where it stated that: "Although the Church is the new people of God, the Jews should not be presented as rejected or accursed by God, as if this followed from the Holy Scriptures."[39] While *Nostra Aetate* does not explicitly state that the covenant with Judaism is still valid, it does refer to Paul saying that "the gifts and the calling of God are irrevocable" (Rom 11:29). Yet no clarification is given as to the meaning of God's promises to the Jewish people after Christ.[40] In 1985, the Commission for Religious Relations with the Jews stated explicitly that the Jewish people "remains a chosen people," and added that the permanence of Israel is "a historic fact and a sign to be interpreted within God's design."[41]

38 The Commission on Faith and Order of the World Council of Churches, "The Church and the Jewish People," 1967, sec. 3.

39 Vatican Council II, *Nostra Aetate*.

40 See André Villeneuve, "Israel's Eschatological Destiny in the Catholic Interpretation of the Prophets," *Josephinum Journal of Theology* 23 (2016): 80.

41 Commission for Religious Relations with the Jews, *Notes on the Correct Way to Present Jews and Judaism in Preaching and Catechesis in the Roman Catholic Church*, 1985, https://www.christianunity.va/content/unitacristiani/en/commissione-per-i-rapporti-religiosi-con-l-ebraismo/commissione-per-i-rapporti-religiosi-con-l-ebraismo-crre/documenti-della-commissione/en2.html.

The most recent document on this subject, released in 2015 to commemorate the fiftieth anniversary of *Nostra Aetate*, provides the Catholic Church's definition of supersessionism as the theological concept that God's promises and commitments would no longer be applicable to Israel.[42] From this viewpoint, the failure of Israel to acknowledge Jesus as the Messiah and the Son of God resulted in the covenant being transferred to the church of Jesus Christ, which then became the "new Israel," the newly chosen people of God.[43] In this document, the term *supersessionism* relates mainly to the category that Soulen has defined as "punitive supersessionism."[44] This can also be seen in the document's emphasis on the church as the fulfillment of the old covenant. In this document it is declared that "the Church is the definitive and unsurpassable locus of the salvific action of God," but nonetheless, this does not imply that Israel, as the people of God, has been rejected or has forfeited its purpose.[45] For Christians, the new covenant, according to this document, is not the nullification or replacement of the old covenant but rather the realization of the promises made in the old covenant.

Marianne Moyaert and Didier Pollefeyt, in the introduction to their book *Nostra Aetate as Ongoing Challenge for Jewish-Christian Dialogue*, pointed to an internal contradiction or paradox that emerges in Catholic theology in this context: While the church argues that the first covenant has never been revoked, it still insists that Jesus fulfilled this same covenant (what the authors call "fulfillment thinking").[46] Therefore, they argued that the theological meanings of the first covenant

42 Commission for Religious Relations with the Jews, *Notes on the Correct Way to Present Jews and Judaism*, para. 17.

43 Commission for Religious Relations with the Jews, "'The Gifts and the Calling of God Are Irrevocable' (Rom 11:29): A Reflection on Theological Questions Pertaining to Catholic-Jewish Relations," 2015, para. 17, https://www.christianunity.va/content/unitacristiani/en/commissione-per-i-rapporti-religiosi-con-l-ebraismo/commissione-per-i-rapporti-religiosi-con-l-ebraismo-crre/documenti-della-commissione/en.html.

44 See Matthew Tapie, "Christ, Torah, and the Faithfulness of God: The Concept of Supersessionism in 'The Gifts and the Calling,'" *Studies in Christian-Jewish Relations* 12 (2017): 6.

45 Commission for Religious Relations with the Jews, "Gifts and the Calling of God," para. 32. This fulfilment theology can be found extensively in the theology of Cardinal Joseph Ratzinger, who later became Pope Benedict XVI. See Joseph Ratzinger, *Many Religions—One Covenant: Israel, the Church, and the World* (Ignatius, 1999).

46 Moyaert and Pollefeyt, "Israel and the Church," 165.

are unclear, as this question remains challenging to address within the framework of fulfillment thinking, as fulfillment alone may not adequately acknowledge the intrinsic and enduring value and significance of Judaism. Consequently, the Catholic Church encounters difficulty in completely distancing itself from substitution thinking, which posits that the old covenant has been replaced by the new covenant through Christ. The theological exploration of this issue remains complex and multifaceted.

The Protestant churches have issued multiple statements concerning their relationship with Judaism, most of them published a decade or more after *Nostra Aetate*.[47] While many of these statements contain an admission of guilt for not protesting the Holocaust, there are far fewer official statements that address the churches' attitudes toward supersessionism. The Synod of the Protestant Church of the Rhineland was among the first to publish a statement on the issue, in 1980. This document declared that the churches of the Rhineland believe in the permanent election of the Jewish people as the people of God.[48]

In 1987, the General Assembly of the Presbyterian Church in the U.S.A. published a document titled, "A Theological Understanding of the Relationship Between Christians and Jews."[49] In this document, the authors articulate that the church has been engrafted, that is incorporated, into the people of God, chosen through the covenant with Abraham, Isaac, and Jacob. Thus it is asserted that Christians do not supersede Jews. This concept of engraftment draws from Paul's metaphor in Romans 11:17, where the church is likened to a branch grafted onto the olive tree of Israel. The document posits that the notion of engraftment more aptly captures the essence of Jewish-Christian relations than does supersessionism. It critiques supersessionism as a construct of the second century CE, arguing that it fails to convey the nuances of the biblical texts accurately.

[47] A collection of such statements can be found in *Bridges: Documents of the Christian-Jewish Dialogue*, ed. Franklin Sherman (Paulist, 2011).

[48] Statements of the Synod of the Protestant Church of the Rhineland and of some key theologians were published in "Towards Renovation of the Relationship of Christians and Jews," Rhineland 1980, https://www.bc.edu/content/dam/files/research_sites/cjl/texts/cjrelations/resources/documents/protestant/EvChFRG1980.htm.

[49] The General Assembly of the Presbyterian Church, "A Theological Understanding of the Relationship Between Christians and Jews," 1987, https://pcusa.org/resource/theological-understanding-relationship-between-christians-and-jews.

However, the use of *engrafted* as a term warrants careful consideration, especially given the context of Romans 11:17. The beginning of the verse, which the document largely overlooks, mentions that the church was grafted in place of branches broken off from Israel's tree. Despite this, the document also underscores a recognition of Jews' enduring covenantal bond with God, describing, in Paul's words, the "continued existence of the Jewish people and of the church as communities elected by God" as a "mystery" (Rom 11:25). This acknowledgment reflects a complex theological stance that seeks to navigate the intricate relationship between Christianity and Judaism with respect to historical covenants and contemporary understanding.

In 2001, the Leuenberg Fellowship—later known as the Community of Protestant Churches in Europe—issued a report on Christian-Jewish relations. Although this document does not contain many explicit statements of theology, it does elaborate on the theological challenges that churches face in establishing a stance on Jewish-Christian relations. It highlights the ongoing efforts of the churches to reach a consensus on these complex issues. It also underscores the theological challenge of addressing the coexistence of two groups who both regard themselves as the "people of God." On one hand, when Christians affirm the enduring election of Israel, it implies recognizing the Jewish people as the people of God. On the other hand, it cannot be assumed that the church can unreservedly identify itself as the "people of God."[50] Even when the emphasis on Israel's continuing election is upheld, Jewish individuals may still find it presumptuous for the church to perceive itself as the "people of God." Nevertheless, if the church does view itself in this way, it cannot overlook its unique relationship with and connection to Judaism.[51] The document thus highlights the intricate theological dynamics at play in navigating these complexities. The document offers an overview of various theological approaches that have been proposed to understand the relation between the church and Israel, among them the concept of "two ways"—that "Israel's way to God is not of less value than the Christian

[50] Leuenberg Church Fellowship, "Church and Israel: A Contribution from the Reformation Churches in Europe to the Relationship Between Christians and Jews," 2001, para. 1:1.3, https://www.jcrelations.net/statements/statement/church-and-israel-a-contribution-from-the-reformation-churches-in-europe-to-the-relationship-between-christians-and-jews.html

[51] Leuenberg Church Fellowship, "Church and Israel," para. 1:1.3.

way"—or an "uncancelled covenant," which nonetheless concludes with the admission that all these attempts are an "unfinished process of theological reasoning."[52] This statement reflects the fact that these approaches do not offer a clear understanding of the relation between the church and Israel, because to recognize the Jews as God's people who still have a covenant with him threatens the significance of the Christ event for Christians, and the Christian understanding of salvation history. Therefore, although the document recognizes the necessity for Jewish-Christian dialogue and for Christian engagement with the subject, it acknowledges that an adequate theological approach is still lacking: "The witness of the New Testament teaches that there are limits to theological knowledge and expression which human beings cannot transcend."[53]

It is difficult to ignore the prominent place of the discourse on Jewish-Christian relations in Western Christian thinking, and the efforts invested in trying to cleanse Christian theology of "antisemitic thinking." Yet the theological questions remain open, and there is still fierce disagreement between various factions. The post-Holocaust critique of Christian theology as inherently antisemitic has been largely accepted by Christian churches, and various theologians have offered new approaches that attempt to address this criticism, but no one theological solution has been clearly formulated and fully accepted. This lack of resolution is evident in the conclusion of the Leuenberg Fellowship document "Church and Israel," as well as in the Catholic Church's fulfillment theology, which is ultimately paradoxical—as Pope Benedict XVI himself acknowledged.[54]

This paradox may bring us back to Paul's words when dealing with the question of Judaism's place in Christian thought: "For who has known the mind of the Lord? Or who has been his counselor?" (Rom 11:34).[55] This approach to addressing theological inconsistency, as presented by various churches, seems sustainable only in contexts where the theological concepts in question bear no tangible implications.

52 Leuenberg Church Fellowship, "Church and Israel," para. 2:1.5.

53 Leuenberg Church Fellowship, "Church and Israel," concluding remarks.

54 Ratzinger, *Many Religions—One Covenant*, 40. A more profound analysis of Ratzinger's understanding of this paradox could be found in Moyaert and Pollefeyt, "Israel and the Church," 164.

55 John Pawlikowski, "Reflections on Covenant and Mission Forty Years After *Nostra Aetate*," *CrossCurrents* 56 (2006): 74.

If the idea that God's covenant with Judaism remains valid does not translate into concrete outcomes for Christian practice or belief, then its relevance is confined largely to the realm of apologetics within interfaith dialogue. The discussions surrounding supersessionism and its variations appear to hold significance primarily in the specific context of Christian-Jewish relations.[56]

Thus the discourse in Christian theology around the conception of Judaism and replacement theology has never been truly resolved. In my understanding, the main reason for this is that after the Holocaust, the urgent desire of the Christian world to clear Christian theology from its responsibility for murderous European antisemitism required a rather superficial intervention that left many questions unanswered. A big and aching hole in a "wisdom tooth" of the Christian faith had not undergone a root canal, but rather a temporary filling. A root canal is a delicate and laborious undertaking, requiring many years of consideration and evaluation, and is thus still ongoing.

Christian Reaction to the Establishment of the State of Israel

This paradoxical situation, in which there is widespread agreement that the covenant with the Jewish people has never been revoked but there is no consensus on the current theological significance of that view, caused significant challenges in determining the appropriate engagement—both theological and diplomatic—with the state of Israel. While Christian theologians debated the theoretical meaning of God's covenant with Judaism in the wake of the Holocaust, the establishment of a Jewish state in the Holy Land and the decision to call this state "Israel" transformed the nature of the theological discussion and made it politically meaningful. Some Christian theologians sought to link their understanding of divine election with the establishment of the state of Israel, thereby giving it religious significance, while others avoided coupling their theological deliberations with political queries. But the questions encompassing the establishment of the state of Israel, especially considering the many theological changes undergone in parallel by Western Christianity, are important.

To date, most official churches have chosen not to confront these questions. For instance, the aforementioned WCC document on the Jewish people relates to the establishment of the state of Israel and states

[56] Pawlikowski, "Reflections on Covenant and Mission," 72.

that while this event has instilled a profound sense of self-assurance and security among the majority of Jews, it has concurrently resulted in suffering and injustice for the Arab population. Therefore, it stresses that the WCC "find it impossible to give a unanimous evaluation of its formation and of all the events connected with it."[57] This statement highlights the difficulty that Western Christianity faces when dealing with the establishment of the state of Israel from a theological point of view.

The basis for this difficulty is severalfold. Although many Western Churches have acknowledged the ongoing validity of a divine covenant with Judaism, the contemporary interpretation and implications of this covenant are subjects of significant debate. Consequently, navigating from the concept of divine election to the practical implications of divine promises in the context of current political realities presents a considerable challenge. This process involves addressing not only the traditional belief that the church has superseded Israel but also examining the notion that the church has assumed Israel's role. Such an examination raises critical questions about the Jewish people's rights to realize the divine promises, especially in light of traditional doctrines that posit that all promises were fulfilled in Jesus. This intricate theological discourse necessitates a deep engagement with both historical interpretations and their implications for present-day interfaith relations and political contexts.

The IPC adds another layer of complexity to this theological and political discourse, as highlighted in a statement issued by the Vatican in 1980 titled "Towards Renovation of the Relationship of Christians and Jews."[58] This document underscores that the existence of the state of Israel and its political decisions should not be viewed solely through a religious lens. Instead, they ought to be considered in relation to the universally recognized principles of international law. With that said, it continues in emphasizing that the enduring existence of Israel, a stark contrast to the disappearance of many ancient peoples, is an undeniable historical reality that can be interpreted within the framework of God's

57 The Commission on Faith and Order of the World Council of Churches, "The Church and the Jewish People," 1967, sec. II.

58 Synod of the Evangelical Church of the Rhineland, "Towards Renovation of the Relationship of Christians and Jews," Rhineland 1980, para. 3, https://www.bc.edu/content/dam/files/research_sites/cjl/texts/cjrelations/resources/documents/protestant/EvChFRG1980.htm.

divine plan. It is essential to move away from the traditional notion of Israel as a punished people preserved solely for Christian apologetic purposes. Instead, Israel is recognized as a chosen people and described as "the pure olive tree" onto which the branches of the olive tree were grafted. Thus, as the debate around Judaism and divine election unfolds, the need to consider the establishment of the state of Israel, or at least to explain the failure to address it, takes on increased urgency. For instance, the synod of the Evangelical Church of the Rhineland has embraced the understanding that the ongoing existence of the Jewish people, their return to the Promised Land, and the establishment of the state of Israel are indicative of God's faithfulness to his people.[59]

The theological discourse in Western Christianity on the state of Israel and its theological significance was comprehensively addressed in an article written by the American biblical scholar Gary Anderson, and in the responses he received from three prominent scholars on this issue: Walter Brueggemann, Marlin Jeschke, and Donald Wagner.[60] In this article, Anderson claimed that Zionism should be understood in relation to the divine promises, and that Israel's right to the land is not a national but a supernatural one.[61] He argues that it is possible to advance the idea that the present-day return to Zion is a part of God's providential design. However, he clarified that it is essential to emphasize that embracing this viewpoint does not imply endorsement of all the policies of the modern state. According to Anderson's perspective, the right of the people of Israel to the land of Israel is seen as eternal, contingent on their adherence to God's commandments and their obedience to divine will. This theological stance posits that the enduring sovereignty of the state of Israel over Palestinian territories is directly linked to the moral and religious conduct of its people.

Walter Brueggemann, engaging Anderson's assertions, largely concurs but proposes a shift in focus.[62] He suggests that the biblical narrative's emphasis should not solely rest on the initial promise of the land to Israel but should also consider the theme of the subsequent

59 Synod of the Evangelical Church of the Rhineland, "Towards Renovation of the Relationship of Christians and Jews," para. 3.

60 Gary Anderson, "Israel and the Land: Does the Promise Still Hold?" *Christian Century* 13 (2009).

61 Anderson, "Israel and the Land," 25.

62 Walter Brueggemann, "Three Responses to Gary Anderson / 'Israel and the Land': Does the Promise Still Hold?" *Christian Century* 13 (2009): 26.

loss of the land. This perspective brings to light the conditional nature of the divine promise, highlighting the consequences of failing to live up to the covenant with God. Furthermore, Brueggemann critiques Anderson's approach for overlooking the pragmatic aspects of the IPC. He acknowledges the legitimacy of Israel's existence but stresses that this right exists within a complex network of other rights and realities. Brueggemann argues that claims of a supernatural right to the land struggle to find relevance in the tangible realm of political and military conflict. This critique underscores the need for a balanced understanding that navigates both theological convictions and the practical considerations of the ongoing conflict, advocating for a dialogue that respects the interplay between divine promises and the exigencies of contemporary political realities.

Marlin Jeschke's response to Anderson focused on the universal aspect of the process.[63] Jeschke claimed that in His promise to Abraham, God intended to guide the human nation to a new way of possessing land, a nonviolent way. Therefore, Jeschke reflects on the contemporary state of Israel's approach to land possession, drawing a parallel with the ancient monarchy of Israel. He laments the modern state's adoption of a worldly and violent manner in claiming territory, suggesting a departure from spiritual and ethical ideals.

Donald Wagner underscores the imperative for justice that encompasses all involved parties.[64] He advocates for a theological viewpoint that transcends the exclusive territorial claims of the three monotheistic religions. Wagner envisions a recognition of the Holy Land as fundamentally belonging to God, with humans serving as stewards entrusted with dual responsibilities: to honor God and to safeguard the well-being of their neighbors. This perspective calls for a reevaluation of land claims through the lens of stewardship, mutual respect, and shared responsibility, aiming to foster a more inclusive and harmonious coexistence in the region.

Anderson's claim that Zionism should be seen as part of the divine fulfillment of God's promise to Abraham, and that proof can be seen in the state of Israel's miraculous triumphs, is a well-known view among Christian theologians in the West. Yet this is not the classic claim of

63 Marlin Jeschke, "Three Responses to Gary Anderson / 'Israel and the Land': Does the Promise Still Hold?" *Christian Century* 13 (2009): 27.

64 Donald Wagner, "Three Responses to Gary Anderson / 'Israel and the Land': Does the Promise Still Hold?" *Christian Century* 13 (2009): 29.

"Zionist Christianity." Anderson emphasized that his position does not give a free hand to the state of Israel, as the promise comes with conditions. However, the right to the land belongs to the Jewish people on the basis of the divine promise. The responses to Anderson's article show the other side of the debate. While no respondent claimed that antisemitic or supersessionist views should be legitimized, some have argued that any attempt to understand the theological implications of the promise in our time must consider the rights of the Palestinians. Accordingly, from this perspective, an emphasis should be placed on the universality of the divine message and thus the universal message of the Promises, as well as on the need for justice for all. These three viewpoints represent the main debates surrounding the creation of the state of Israel, which encompass political discussions and actual religious controversies as well. The main challenge for Christian theologians arises when support for Israel on a religious level has political consequences for the Palestinian people.

PCT AND WINDS OF CHANGE IN GLOBAL CHRISTIANITY

PCT has been profoundly shaped by various theological movements emanating from the global South, such as contextual theology, liberation theology, and Black theology in South Africa. These movements have engaged in a critical dialogue with the dominant strands of European theology, integrating postcolonial criticism into Christian theological discourse. By adopting the liberal discourse of human rights and justice and reframing it within a religious context, these movements have significantly influenced Christian theology in the Western world. Critiques of mainstream Western theology and ecclesiastical concepts, perceived by churches in the global South as unjust, have gained widespread acceptance. Palestinian contextual theologians, drawing inspiration from these movements, have developed a theology that is deeply rooted in their unique cultural and historical circumstances. This approach allows them to move beyond the historical baggage of Jewish-Christian relations in Europe, focusing instead on divine justice as a central tenet of Christian theology. This emphasis on justice facilitates a call for transformative change in the political landscape.

Many Palestinian theologians received their professional training in Western countries such as Germany, France, and the United States, and were influenced by theologies that are dominant in the global South, among them Mitri Raheb, Naim Ateek, Munib Younan, Yohanna Katanacho, and Munther Isaac. This background shaped their ability to address theological issues from within their own context. Thus, when Palestinian Christians such as Mitri Raheb encountered interpretations of the Scriptures in the West that were inconsistent with their perspective, they were able to offer alternate interpretations derived from the context of the Palestinian Christian experience. This enabled Palestinian Christian theologians not only to respond to challenges faced by their communities, but also to turn to the Christian world as a whole and offer a contextual interpretation of issues relevant to their communities. For Palestinian theologians, the development of those movements has been crucial because their most pressing concerns, at least in the conversation with the Christian world, and especially regarding Judaism, have been significantly impacted by European responses to WWII.

By engaging theological discourse that underscores the importance of combating poverty, racism, and other forms of injustice—issues that resonate with many Westerners—Palestinian theologians have successfully reframed their struggle in terms that align with other globally recognized movements for justice. Consequently, they have sought to shift the discourse surrounding the Promised Land from a focus on Jewish-Christian relations to broader discussions on divine justice, thereby situating the Palestinian struggle within a larger framework of legitimate quests for justice and equity.

In the following sections, I will provide a brief overview of various theological movements and their impact on PCT. These movements, originating from different cultural and historical contexts, have each contributed to shaping the discourse and practice of PCT, infusing it with diverse perspectives and priorities. By examining these influences, we can gain insight into the ways in which PCT has been enriched and challenged by global theological thought, ultimately forging a theology that is both contextually grounded and universally resonant.

Contextual Theology: Old Approach, New Category

Contextual theology emerges as a pivotal approach that acknowledges and incorporates the diverse cultural and political contexts of Christians globally. This theological perspective gained momentum alongside a significant transformation within the Christian world throughout the twentieth century, a shift articulated by Harvey Cox as "the rapid de-Europeanization" of Christianity.[65] This transformation challenges the longstanding notion of Christendom, which for centuries was predominantly defined by European perspectives and experiences.

As the number of Christians in Asia, Africa, and Latin America rose, an increasing number of Christians felt that traditional Christian theological approaches did not address their daily lives or coincide with their understanding of reality. With the development of postcolonial thinking and nationalism in the global South, the gap between local communities and traditional Christian theology has widened.[66] Thus, starting in the late 1950s, theologians from a variety of denominations have turned to contextual models of theology.[67] Although contextual theology mainly emerged in the global South, the issue of the contextualization of theology has been discussed at length by prominent theologians in Europe and the United States.[68]

The relationship between theology and culture was a pressing concern for the Catholic Church at the time of the Second Vatican Council. Consequently, the themes of engagement with the world, and of inculturation, gained prominence in various church documents.[69] The decade following the Council, however, saw the church divided on these issues, and the broadly worded conclusions of the council were interpreted in a variety of ways.[70] An important figure in this context was the German Jesuit priest Karl Rahner (1904–84). In discussing the conference, Rahner wrote that "the Church recalls to the mind of all that culture is to be subordinated to the integral perfection of the human person, to the good of the community and of the whole

[65] Harvey Cox, *The Silencing of Leonard Buff: The Vatican and the Future of World Christianity* (Collins, 1988), 12.

[66] Paul Duane Matheny, *Contextual Theology: The Drama of Our Times* (Pickwick, 2011), xi.

[67] See, for example, the Association of Theological Education in South-East Asia from 1956; the Rockefeller fund for "Contextualizing of the Gospel" from 1957; and the Ecumenical Association of Third World Theologians that was established in 1976.

[68] For example, James Cone and Jürgen Moltmann. See Paul Duane Matheny, *Contextual Theology*.

[69] See, for example, *Gaudium et Spes* (Pastoral Constitution of the Church in the Modern World, December 1965), in which there is also the church's definition of culture (para. 53); *Lumen Gentium* (Dogmatic Constitution on the Church), para. 17, and *Ad Gentes* (Decree on the Missionary Activity of the Church), para. 10.

[70] Dennis Doyle, "The Concept of Inculturation in Roman Catholicism: A Theological Consideration," *U.S. Catholic Historian* 30 (2012): 4–5.

society."[71] Pope John Paul II, offers his own understanding of the implications of the Second Vatican Council, emphasizing the importance of inculturation and the council's theological understanding of the incarnation.[72] For him, "inculturation [is] the incarnation of the Gospel in native cultures and also the introduction of these cultures into the life of the Church."[73]

The Taiwanese theologian Shoki Coe (1914–88) was among the first to define the term *contextualization* in relation to theology. In his contributions to the *Theological Education Fund* of the World Council of Churches (WCC) in 1976, he wrote that contextualization involves a critical evaluation of the elements that render a context truly significant, viewed through the lens of the Missio Dei, or the mission of God.[74] This process seeks to discern and articulate how God's mission unfolds within specific cultural, social, and historical settings. Twenty years later, when the concept of contextual theology had gained a great deal of traction, the American Catholic theologian Stephen Bevans (b. 1944) offered a more comprehensive explanation.[75] According to Bevans, contextualization is a method of engaging in theology that meticulously considers several key factors: the spirit and message of the gospel, the enduring tradition of the church, the specific culture within which theological reflection is occurring, and the dynamics of social change happening within that culture. This approach emphasizes the importance of integrating the foundational truths of Christianity with the lived experiences and realities of the community, ensuring that theological discourse remains both relevant and transformative in addressing contemporary challenges and aspirations.

Contextual theology, despite being a significant theological approach, engenders debate and controversy among scholars. Some leading theologians question the distinctiveness of the term, suggesting that all theology is inherently contextual by virtue of addressing

[71] Karl Rahner, "Toward a Fundamental Theological Interpretation of Vatican II," *Theological Studies* 40 (December 1979): 716–27.

[72] For further reading on incarnation and inculturation see Aylward Shorter, *Toward a Theology of Inculturation* (Orbis, 1988), 75–88.

[73] John Paul II, *Slavorum Apostoli* (1985), 21.

[74] Shoki Coe, "Contextualizing Theology," *Mission Trend* 3 (1976): 21–22.

[75] Stephen Bevans, *Models of Contextual Theology* (Orbis, 1992), 1.

and emerging from specific historical, cultural, and social settings.[76] Complicating the discussion is the observation that the majority of theologians advocating for contextual theology hail from the global South, crafting their theological reflections as a counternarrative to the predominance of Eurocentric Christianity.[77] This dynamic has led to a perception that European theological frameworks are considered universal, whereas theologies emerging from the global South are labeled as "contextual," potentially reinforcing a dichotomy between the two.

Despite these challenges, proponents of contextual theology emphasize its capacity to address universal themes and connect with broader audiences beyond their immediate cultural or regional contexts. This perspective underscores the belief in a universal dimension within theology that transcends geographical and cultural boundaries, allowing for a dialogue that is both particular and global. Coe's insight into the practice of contextual theology highlights the importance of maintaining an awareness of the gospel's catholicity—its universal nature and appeal—while engaging in contextual theological reflection.[78] This balance ensures that the specificity of local experiences and challenges does not eclipse the broader, unifying truths of the Christian faith. Furthermore, some scholars argue that contextual theology is synonymous with liberation theology, while others see it as a broader category encompassing a wider range of theological concerns beyond those typically associated with liberation theology. This debate reflects the ongoing effort to define and understand the nuances of contextual theology within the larger theological landscape, indicating both its complexity and its critical role in fostering a more inclusive and representative global Christian discourse.

Leaving aside the debates about its definition, the development of contextual theology itself holds significance. While theology has always been formulated within a specific context, contextual theology proposes to recognize these contexts openly and directly.[79] In contextual

[76] Christopher Rowland, foreword to *The Cambridge Companion to Liberation Theology*, ed. Christopher Rowland, 2nd ed. (Cambridge University Press, 2007), xv.

[77] John R. Franke, "Reforming Theology: Toward a Postmodern Reformed Dogmatics," *Westminster Theological Journal* 65 (2003): 27–28.

[78] Shoki Coe, *Recollections and Reflections*, 2nd ed. (Dr. Shoki Coe Memorial Fund, 1993), 274.

[79] Susan Abraham, "What Does Mumbai Have to Do with Rome? Postcolonial Perspective on Globalization and Theology," *Theological Studies* 69 (2008): 377.

theology, the subjective nature of theological reflection is acknowledged, recognizing that theologians, much like any other individuals, engage with faith and scripture through lenses shaped by their cultural background, social environment, and personal experiences. The biblical scholar Charles Kraft articulates this perspective, noting that individuals are shaped by their culture, subculture, and psychological makeup, conditioning them to perceive and interpret their reality in ways that align with these influences.[80] In this sense, we can understand theology as part of a specific context that exists in a certain space and at a certain time.

The development of contextual theology has had a dramatic effect on the ability of Palestinian theologians to create a theology that represents them and relates to their political context. But PCT cannot be fully understood without a discussion of the key concepts developed in two specific theological movements in the global South, namely, South American liberation theology and South African theology—and perhaps most importantly, the publication of the *Kairos Document* in 1985.

Palestinian Liberation Theology: From Jewish-Christian Relations to Divine Justice

The term *theology of liberation* was coined by Gustavo Gutiérrez, a Peruvian Catholic priest, who articulated this concept in his seminal book titled *Theology of Liberation*, published in 1971.[81] Liberation theology, originating within the Catholic Church in Latin America during the 1960s, centralizes the concept of liberation for society's oppressed.[82] This theological movement emerged in the aftermath of WWII and the transformative Second Vatican Council, which addressed the church's role in the global quest for justice, peace, and poverty alleviation.[83]

Following the Council, two significant conferences in South America, in Colombia (1968) and Mexico (1979), propelled the movement forward, echoing the Council's themes but with a sharper focus on

80 Charles Kraft, *Christianity in Culture: A Study in Biblical Theologizing in Cross-Cultural Perspective* (Orbis, 1979), 300.

81 Gustavo Gutiérrez, *A Theology of Liberation: History, Politics, and Salvation*, trans. John Eagleson (Orbis, 1973).

82 Gustavo Gutiérrez, "The Task and Content of Liberation Theology," trans. Judith Condor, in Rowland, *Cambridge Companion to Liberation Theology*, 19.

83 The most important document in this matter is *Gaudium et Spes*, where there is a major emphasis on "transforming the world" and encouraging activism "toward justice and love."

poverty and justice.[84] These conferences particularly emphasized addressing the needs and injustices faced by the poor and oppressed, setting a distinct path for liberation theology.[85] This movement was notably shaped by the socioeconomic contexts of South American Christian communities, often characterized by poverty and the lingering impacts of colonialism.[86] The intertwining of postcolonial sentiments and Marxist ideologies with Christian doctrine marked liberation theology's unique approach to addressing these systemic issues.[87] Following those conferences, several theologians from different countries in South America published their understanding of the concept of liberation theology.[88]

The development of liberation theology was significantly shaped by various transformations within the Christian world, particularly the Catholic and Protestant Churches' engagement with issues of poverty and colonialism.[89] The discourse around justice and its political implications, previously explored by European political theologians like Johannes Metz (1928–2019) and Jürgen Moltmann (1926–2024), highlighted the church's responsibility to champion justice globally.[90] These theologians laid foundational work that emphasized the imperative of the church's active involvement in advocating for justice.

84 Arthur McGovern, *Liberation Theology and Its Critics: Toward an Assessment* (Wipf and Stock, 1989), 7–8.

85 Christopher Rowland, "Introduction: The Theology of Liberation," in Rowland, *Cambridge Companion to Liberation Theology*, 7.

86 McGovern, *Liberation Theology and Its Critics*, 7–8.

87 Gutiérrez, "Task and Content of Liberation Theology," 21–23. For further reading on the influence of Marxist thought on Latin America Liberation Theology, see Arthur McGovern, "Dependency Theory, Marxist Analysis, and Liberation Theology," in *The Future of Liberation Theology: Essays in Honor of Gustavo Gutiérrez*, ed. Marc H. Ellis and Otto Maduro (Orbis, 1989), 272.

88 For example, Gutiérrez, *Theology of Liberation*; Juan Luis Segundo, *Liberation of Theology*, trans. John Drury Maryknoll (Orbis, 1976); Jon Sobrino, *The True Church and the Church of the Poor* (Orbis, 1985); Leonardo Boff, *Church, Charism and Power: Liberation Theology and the Institutional Church*, trans. John Diercksmeier (Wipf and Stock, 1985).

89 For example, Pope John XXIII published several documents on the status of the poor in the world, as has Pope Paul VI, both relating to the effect that colonialism had on the colonialized countries. See McGovern, *Liberation Theology and Its Critics*, 5.

90 McGovern, *Liberation Theology and Its Critics*, 6. For further reading on European political theology see Jürgen Moltmann, "European Political Theology," in *The Cambridge Companion to Christian Political Theology*, ed. Craig Hovey and Elizabeth Phillip (Cambridge University Press, 2015), 3–22.

However, liberation theology introduced a profound shift in Christian thought across both the Western and global South contexts, challenging entrenched perceptions of how theology should be practiced. It called for a critical reevaluation of the traditional interplay between faith and politics, positing that a fresh theological approach was necessary.[91] Central to the discourse of liberation theology are two pivotal inquiries: the identity of those crafting theological narratives and the ultimate objectives of theological endeavor. Advocates for liberation theology, drawing on insights from figures like Gustavo Gutiérrez, argue that theological reflection must originate from the lived experiences of the impoverished and oppressed, who strive to "claim God in a world that is inhuman."[92] This perspective underscores a theology rooted in the realities of the most marginalized, advocating for a redefinition of theological priorities and methods to reflect and address the injustices they face more accurately.

Liberation theologians view their work as a grassroots initiative that voices the experiences of the ordinary, often uneducated believer. They prioritize the lived experiences of the oppressed over abstract theological discussions, grounding their theological reflections in the realities of those who suffer injustice.[93] This approach shifts the focus from a purely scriptural analysis to the tangible, often painful circumstances of the marginalized. Central to liberation theology is the concept of praxis, which emphasizes action informed by and integrated with theological reflection. This praxis is approached from a sociological perspective, viewing acts of service "for the poor" as inherently political, with the potential to transform social structures.[94] Gustavo Gutiérrez writes that the primary aim of theology should be guiding believers in navigating their faith amid the complexities of a tumultuous world.[95] This perspective insists on a seamless integration of faith with the pursuit of social justice, asserting that theology's first concern should be liberation, with doctrinal considerations following.[96]

91 Christopher Rowland and Mark Corner, *Liberating Exegesis: The Challenge of Liberation Theology to Biblical Studies* (Westminster John Knox, 1989), 4.

92 Gustavo Gutiérrez, *The Power of the Poor in History*, trans. Robert Barr (SCM, 1983), 57.

93 Rowland, "Introduction: The Theology of Liberation," 2.

94 Samuel Escobar, "Liberation Theology," in *The Blackwell Encyclopedia of Modern Christian Thought*, ed. Alister E. McGrath (Blackwell, 1993), 333.

95 Gutiérrez, "Task and Content of Liberation Theology," 29.

96 McGovern, "Dependency Theory," 272; Samuel Kuruvilla, "Theologies of Liberation in Latin America and Palestine-Israel in Comparative Perspective: Contextual Differences and Practical Similarities," *Holy Land Studies* 9 (2010): 57.

At the core of this liberation-focused approach is the principle of justice. Liberation theology seeks to meld liberal values—such as equality, freedom, and human rights—with the Christian ethic of solidarity, thereby infusing Christian theology with a commitment to address and rectify social injustices.[97] This synthesis allows liberal principles to enrich and challenge traditional theological frameworks, advocating for a theology that is both deeply Christian and profoundly responsive to the demands of justice in the contemporary world. By focusing on justice, liberation theology aims to combine a liberal set of values with the traditional Christian understanding of human solidarity. In this way, liberal discourse is allowed to penetrate Christian theology.

The backdrop of Christian communities in South America played a pivotal role in shaping liberation theology. Many of these communities were impoverished, bearing the brunt of colonial legacies and the volatile shifts of nascent capitalist economies. This setting, influenced by postcolonial ideologies and Marxist thought, became fertile ground for the emergence of liberation theology, which sought to address the systemic injustices faced by these marginalized groups.[98]

A significant critique of liberation theology centers on its engagement with political theology, particularly the debate over the extent of the church's involvement in political activities, movements, and discourse. Leonardo Boff (b. 1938), a renowned Brazilian theologian, champions the idea that discussions about justice inherently necessitate engagement with political issues.[99] He contends that avoiding political discourse under the pretext of maintaining neutrality only serves the interests of reactionary elements within both the church and broader society. For Boff, the concept of politics carries inherent ambiguity, an ambiguity that conservative forces exploit to distance themselves from the imperative of fighting for justice. This perspective underscores the belief that genuine commitment to justice requires active participation in the political realm, challenging the notion that the church should remain apolitical.

The concept of Palestinian liberation theology was introduced by Naim Ateek in his pivotal 1989 work, *Justice and Only Justice: A*

[97] Russel Hittinger, "Justice," in *The Blackwell Encyclopedia of Modern Christian Thought*, ed. Alister E. McGrath (Blackwell, 1993), 291.

[98] McGovern, "Dependency Theory," 272.

[99] Boff, *Church, Charism and Power*, 26.

Palestinian Theology of Liberation.[100] Following the book's publication, a seminal conference dedicated to Palestinian liberation theology took place at the Tantur Ecumenical Institute in Jerusalem in 1990. This gathering catalyzed the founding of the Sabeel Center, an organization committed to cultivating Palestinian liberation theology.[101]

While Ateek is often associated with liberation theology, theologians such as Mitri Raheb and Rafiq Khoury prefer to describe their approach as contextual theology.[102] They view it as a broader hermeneutical framework applicable not only to Christianity but also to Judaism and Islam. Despite these distinctions, liberation theology has significantly influenced numerous Palestinian theologians. It empowers them to bring the realities of Palestinian life to the forefront of theological discourse, enabling a transformation of the Palestinian national struggle into a language of faith. This synthesis of political concerns with theological reflection is a recurring theme among these theologians, driven by a necessity to address the use of the Bible for political ends by others. The rationale behind engaging theology with politics varies among Palestinian theologians. A common assertion is the need to counteract the political misuse of biblical texts. However, explanations drawing parallels to the logic of South American theologians also emerge. Geries Khoury, for instance, has said that aspirations for a normal life and security transcend political discourse, aligning instead with fundamental human rights integral to peace—echoing Jesus's call for "the things that make for peace" (Luke 19:42).[103] Thus, advocating for peace—a core Christian principle—inherently involves addressing political and theological issues concurrently.

Liberation theology places a strong emphasis on the concept of justice, a principle that Naim Ateek highlights as particularly pertinent in Palestinian society today, transcending religious divides.[104] This focus on justice, coupled with the pursuit of national freedom and equal rights, enables Palestinian Christians to shift the Western Christian

[100] Naim Ateek, *Justice and Only Justice: A Palestinian Theology of Liberation* (Orbis, 1989).

[101] Laura Robson, "Palestinian Liberation Theology, Muslim-Christian Relations, and the Arab-Israeli Conflict," *Islam and Christian-Muslim Relations* 21 (2010): 40.

[102] Kuruvilla, "Theologies of Liberation in Latin America," 52.

[103] Geries Khoury, "Olive Tree Theology: Rooted in the Palestinian Soul," *Al-Liqa' Journal* 26 (2006): 85.

[104] Ateek, *Justice and Only Justice*, 75.

narrative surrounding the Promised Land from a discourse primarily concerned with Jewish-Christian relations to one that foregrounds the theme of divine justice. This justice-oriented discourse, aligned with postcolonial thought, positions the Palestinian theologians' efforts as part of a broader struggle by the non-Western Christian world against injustices and wrongdoings perpetrated by the Western world, particularly in the context of colonialism. The linkage between Zionism and colonialism, as articulated by influential Palestinian thinkers like Edward Said—who regarded Zionism as a colonialist movement—further underscores this perspective.[105]

Another key element of liberation theology that deeply influences PCT is the theological emphasis on the persecuted and oppressed. This focus crafts a new understanding of who constitutes God's chosen people, extending a preferential option for the poor and oppressed. Given that both the historical people of Israel and Jesus Christ himself were among the oppressed, this theological viewpoint posits that God invariably sides with the oppressed against their oppressors.[106] Within this interpretive framework, the oppressors are identified with contemporary entities, including the state of Israel, challenging traditional narratives, and inviting a reevaluation of theological and ethical commitments in light of present-day realities. This approach not only redefines the identity of God's chosen but also calls for a reflection on the nature of justice, solidarity, and divine preference in the ongoing struggle for liberation and dignity.

The application of biblical hermeneutics, a cornerstone of liberation theology, represents a critical facet of Palestinian theology. What distinguishes the hermeneutical approach of liberation theology is the grassroots involvement of worship communities and lay leaders in its development.[107] Unlike traditional academic biblical studies, this theology begins with the lived experiences of practicing Christians, interpreting the Bible not to unearth historical truths but to shed light on present circumstances and discern God's active presence within them.[108] Over

[105] Edward Said, *The Palestinian Problem* (Times Books, 1979), 69.

[106] Miguel De La Torre, "Liberation Theology," in Hovey and Philip, *Cambridge Companion to Christian Political Theology*, 31.

[107] Barbara Reid, "The Charism of the Exegetes: Unleashing the Power of the Word," in *Retrieving Charisms for the Twenty-First Century*, ed. Doris Donnelly (Liturgical, 1999), 67.

[108] Rowland and Corner, *Liberating Exegesis*, 34–38.

time, theologians have refined these community-based interpretations into a systematic approach to biblical reading.[109] A notable figure in this respect is the Uruguayan theologian, Juan Luis Segundo (1925–96), who proposed the "hermeneutic circle" methodology.[110] Drawing from scholars like Bultmann, Ricoeur, and Gadamer, Segundo posited that each new social reality necessitates a fresh interpretation of God's word, which in turn demands subsequent reinterpretations in a continual process. He argued for the inextricability of scripture interpretation from historical context, advocating for a dynamic approach to biblical hermeneutics. This hermeneutic approach has been especially applied to the exodus narrative within liberation theology, positioning it as a central story that symbolizes liberation from oppression and highlights God's commitment to justice.[111] For Gustavo Gutiérrez, the exodus story underscores the image of God as an active liberator in history, beyond just being the creator of nature.[112] Thus the significance of the book of Exodus lies not in its historical or eschatological implications but in its relevance to the personal liberation experiences of contemporary readers.

For Palestinian theologians, this hermeneutic methodology allows for a renewed engagement with biblical texts, free from the constraints of traditional interpretations. It enables them to juxtapose biblical stories, like the Exodus, against their own struggle for liberation from contemporary forms of oppression. Given the frequent invocation of the Bible in the IPC to justify the state of Israel's establishment through historical claims, a hermeneutic that emphasizes the Bible's spiritual relevance to present struggles offers Palestinian Christians a powerful tool to reinterpret the Bible for their liberationist ends. This approach empowers Palestinian Christians to reclaim the Bible from Zionist interpretations that equate biblical Israel with the modern state of Israel. Naim Ateek has emphasized the importance of challenging theologies that endorse militarism, domination, and injustice as distortions of the Bible, advocating instead for a biblical message centered on justice, mercy, and peace.[113]

[109] Rowland, "Introduction: The Theology of Liberation," 7.

[110] Segundo, *Liberation of Theology*, 8.

[111] Peter Hebblethwaite, "Let My People Go: The Exodus and Liberation Theology," *Religion, State and Society* 21 (1993): 106.

[112] Gutiérrez, *Theology of Liberation*, 88.

[113] Naim Ateek, *A Palestinian Christian Cry for Reconciliation* (Orbis, 2008), 10.

PCT and the South Africa *Kairos Document*: A New Anti-Apartheid Struggle

South African Theology is a key component in the development of Palestinian contextual theology. The method of resistance adopted by theologians in South Africa against the apartheid regime and the theological approaches they developed for this purpose were later adopted by many Palestinian theologians.

Contextual theology or postcolonial theology in South Africa developed in parallel with various contextual movements, and later followed the influence of liberation theology in South America and of Black theology in the United States.[114] While Latin American Christian liberationists sought to fight on behalf of those who were poverty-stricken by colonialism, the South African struggle was against racism and the apartheid regime that had begun in the late 1940s.[115] Although Palestinian theologians were deeply influenced by the principles of liberation theology that developed in South America, the theology developed in South Africa had an even greater impact on the development of their theology, as they felt that the type of theological discourse in South Africa, and the methods of action taken there, were more relevant to them.

Ateek draws attention to the similarities between the South African and Palestinian struggles, highlighting their shared themes and mutual challenges concerning the legitimacy of their respective fights for justice.[116] He raises critical questions about the fairness of equating the oppressive actions carried out by the state with the defensive measures taken by the people in their desperate bid for self-preservation, under a uniform denunciation of "violence." This inquiry underscores the complexities of resistance movements and the moral quandaries they navigate, especially in contexts marked by stark power imbalances and systemic injustices.

As far as Ateek was concerned, the two peoples not only were fighting for the same basic human rights against a regime that oppressed

[114] Peter Walshe, "South Africa: Prophetic Christianity and the Liberation Movement," *Journal of Modern African Studies* 29 (1991): 34; Matthew Schoffeleers, "Black and African Theology in Southern Africa: A Controversy Re-Examined," *Journal of Religion in Africa* 18 (1988): 100–101.

[115] Isabel Phiri, "Southern Africa," in *An Interaction to Third World Theologies*, ed. John Parratt (Cambridge University Press, 2004), 143.

[116] Ateek, *Justice and Only Justice*, 137–38.

them but also suffered unreasonable criticism due to their very will to struggle. The comparison between the Palestinian situation to that of apartheid in South Africa was not invented by Ateek or the other Palestinian theologians. This comparison was frequently made by Palestinian and Western scholars beginning in the 1970s, as well as by some Israeli ones.[117] With the fall of the South African apartheid regime in 1994, demonstrating that an unjust reality could be changed, the comparison became much more common.[118] The opposition to apartheid in the West had been significant, albeit generally passive in nature. The term *apartheid*, when applied to the IPC, had a delegitimizing effect on the Israeli presence in Judea and Samaria.[119] The culmination of the equation between the state of Israel and the apartheid regime in South Africa was the establishment of the BDS movement in 2001, which uses the language of the South African struggle as the basis for recruiting supporters for boycotting Israel.[120]

Both South African theology and PCT share a critical theological concern: the use of the Bible to legitimize the policies of the apartheid regime in South Africa and Israel, respectively. In South Africa, this theological justification manifested through Afrikaner Calvinism, which interpreted the separation of races as divinely ordained.[121] Similarly, Palestinian theologians observe that in Israel, Zionist interpretations of biblical texts, embraced by both Jewish and Christian Zionists, have been used to legitimize the occupation of the Promised Land, underpinned by post-Holocaust theological narratives.[122] South African theologians' efforts to emancipate the Black population from systemic injustice encompassed a theological critique against racism and

[117] Andy Clarno, *Neoliberal Apartheid: Palestine/Israel and South Africa After 1994* (University of Chicago Press, 2017), 3.

[118] Clarno, *Neoliberal Apartheid*, 3.

[119] Atalia Omer, "'It's Nothing Personal': The Globalization of Justice, the Transferability of Protest, and the Case of the Palestine Solidarity Movement," *Studies in Ethnicity and Nationalism* 9 (2009): 497–518.

[120] Claudia Baumgart-Ochse, "Claiming Justice for Israel/Palestine: The Boycott, Divestment, Sanctions (BDS) Campaign and Christian Organizations," *Globalizations* 14 (2017): 1177. On the Palestinian BDS movement see https://bdsmovement.net/.

[121] For further reading, see Andre du Toit, "Puritans in Africa? Afrikaner 'Calvinism' and Kuyperian Neo-Calvinism in Late Nineteenth-Century South Africa," *Comparative Studies in Society and History* 27 (1985): 209–40.

[122] See, for example, Ateek, *Justice and Only Justice*, 62–67; Mitri Raheb, *I Am a Palestinian Christian* (Fortress, 1994), 57–59.

the misuse of scripture to support such ideologies. This critique catalyzed the development of South African confession theology, which underscores the merging of faith affirmations with social and political actions, urging Christians to confront and address prevailing injustices and inequalities. This theological approach draws from the influential works of Karl Barth and Dietrich Bonhoeffer, who notably opposed the Nazi regime and its antisemitic ideologies through the Barmen Declaration.[123] A seminal document in this theological tradition, "The Message to the People of South Africa" (South African Council of Churches, 1968), asserted the incompatibility of racial and national barriers with the Christian ideal of universal brotherhood.[124]

In the United States, confession theology further evolved within the Black theology movement into a form of political praxis. James Cone, a prominent American theologian, integrated confession theology into Black theology, extending its scope to not only denounce racist theological interpretations but also align the gospel with historical-political movements advocating for justice.[125] Cone's approach marked a significant shift, refusing to allow theological discourses to obscure God's solidarity with human endeavors for justice.[126]

A pivotal element of South African theology, championed by Anglican Bishop Desmond Tutu (1931–2021), is the principle of reconciliation.[127] Tutu articulated that Jesus's primary mission was to reconcile humanity with God and to foster reconciliation among individuals.[128] Consequently, Black theology aims not only to liberate the oppressed but also to encourage the repentance and transformation of oppressors.[129]

These themes from South African theology have profoundly influenced Palestinian theologians, with confession theology and its asso-

123 Phiri, "Southern Africa," 143.

124 Vuyani Vellem, "Prophetic Theology in Black Theology, with Special Reference to the Kairos Document," *HTS Theological Studies* 66 (2010).

125 James Cone, *My Soul Looks Back* (Abingdon, 1982), 45.

126 Cone, *My Soul Looks Back*, 45. For more on Cone's influence on South African theology see Orji Kalu, "James Cone's Legacy in Africa: Confession as a Political Praxis in the Kairos Document," *Verbum et Ecclesia* 27 (2006): 576–92.

127 Charles Haws, "Suffering, Hope and Forgiveness: The Ubuntu Theology of Desmond Tutu," *Scottish Journal of Theology* 62 (2009): 477–89.

128 Desmond Tutu, *Hope and Suffering* (Eerdmans, 1984), 155.

129 Timothy van Aarde, "Black Theology in South Africa: A Theology of Human Dignity and Black Identity," *HTS Theological Studies* 72 (2006): 8–9.

ciated call for political change becoming central to PCT. Likewise, the focus on reconciliation is crucial within Palestinian contextual theology, bridging the theological dialogue with themes of divine election and the Promises, which are particularly delicate topics in Western Christianity post-Holocaust. The reconciliation discourse enables Palestinian theologians to articulate more nuanced statements that offer hope for a constructive and peaceful future for all involved parties.

A pivotal moment for South African theology was the publication of the South African *Kairos Document* in 1985, signifying a major leap in theological discourse. Inspired by Desmond Tutu's Black liberation theology and confession theology, this document heralded the rise of a prophetic theology in South Africa that addressed injustices with a direct, prophetic voice.[130] Released by the Institute for Contextual Theology, the *Kairos Document* articulated a clear, public declaration of this theological stance, structured into four distinct parts:[131]

(1) "The Moment of Truth" underscored the Kairos—the critical moment—necessitating a truthful engagement with South Africa's realities and a thorough examination of the prevalent theologies within the church, advocating for a bold proclamation of their true implications.

(2) "Critique of State Theology" exposed how the state exploited biblical texts to legitimize the existing oppressive social order, characterized by racism, capitalism, and totalitarianism.

(3) "Critique of Church Theology" examined the theological responses of "English-speaking churches" to South Africa's situation, critiquing their inadequate action against apartheid as superficial and ultimately counterproductive.

(4) "Towards a Prophetic Theology" envisioned a theology that was simultaneously spiritual, pastoral, and prophetic. It emphasized the necessity for social analysis, critical biblical interpretation to challenge oppressive narratives within scripture, a critique of the tyranny within Christian tradition, and a potent message of hope.

This document's publication marked a critical juncture in theological thought, offering a template for engaging with oppression through a

130 Phiri, "Southern Africa," 143.

131 *Kairos Document* (South Africa), Soweto, 1985, https://kairossouthernafrica.wordpress.com/2011/05/08/the-south-africa-kairos-document-1985.

prophetic lens that has significantly influenced Palestinian theological discourse.[132]

The prophetic theology that emerged in South Africa, notably through the publication of the *Kairos Document*, captivated the global Christian community, sparking widespread discussions on its theological propositions and the critique it offered to the ecclesiastical establishment.[133] Its reach and impact were amplified by significant media coverage, garnering substantial popular support internationally.[134]

The influence of South African theology on Palestinian Christian Theology extends beyond mere academic or theoretical engagement; it involves direct interaction and collaboration between the two theological communities. In the 1990s, a delegation of Palestinian theologians traveled to South Africa for study, marking a significant exchange of ideas and experiences.[135] Desmond Tutu's active involvement with the Sabeel Center, serving as its international patron from 2003, further exemplifies this deep connection.[136] The publication of the Palestinian *Kairos Document* in 2009 stands as a testament to the profound relationship and mutual influence between South African and Palestinian theological thought.[137]

A pivotal aspect of South African theology that resonated with Palestinian theologians is its ecumenical nature. This approach allowed theologians to transcend denominational boundaries, granting them a degree of autonomy from denominational authorities and the constraints they impose.[138] Such ecumenical engagement facilitated bold statements against the South African regime, which individual

132 Felipe Buttelli, "Public Theology as Theology on Kairos: The South African Kairos Document as a Model of Public Theology," *Journal of Theology for Southern Africa* 143 (2012): 96–98.

133 Vellem, "Prophetic Theology in Black Theology."

134 Wesley Mabuza, "Kairos Revisited: Investigating the Relevance of the Kairos Document for Church-State Relations Within a Democratic South Africa" (PhD diss., The University of Pretoria, 2009), 103–9.

135 Samuel Kuruvilla, *Radical Christianity in the Holy Land: A Comparative Study of Liberation and Contextual Theology in Palestine-Israel* (University of Exeter, 2009), 76.

136 Kuruvilla, *Radical Christianity in the Holy Land*, 156.

137 *Kairos Document* (Palestine), 2009, https://www.kairospalestine.ps/index.php/about-kairos/kairos-palestine-document.

138 Walshe, "South Africa," 59–60.

churches might have hesitated to make due to internal disagreements or diplomatic concerns.[139]

Inspired by the South African experience, Palestinian theologians aspired to establish a Palestinian ecumenical theology, fostering unity among the diverse Palestinian Christian community. The ecumenical movement enabled these religious leaders to find common ground, minimizing denominational differences in favor of a unified voice. This unity is exemplified in the preface of a document on Theology and the Local Church of the Holy Land, published by the Al-Liqa' Center in 1988.[140] In this document, theologians like Geries Khoury, Rafiq Khoury, and Munib Younan highlighted the collective endeavor of clergy and laity from various denominations to reflect on the church's mission, purpose, and witness within their unique historical and contemporary context. This collaboration, rooted in a shared responsibility and ecumenical spirit, illustrates the potential for theological discourse to bridge divides and articulate a collective vision for justice and peace in the Holy Land.

Rafiq Khoury highlighted that ecumenical cooperation emerged as a defining feature of PCT due to the division among churches in the Holy Land.[141] This ecumenical aspect is pivotal for PCT, as it enhances the cohesion of Palestinian Christians, fostering a sense of unity within the community. Khoury emphasized that this unity enabled the incorporation of theological insights from both Protestant and Catholic traditions, enriching PCT with a diverse spectrum of Christian thought aimed at serving the collective interests of the churches in the Holy Land.

PCT has been shaped by a confluence of postcolonial theological movements originating in the global South, including contextual theology, liberation theology, and South African or Black theology. While pinpointing the specific influences on Palestinian theologians is challenging, the affinity with South African theology is notable, especially given the connections between theologians from both contexts. The concurrent development of PCT with the apex of South African theology—marked by the *Kairos Document* of 1985 and the subsequent fall of apartheid in 1994—suggests a significant, albeit complex, interplay of influences. Despite the profound impact of local events such as

139 Kiran Lalloo, "The Church and State in Apartheid South Africa," *Contemporary Politics* 4 (1998): 39–55.

140 Al-Liqa' Center, *Theology and the Local Church in the Holy Land*, 1988.

141 Al-Liqa' Center *Theology and the Local Church in the Holy Land*, 1988.

the Intifada on PCT, the similarities and influences of South African theology on Palestinian Christians are undeniable. The shared themes of liberation, justice, and ecumenical collaboration between these movements underscore a mutual dedication to articulating a theology that addresses the realities of oppression and seeks to empower marginalized communities within their respective sociopolitical contexts.

PCT BETWEEN AND BETWIXT

PCT grapples with a unique challenge: its identification of oppressors, specifically Jews, who also historically exist as a marginalized group suffering under Western Christianity. This complexity is further intensified by Rosemary Ruether's observation that the Christian Zionist movement employs a version of liberation theology akin to PCT, creating a scenario where two forms of liberation theology appear to be in contention.[142] This suggests the intriguing possibility that the ascendancy of Christian Zionism, or post-Holocaust theology, indirectly facilitated the conditions leading to the Palestinian plight and consequently the genesis of PCT. The post-Holocaust interpretive approach to Judaism has significantly influenced the Christian endorsement of the state of Israel's legitimacy, drawing on biblical narratives.

However, the competition faced by PCT extends beyond a singular alternate liberation theology. After all, liberation theology as it evolved in South America does not claim superiority over iterations developed in Africa or Asia. The narrative approach to the Bible fosters the creation of diverse contextual theologies that resonate with different communities. Yet, the confrontation between PCT and Zionism is not merely about competing interpretations but also engages with broader theological and historical complexities. This is further complicated by the intersection of postcolonial theologies with new Western Christian discourses on Judaism. These two theological movements emerge from a similar critique of Western attitudes toward "the other," reflecting shared principles established in Western Christianity post-WWII, such as pluralism, nuanced historical understanding, suspicion toward authority, and advocacy for the oppressed. This shared foundation underscores the intricate relationship between these movements, illustrating the nuanced challenges PCT faces in articulating its stance

[142] Rosemary Ruether, "Foreword," in Naim Ateek, *Justice, and Only Justice: A Palestinian Theology of Liberation* (Orbis, 1989), xii.

within the broader landscape of contemporary Christian theology and political discourse.

The concept of a "theology of resistance," integral to liberation theology, finds its roots in the German theological response to the Nazi regime and the Holocaust.[143] The work of Karl Barth and Dietrich Bonhoeffer, particularly their theologies of confession, and subsequently the contributions of Jürgen Moltmann and Johannes Metz—who are recognized as pivotal figures in post-WWII European political theology and instrumental in shaping liberation theology—centered on addressing the injustices experienced by the Jewish people.[144] Moltmann further elaborates that each culture or region confronts its unique liberation needs, such as capitalism in South America, apartheid in South Africa, and racism in the United States, with the Holocaust being a focal point of liberation for Europeans. In this context, Judaism occupied a position as the "ultimate other" for Christianity. However, the postwar era's emphasis on reconciliation fostered a theoretical embrace of Judaism, serving as a precursor for the acceptance of other marginalized groups. As European theologians endeavored to reformulate their theological frameworks to acknowledge and integrate the "ultimate other" in their resistance against injustice, this process also opened avenues for recognizing and humanizing other "nearer" marginalized groups. This evolution in theological thought underscores a broader shift toward inclusivity and recognition of diverse identities within the Christian theological tradition, motivated by the imperative to address and rectify historical and contemporary injustices.

This analysis suggests that there isn't an inherent conflict between post-Holocaust theology and postcolonial theology; both emerged from a critique of historical injustices and sought to rectify the exclusion of marginalized groups. However, for PCT, a tension arises due to the political ramifications of post-Holocaust discourse, particularly its role in legitimizing the state of Israel through biblical narratives. This stance is seen as conflicting with a universalist interpretation of the

143 See Werner Jeanrond, "From Resistance to Liberation Theology: German Theologians and the Non/Resistance to the National Socialist Regime," in *Resistance Against the Third Reich, 1933–1990*, ed. Michael Geyer and John Boyer (University of Chicago Press, 1994), 295–311.

144 Moltmann, "European Political Theology," 3–4.

Bible that emphasizes the broad applicability of its messages beyond specific historical or ethnic contexts.

Critics, on the other hand, have raised concerns that liberation theology or postcolonial theologies may harbor antisemitic elements or fail to adequately address Jewish concerns. The English Catholic theologian Paul Gallagher (b. 1953) points out that the framing of history by postcolonial theologies as a binary struggle between oppressor and oppressed could inadvertently marginalize the Jewish narrative by replacing it with the plight of contemporary oppressed groups.[145] This, in turn, might dilute the specificity of God's relationship with the Jewish people as depicted in the Bible. The feminist Jewish theologian Amy-Jill Levine adds another dimension to the critique, focusing on the postcolonial theologians' skeptical stance toward historical-critical methods of biblical interpretation.[146] Such skepticism, which views historical criticism as a colonial imposition, may inadvertently foster a form of ahistoricism that sidelines Jewish perspectives and contributions to biblical interpretation. Levine suggests that an ideologically driven reading of the Bible, aimed at supporting postcolonial narratives, risks excluding Judaism from its historical and theological context. Conversely, interpreting the Bible solely within the confines of Jewish history may alienate non-Western communities from accessing and finding relevance in the scriptures. Therefore, the challenge lies in navigating the delicate balance between acknowledging the unique historical relationship between God and the Jewish people, as articulated in the Bible, and recognizing the universal dimensions of biblical messages that transcend specific historical contexts. This tension reflects broader debates within theological discourse about how to interpret sacred texts in a way that honors their origins while also making them relevant to contemporary global issues and diverse communities.

The evolution of post-Holocaust theology and postcolonial theology reflects a postmodern relativist shift in understanding history and religious thought, moving from an emphasis on historical accuracy to theological interpretation. Both movements emerge from a critical reassessment of Christian claims to universality and the traditionally Eurocentric orientation of Western Christianity, challenging the exclu-

[145] Paul Gallagher, "Salvation from the Jews? Israel in Liberation Theology," *Asia Journal of Theology* 23 (2009): 281–96.

[146] Amy-Jill Levine et al., "Roundtable Discussion: Anti-Judaism and Postcolonial Biblical Interpretation," *Journal of Feminist Studies in Religion* 20 (2004): 96.

sion of non-European perspectives from the narrative of salvation history. They advocate for recognizing the multifaceted nature of history, proposing that multiple narratives can coexist without necessarily contradicting one another—a concept to be further explored in the following chapter.

However, the coexistence of post-Holocaust and postcolonial theologies is fraught with inherent contradictions, particularly in their entwining of religion, identity, and history. This tension places Palestinian theologians, who respond to both movements, at the heart of a moral and theological dilemma central to Western Christian theology: How does one reconcile the rights of different groups to interpret the Bible from their unique perspectives when those interpretations may conflict?

This dilemma also poses a significant challenge to Western theologians. Rosemary Ruether exemplifies this challenge; as a theologian who vigorously opposed antisemitism within Christian thought, Ruether has also been a sympathetic voice introducing Palestinian theology to a Western audience, particularly in her book *The Wrath of Jonah*.[147] Her work underscores the complex interplay between advocating for justice within theological discourse while navigating the sensitive intersections of religion, history, and cultural identity.

147 Rosemary Ruether and Herman J. Ruether, *The Wrath of Jonah: The Crisis of Religious Nationalism in the Israeli-Palestinian Conflict* (Harper & Row, 1989).

3
Mind the Gap
Bible, Faith, and History in PCT

INTRODUCTION

In drawing on various postcolonial theological movements, PCT has effectively reoriented its discourse from primarily focusing on the IPC, the formation of the state of Israel, and Jewish-Christian dynamics, to centering on its own political realities. This shift underscores the unique challenges Palestinian theologians face, particularly in the realm of biblical hermeneutics, within the broader context of Jewish-Christian relations. The shared sacred text of the Bible becomes a battleground for narratives and origins, influencing Palestinian theologians' efforts to carve out their identity within the global Christian conversation.

The endorsement by liberal and left-leaning Christian groups in Europe and North America of a Jewish homeland in response to the Holocaust has legitimized the Jewish interpretation of scriptures. These same circles, grounded in religious-humanist principles, have also championed the ideals of liberation theology, advocating for the diverse interpretative rights of scriptures across different cultures and contexts. However, the quandary arises when the Jewish biblical interpretation exerts political ramifications on the rights of the Palestinians. This pivotal question, central to the hermeneutical approach of

PCT, highlights the perceived disjunction between faith and history in certain Christian interpretations of the Bible and the linkage made between biblical Israel and the modern state of Israel. The core of PCT and its hermeneutical challenge lies in navigating this gap and addressing the implications of biblical interpretations that impact the lived realities of the Palestinian people. This tension between faith, history, and contemporary political contexts forms a critical aspect of PCT's endeavor to articulate a theology that is both faithful to its religious heritage and responsive to its current sociopolitical circumstances. In what follows I examine how PCT developed its hermeneutics from the encounter between post-Holocaust and postcolonial theology.

Considering PCT as an "apologetic theology," in the manner articulated by theologian Paul Tillich, provides a useful lens for understanding its objectives and challenges.[1] Tillich conceptualizes apologetic theology as responding to the implicit questions posed by the prevailing "situation," rather than merely defending doctrine. Theologian Judith Gruber further expands on this idea, suggesting that apologetic theology acknowledges the influence of external discourses on Christian traditions and leverages the complexity of Christian practices as a foundation for exploring divine knowledge.[2] This approach embraces the deep theological inquiries emerging from a critical examination of Christian tradition.

The pivotal question for Palestinian theologians, as highlighted by Michel Sabbah, centers on the relationship between ancient biblical history and contemporary history.[3] This inquiry delves into the heart of Palestinian theological challenges, examining the tension between the historical context of biblical narratives and their significance as sacred texts of faith. Sabbah's articulation of this dilemma brings to light several critical questions:

(1) The correlation between ancient biblical history and the current historical moment;
(2) the comparison of biblical Israel with the modern state of Israel;

[1] Paul Tillich, *Systematic Theology*, vol. 1 (University of Chicago Press, 1951), 6.

[2] Judith Gruber, "Doing Theology with Cultural Studies Rewriting History—Reimagining Salvation—Decolonizing Theology," *Louvain Studies* 42 (2019): 105.

[3] Michel Sabbah, *Fourth Pastoral Letter: Reading the Bible Today in the Land of the Bible* (Jerusalem, 1993), para. 7.b.

(3) the theological implications of the promises, election, covenant, and the "promise and gift of the land";
(4) the role of the Bible in justifying contemporary political claims;
(5) the perceived position of Palestinian people within the narrative of salvation history, which appears to privilege the Jewish people; and
(6) the question of divine will and the ethical considerations it raises regarding the rights and claims of different peoples.

These inquiries underscore the intricate challenges at the confluence of history, faith, and contemporary politics, particularly in the context of the IPC. Sabbah suggests that the core issue lies in the connection between historical biblical events, the present-day reality, and the prophetic or eschatological future.

Against the backdrop of the IPC, the Bible's dual identity as both a historical record and a sacred text amplifies its relevance and contention. The Bible's narrative, predominantly seen as the history of the Jewish people, becomes central to the territorial disputes in the Holy Land. Concurrently, concepts like divine election and the biblical promises acquire immediate political relevance, interwoven with messianic expectations from both Jewish and Christian perspectives. These expectations frame the convergence of biblical history and contemporary political scenarios in the Holy Land with profound eschatological significance. This complex interplay highlights the pressing need for Palestinian theologians to navigate these theological and historical tensions while seeking a path that honors their faith and responds to their lived reality.

Mitri Raheb's critique, in his essay "Displacement Theopolitics," on the simplification of biblical narratives by European Christians offers a profound entry into the discussions at the heart of PCT.[4] Raheb reflects on an encounter with a German reformed pastor who, during a ceremony in Bethlehem aimed at fostering Jewish-Christian dialogue, made statements that described his mission as an effort to "bring the children of Isaac and the children of Ishmael together." Raheb's frustration with the pastor's remarks underscores a critical issue in the interpretation of the Bible: the conflation of religious narratives with

[4] Mitri Raheb, "Displacement Theopolitics: A Century of Interplay Between Theology and Politics in Palestine," in *The Invention of History: A Century of Interplay Between Theology and Politics in Palestine*, ed. Mitri Raheb (Diyar, 2011), 9–11.

historical realities without accounting for the complex historical, cultural, and political developments that have occurred over millennia. Raheb challenges the simplistic binary categorizations employed by the pastor, questioning the basis upon which contemporary individuals and groups are identified with ancient biblical figures. His inquiry into whether these associations were determined by DNA, race, ethnicity, religion, or some other criteria highlights the problematic nature of interpreting modern identities through purely biblical lenses. Furthermore, Raheb's questioning of where a Christian pastor from Germany fits within this biblical genealogy, asking, "If those three rabbis were considered the descendants of Isaac, and I a descendant of Ishmael, then who was he, as a Christian from Germany?"[5]

This reflection serves as a springboard for PCT's reexamination of the relationship between biblical Israel and the modern state of Israel. Raheb's critique moves beyond questioning the historicity of biblical accounts to probing their significance in the current era, as proclaimed by Jesus Christ. This approach raises essential questions about the nature of the Bible itself: Is it a historical document, a religious text, or both? And how should the historical context inform contemporary faith? How does faith reinterpret history? These inquiries are pivotal in the context of PCT, as they navigate the "four thousand years of history" gap, striving to understand the relevance of ancient biblical narratives in today's geopolitical realities.[6] The dialogue between history and faith becomes a crucial aspect of PCT, challenging both the theological community and believers to consider the implications of their scriptural interpretations on the lived experiences of people in the Holy Land and beyond.

In Christian theology, there exists a foundational tension between viewing the Bible as a historical document and a sacred text.[7] This tension arises from Christianity's roots in specific historical events that

5 Raheb, "Displacement Theopolitics," 9–10

6 Raheb, "Displacement Theopolitics," 10.

7 See, for example, Gordon Michalson, "Faith and History," in *The Blackwell Encyclopedia of Modern Christian Thought*, ed. Alister McGrath (Blackwell, 1993), 210; John Goldingay, "The 'Salvation History' Perspective and the 'Wisdom' Perspective Within the Context of Biblical Theology," *Evangelical Quarterly* 51 (1979): 196; Carl Braaten, *History and Hermeneutic* (Wipf and Stock, 1966), 17. On the Bible as literature or historical book, see James Barr, "Story and History in Biblical Theology: The Third Nuveen Lecture," *Journal of Religion* 56 (1976): 1–17; Hans Frei, *The Eclipse of Biblical Narrative* (Yale University Press, 1974), chap. 1.

occurred in a defined place and time, juxtaposing its universal and global religious claims. Joseph Weber, an American biblical scholar, articulates the challenge facing Christian theology: It must reconcile the faith's grounding in a unique historical event with the understanding that this event, while subject to modern historiography, cannot be fully equated with divine revelation itself.[8] This dichotomy prompts critical inquiries into the possibility of establishing a relationship between faith and history, especially regarding events foundational to Christian faith. Questions emerge about how these historical events, which inherently belong to the past and are subject to the relativity of historical interpretation, can continuously serve as a source of faith across all human history.

The debate around the intersection of faith and history has long been a part of Christian discourse, but it gained prominence in the modern era, influenced significantly by the Reformation and the Enlightenment. These movements prompted a reevaluation of the biblical text and its interpretations, urging a reconsideration of how historical events are understood within the framework of faith.[9] This reevaluation challenges believers and theologians alike to navigate the complexities of interpreting a text that is at once a record of historical events and a testament of faith, questioning how these two aspects can coexist and inform one another within the broader context of Christian theology.

Gotthold Lessing, an eighteenth-century German theologian, profoundly addressed the challenges of modernity in biblical studies through his metaphor of the "ugly ditch," highlighting the gap between faith and history.[10] Lessing identified three critical aspects of this divide: temporal, metaphysical, and existential, each presenting unique challenges to the integration of historical events and religious faith.[11]

[8] Joseph Weber, "Dogmatic Christology and the Historical-Critical Method: Some Reflections on Their Interrelationship," *Christian Scholar* 47 (1964): 316.

[9] Kevin Vanhoozer, "Scripture and Tradition," in *The Cambridge Companion to Postmodern Theology*, ed. Kevin Vanhoozer (Cambridge University Press, 2003), 149–51.

[10] Gotthold Lessing, *Über den Beweis des Geistes und der Kraft* [Lessing's Theological Writing], trans. Henry Chadwick (Stanford University Press, 1956).

[11] See also Gordon Michalson, "Faith and History: The Shape of the Problem," *Modern Theology* 1 (1985): 278; Matthew Benton, "The Modal Gap: The Objective Problem of Lessing's Ditch(es) and Kierkegaard's Subjective Reply," *Religious Studies* 42 (2006): 28–32.

(1) Temporal Gap: This aspect concerns the historical veracity of biblical stories. Lessing pointed out the difficulty in believing in events, especially supernatural ones like miracles and prophecies, that happened millennia ago based on the testimony of others. He questioned how events believed in the past on substantial grounds could hold the same validity for individuals today on much lesser grounds.[12]

(2) Metaphysical Gap: Lessing's second point addresses the division between historical facts and religious truths. He argued that "accidental truths of history can never become the proof of necessary truths of reason," challenging the notion that faith can be proven through history.[13] This gap underscores the tension between empirical evidence of historical events and the transcendent truths of religious belief.

(3) Existential Gap: The third aspect Lessing introduced pertains to the distance or conflict between the gospel's world and modern humanity. This gap probes the relevance and personal significance of religious messages from the past in contemporary life. It encapsulates the struggle of modern individuals to find personal meaning and obligation in ancient religious narratives.[14]

American philosopher Matthew Benton further elucidates these gaps, summarizing the temporal gap as a question of the "what" and "when" of historical revelation, the metaphysical gap as a question of the "how" of correlating the historical with the religious, and the existential gap as questioning the "why."[15] This final question, "Why should I embrace and make this unfamiliar religious message my own?" captures the essence of the existential gap, highlighting the individual's challenge in finding personal relevance and commitment in religious teachings that originate from a distant past.

This existential ditch or gap that Lessing referred to, and which Raheb and Sabbah addressed, gave rise to various biblical studies and theological responses, among them liberation theology, which will be the focus of this chapter. I examine PCT through the "hermeneutical circle," an approach developed by the Uruguayan liberation theologian Juan Luis Segundo.[16] Using Segundo's method, I attempt

12 Lessing, *Lessing's Theological Writing*, 51.

13 Lessing, *Lessing's Theological Writing*, 51.

14 Michalson, "Faith and History," 283.

15 Benton, "Modal Gap," 31.

16 Juan Luis Segundo, *Liberation of Theology*, trans. John Drury Maryknoll (Orbis, 1976).

to demonstrate how PCT shapes its reading of the Bible in order to respond to the different discourses and power circles that construct the way Christians relate to the Bible in the context of the IPC, and how PCT attempts to navigate between perceiving the biblical texts as narratives of faith and/or history.

THE LIBERATION OF THE BIBLE AND THE HERMENEUTICAL CIRCLE

The emergence of liberation theology's biblical hermeneutics can be directly traced to the need to address the profound gap between faith and history as depicted in the Bible. This gap, highlighting the intricate relationship between historical events and their theological implications, is of paramount importance to liberation theologians and other postcolonial thinkers. In Western contexts, the historical narratives of the Bible are often intertwined with the identity and history of believers and so do not significantly impede their engagement with the text. However, for communities outside the West, such as those in Latin America or Africa, the situation differs markedly. For these communities, the Bible's historical narratives, rooted in distant lands and times, may seem alien and disconnected from their lived experiences.

This disconnection is not solely temporal but also spatial and cultural, necessitating these communities to bridge a substantial divide to incorporate biblical history meaningfully into their lives and faith. Liberation theologians, recognizing the alienation that can arise from conventional historical-critical interpretations of the Bible, sought to develop a hermeneutical approach that resonates with their contemporary sociopolitical contexts. They critique the traditional biblical interpretation as reflective of Western, Judeo-Christian norms that perpetuate Western cultural hegemony.[17] Sergio Torres and Virginia Fabella have underscored the dominance of European and North American theologies within Christian discourse, pointing out the cultural

[17] Gustavo Gutiérrez, *A Theology of Liberation: History, Politics, and Salvation*, trans. John Eagleson (Orbis, 1973), 12; Gerald West, "The Bible and the Poor: A New Way of Doing Theology," in *The Cambridge Companion to Liberation Theology*, ed. Christopher Rowland, 2nd ed. (Cambridge University Press, 2007), 159. On the importance of experience in liberation theology, see, for example, Gutiérrez, *Theology of Liberation*, ix.

dominance these theologies exert.[18] They argue against adopting these theologies uncritically, without considering their relevance and applicability to the specific realities of non-Western communities. They call for deep reflection on the specific realities of one situation and to interpret the word of God in light of these contextual realities. This approach champions a reading of the Bible that not only acknowledges but is also informed by the experiences, struggles, and aspirations of communities marginalized by global power dynamics. Through this lens, liberation theology seeks to reinterpret the biblical narrative in a manner that empowers these communities, advocating for justice and liberation in a contextually relevant and meaningful way.

In their pursuit of interpreting the Bible through the lens of their lived experiences, liberation theologians adopted a novel historical perspective deeply rooted in the dialectical theories of Hegel and Marx, with theological expansion by Jürgen Moltmann.[19] This dialectical method suggests that the progression of history and societal evolution is propelled by the conflict between opposing forces or contradictions. These conflicts are dynamic, rather than static or intractable, leading to the creation of new conditions or realizations—known as syntheses.

In the framework of South American liberation theology, heavily influenced by Marx's ideas, the dialectic is conceptualized as a conflict between social classes: on one side, the oppressed or economically disadvantaged poor, and on the other, their oppressors or the economically privileged elite.[20] This perspective is fundamentally geared toward achieving liberation, aligning with Jürgen Moltmann's "theology of hope," where the end goal is the emancipation from oppressive structures.[21]

[18] Sergio Torres and Virginia Fabella, *The Emergent Gospel: Theology from the Underside of History* (Orbis, 1978), 269.

[19] Samuel Escobar, "Liberation Theology," in *The Blackwell Encyclopedia of Modern Christian Thought*, ed. Alister E. McGrath (Blackwell, 1993), 333; Robert Cornelison, "The Development and Influence of Moltmann's Theology," *Asbury Theological Journal* 55 (2000): 25; Rebecca Chopp and Ethna Regan, "Latin American Liberation Theology," in *The Modern Theologians: An Introduction to Christian Theology Since 1918*, ed. David Ford and Rachel Muers (Blackwell, 2005), 470.

[20] Leonardo Boff and Clodovis Boff, *Introducing Liberation Theology*, trans. Paul Burns (Orbis, 1989), 27–29; Enrique Dussel, *Beyond Philosophy: Ethics, History, Marxism, and Liberation Theology* (Rowman & Littlefield, 2003), 85–87.

[21] Randall Otto, "God and History in Jürgen Moltmann," *Journal of the Evangelical Theological Society* 35 (1992): 375–76.

Within this theological approach, the interpretation of biblical history is imbued with this dialectical conflict, emphasizing the narrative of liberation as its core promise.[22] Moltmann posits that the essence of understanding history lies not merely in the factual recounting of events but in the acknowledgment of divine promises made within these historical contexts.

Gustavo Gutiérrez, a pivotal figure in liberation theology, further elucidates this idea by suggesting that faith is perpetuated not by merely recalling historical events but by reinterpreting these events in the context of present circumstances and God's ongoing promises.[23] This approach underscores the dynamic nature of faith, which is continually redefined and rejuvenated by current realities and the hopeful anticipation of liberation, aligning historical biblical narratives with the lived experiences of contemporary communities struggling for justice and freedom.

The approach to biblical interpretation within liberation theology is deeply rooted in this dialectical understanding of history, emphasizing the importance of recognizing social categories and the belief that the Bible's redemptive message is fundamentally one of liberation and justice, intricately linked to the interplay between historical events and the concept of salvation.[24] This perspective posits that the Bible's relevance and meaning are derived specifically from this context of liberation, focusing not on individual salvation but on the collective emancipation of peoples, nations, or societies.[25]

Liberation theology advocates for the application of social science methodologies in interpreting the Bible, aiming to situate its message within a contemporary, expansive context.[26] This approach highlights, for example, the biblical narrative of the exodus not merely as a historical event but as a paradigmatic example of divine intervention in

22 Jürgen Moltmann, *Theology of Hope: On the Ground and the Implications of a Christian Eschatology*, trans. James Leitch (SCM, 1967), 107.

23 Gustavo Gutiérrez, *The Power of the Poor in History*, trans. Robert Barr (SCM, 1983), 6.

24 Boff, *Introducing Liberation Theology*, 27. David Tombs, "The Hermeneutic of Liberation," in *Approaches to New Testament Study*, ed. Stanley E. Porter and David Tombs (Sheffield Academic, 1995), 317.

25 Pablo R. Andiñach and Alejandro F. Botta, introduction to *The Bible and the Hermeneutics of Liberation*, ed. Pablo R. Andiñach and Alejandro F. Botta (Society of Biblical Literature, 2009), 6–7.

26 Peter Phan, "Method in Liberation Theology," *Theological Studies* 61 (2000): 43–46.

history for the purpose of liberating an oppressed people.[27] Such narratives provide a lens through which the oppressed of today can interpret their own circumstances, making personal and collective human experiences within history crucial hermeneutical keys. This theological strand integrates the method of historical critique while bringing to the fore discussions on social classes, particularly the poor, who have been marginalized in traditional theological discourses. Gutiérrez emphasizes the newfound visibility and presence of those historically excluded from society and the church, marking a significant shift toward inclusivity.[28]

A critical component of liberation theology is the adoption of a "hermeneutic of suspicion," inspired by the works of the "masters of suspicion"—Marx, Freud, and Nietzsche.[29] This approach is grounded in the understanding that all interpretations are inherently influenced by underlying ideologies.[30] Consequently, liberation theology operates with the awareness that the act of biblical interpretation is never neutral but is always colored by the interpreter's perspectives and biases. This acknowledgment encourages a critical examination of texts, urging theologians and believers alike to remain vigilant of the ideological influences that shape their understanding of scripture, ensuring that the pursuit of liberation and justice remains central to their interpretive efforts.

Juan Luis Segundo's "Hermeneutical Circle"

In his book *Liberation of Theology*, Juan Luis Segundo presents a scheme of the hermeneutical method of liberation theology, and the following discussion is heavily based on his insights.[31] For Segundo, liberation

[27] See M. J. Oosthuizen, "Scripture and Context: The Use of Liberation Theology in the Hermeneutics of Liberation Theology," *Scriptura* 25 (1988): 7–22; Enrique Dussel, "Exodus as a Paradigm in Liberation Theology," in *Exodus: A Lasting Paradigm*, ed. Bas van Iersel and Anton Weiler (T&T Clark, 1987), 83–92.

[28] Gustavo Gutiérrez, "The Task and Content of Liberation Theology," trans. Judith Condor, in Rowland, *Cambridge Companion to Liberation Theology*, 20.

[29] Susan Brooks and Mary Engel, "Lift Every Voice," in *Lift Every Voice: Constructing Christian Theologies from the Underside*, ed. Susan Brooks and Mary Engel (Harper & Row, 1990), 11. The term "hermeneutic of suspicion" was coined by Paul Ricoeur in *Freud and Philosophy: An Essay on Interpretation*, trans. Denis Savage (Yale University Press, 1970), 32–36.

[30] See Segundo, *Liberation of Theology*, 8.

[31] Segundo, *Liberation of Theology*, 7–38.

theology, unlike other traditional academic theologies, aims not only to "open up the past, but also to explain the present."[32] Liberation theologians propose a method to contextualize the divine message, making it relevant to our current times.[33] This method, referred to by Juan Luis Segundo as the "hermeneutic circle," emphasizes the dynamic nature of biblical interpretation, which evolves in response to contemporary societal changes. Segundo points out that while Rudolf Bultmann also employs the term "hermeneutic circle," its origins can be traced back to Friedrich Schleiermacher, with Hans-Georg Gadamer being its most notable proponent in recent times. This hermeneutical approach underlines the necessity of continually revisiting and reinterpreting scripture to ensure its messages remain pertinent to the challenges and realities faced by communities today.[34]

In presenting his hermeneutic circle, Segundo mentions four main points:[35]

(1) Our unique perspective on reality, which fosters ideological suspicion;
(2) the extension of this ideological suspicion to the broader ideological framework, including theology;
(3) the emergence of a fresh perspective on theological reality, leading to exegetical suspicion (this entails doubting whether the prevailing interpretation of the Bible has adequately considered crucial information); and
(4) the development of a novel hermeneutic, a fresh approach to interpreting our foundational faith source (scripture) while incorporating new elements into our understanding.

Juan Luis Segundo's hermeneutic circle begins with an analysis of the current context of the community, emphasizing the importance of interpreting one's own reality before consulting scripture.[36] This process aims to discern the biblical message relevant to transforming the present condition of existence. According to Segundo, this approach

[32] Segundo, *Liberation of Theology*, 8. By "traditional academic theology" he means mainly the critical-historical approach.

[33] Segundo, *Liberation of Theology*, 8.

[34] See Wallace Martin, "The Hermeneutic Circle and the Art of Interpretation," *Comparative Literature* 24 (1972): 97–117.

[35] Segundo, *Liberation of Theology*, 39.

[36] Rasiah Sugirtharajah, *The Bible and the Third World: Precolonial, Colonial and Postcolonial Encounters* (Cambridge University Press, 2001), 207.

inherently results in a liberation theology that is partial, aligning theology with the dynamic, ever-evolving reality of life.[37] This partiality, however, is justified as it seeks to identify and prioritize aspects of divine revelation that are most pertinent for liberation in the current historical moment.[38] The hermeneutic circle also serves to uncover the ideological underpinnings of theology, highlighting how oppression often masquerades behind ideologies that distort the true nature of human experiences.[39] Recognizing the ideology that perpetuates oppression is crucial, as it allows for the development of a new hermeneutics—a fresh way to engage with scripture that directly informs practical action toward liberation.[40]

Segundo posits two critical conditions for theology to qualify as liberation theology: first, it must address questions broad and fundamental enough to prompt significant shifts in societal, political, and global perceptions; second, it must acknowledge the need for a profound transformation in worldviews.[41] The resolution of such questions necessitates a reinterpretation of scripture that keeps pace with evolving challenges. If theological interpretations do not evolve alongside these problems, the issues at hand remain unresolved.[42] This innovative hermeneutical framework enables theologians to explore the identity and aspirations of their communities during times of turmoil. Segundo echoes James Cone's perspective on Black theology, which seeks "new ways of talking about God" that enhance self-understanding and empowerment among the oppressed.[43] By severing the link between God and the oppressor, this approach fosters a reinterpretation of divine narratives in a manner that advocates for the liberation and dignity of the oppressed.

Using Juan Luis Segundo's hermeneutic circle in analyzing PCT offers profound insights, especially when placed within the ambit of

37 Alfred Hennelly, "The Challenge of Juan Luis Segundo," *Theological Studies* 38 (1977): 126–27.

38 Segundo, *Liberation of Theology*, 33.

39 Segundo, *Liberation of Theology*, 27.

40 Ann Wansbrough, "The Relationship Between Theology and Reality," in *Reliving Our Faith Today*, ed. Antone Hope and Yong Ting Jin (World Christian Federation, Asia-Pacific Region, 1992), 116.

41 Segundo, *Liberation of Theology*, 8–9.

42 Segundo, *Liberation of Theology*, 9.

43 Segundo, *Liberation of Theology*, 29; James Cone, *A Black Theology of Liberation* (Lippincott, 1970), 40.

liberation theology's dialogue with biblical texts and historical contexts. The hermeneutic circle's critical features greatly enhance our understanding of PCT by emphasizing the need for a hermeneutics of suspicion, which scrutinizes the underlying ideologies shaping theological discourse. This approach foregrounds the dynamics between the oppressed and the oppressor, casting PCT as a marginalized theology that provides a counterpoint to conservative interpretations by emphasizing the lived experiences of the oppressed. Central to this analysis is the notion that redemption is synonymous with liberation, imbuing PCT with a social and political dimension that challenges conventional notions of salvation. By acknowledging the inherent bias in all theological endeavors, the hermeneutic circle allows for an interpretation of scripture that is reflective of specific communal experiences without the pretense of universality. This framework not only situates PCT within a broader theological discussion but also underlines its unique contributions to understanding the interplay between faith, oppression, and the quest for liberation.

THE PALESTINIAN HERMENEUTIC CIRCLE

Using the hermeneutic circle to examine PCT necessitates acknowledging the diversity within PCT itself, which encompasses a broad spectrum of theologians from various denominations predominantly linked to Western Christianity, each rooted in distinct theological traditions. This raises a crucial question: Is it viable to treat PCT as a unified category for analysis? My approach aims to provide a generalized analysis of PCT while acknowledging the variances among its theologians and their respective traditions. PCT embodies both a contextual and ecumenical theological perspective, thereby uniting Palestinian theologians in confronting a shared set of challenges, predominantly stemming from the ongoing IPC. This shared struggle against the backdrop of conflict is highlighted by Michel Sabbah, who underscores the collective plight of Palestinian Christians in his preface to *Christian Theology in the Palestinian Context*, noting that the theologians discussed are inherently shaped by the tribulations of their contemporary circumstances.[44]

The core inquiry of PCT regarding the connection between biblical Israel and modern Israel, or between ancient biblical narratives

[44] Michel Sabbah, preface to *Christian Theology in the Palestinian Context*, ed. Rafiq Khoury and Rainer Zimmer-Winkel (AphorismA, 2019), 8.

and today's political landscape, hinges on the interpretative strategies applied to the biblical text and the conceptualization of religious history. Liberation theology empowers Palestinians to craft an interpretation of the Bible that transcends mere historical context, instead positioning their contemporary experiences within a broader narrative of struggle and eventual liberation from oppression. Through Juan Luis Segundo's hermeneutic circle, a nuanced interpretation of PCT emerges, facilitating a thorough analysis of the challenges PCT faces. This framework enables the deconstruction of arguments posited by those perceived as oppressors and the construction of a theology that authentically represents the Palestinian people and their aspirations. Thus, liberation theology serves as a critical tool for Palestinian theologians, allowing them to bridge historical divides by casting a critical eye on traditional reconciliatory efforts, thereby fostering a theology deeply rooted in the quest for liberation.

Experience of Reality

Reflecting the approach of Juan Luis Segundo's hermeneutic circle, which emphasizes starting theological reflection from one's own lived experience, numerous Palestinian theologians initiate their works by sharing personal narratives and insights into the IPC.[45] These stories include the personal, often difficult tales of their families, which are presented as part of the tragic dispossession of many Palestinians during the 1948 and 1967 wars. The personal stories are usually followed by a historical survey of the presence of Christians in the Holy Land and a description of the IPC.[46] With the narrative of their own experience of reality, the Palestinian theologians can, in the words of

[45] See, for example, Munib Younan, *Witnessing for Peace: In Jerusalem and the World* (Fortress, 2003), chapter 1, "The Younan Family Story;" Mitri Raheb, *I Am a Palestinian Christian* (Fortress, 1994), 3–5, 55–64; Naim Ateek, *Justice and Only Justice: A Palestinian Theology of Liberation* (Orbis, 1989), 7–12; Yohanna Katanacho, *The Land of Christ: A Palestinian Cry* (Pickwick, 2013), 2–6.

[46] On the history of Christians in the Holy Land, see, for example, Ateek, *Justice and Only Justice*, 50–57; Raheb, *I Am a Palestinian Christian*, 6–12; Rafiq Khoury, "Palestinian Contextual Theology: A General Survey," in Khoury and Zimmer-Winkel, *Christian Theology in the Palestinian Context*, 9–15. For survey on the conflict see Ateek, *Justice and Only Justice*, 30–49; Raheb, *I Am a Palestinian Christian*, 15–25; *Kairos Palestine Document: A Moment of Truth. A Word of Faith, Hope and Love from the Heart of Palestinian Suffering* (Kairos Palestine, 2009), available at https://www.kairospalestine.ps, para. 1.

Rafiq Khoury, "express their attachment to the land, their people, and their faith."[47] These narratives intertwine personal experiences, the historical trajectories of Christian communities, and the broader history of the IPC, highlighting a deeply woven relationship between Christian faith, the Palestinian people, and their attachment to the land. This intricate linkage underscores the heightened tensions and realities of living under occupation, positioning their theological reflections within a contextual framework. Through the lens of liberation theology, their theology becomes an immediate response to their current circumstances, advocating for a reading of faith that is both grounded in the present struggles and aspirational toward liberation and justice.

The Palestinian *Kairos Document* begins with an introduction that articulates the profound suffering and enduring hope of the Palestinian Christian community amid the challenges of Israeli occupation.[48] This portrayal encapsulates a fervent cry, born from the depths of suffering yet imbued with hope and unwavering faith in the watchful presence and providential care of God for all residents of the land. Following this opening, the document delves into a description of the "reality on the ground" faced by Palestinians living under occupation.[49] It paints a vivid picture of the constraints on Palestinian freedom, the fragmentation of Palestinian society, the dire conditions in the Gaza Strip, the humiliation endured by the people, and the ongoing refugee crisis. Central to the narrative constructed by Palestinian theologians within this document are two pivotal historical events that have significantly shaped the Palestinian reality and consciousness: the Nakba, referring to the 1948 war and the subsequent founding of the state of Israel, and the Naksa, denoting the 1967 war which led to Israeli occupation over the Gaza Strip and the territories of Judea and Samaria. These events are not merely historical footnotes but have become foundational elements of Palestinian theological reflection and political discourse, illustrating the deep interconnection between faith, history, and the struggle for justice and liberation.

Ateek offered a threefold scheme of the catastrophe of the Palestinian people following the Nakba: human Nakba, identity Nakba, and faith Nakba.[50] For him, the Nakba was not only a catastrophe that

47 Rafiq Khoury, "Palestinian Contextual Theology," 34.

48 *Kairos*, introduction.

49 *Kairos*, paras. 1.1–1.5.

50 Naim Ateek, *A Palestinian Theology of Liberation* (Orbis, 2017), 26–29.

"affected Palestinians economically, ruptured Palestine's social fabric, and caused significant human trauma,"[51] but also an event that led to an identity crisis. Ateek contends that Israel's actions have aimed at obliterating Palestinian culture, history, and collective memory.[52] He highlights the unique trauma experienced by Palestinian Christians during the Nakba, noting the vacuum of theological responses and spiritual guidance from their churches amid the turmoil. This crisis of faith, described by Ateek as a "faith Nakba," emerges as a recurring theme in PCT.[53] It reflects the dissonance between the traditional understanding of the Bible and the lived experience of the Bible and God within the IPC. A critical focus of PCT is not solely on Israeli policies but on the broader question of Christian endorsement or legitimation of the state of Israel. This scrutiny stems from witnessing direct support for Israel by certain churches and the silence of others concerning the political reality. The Palestinian *Kairos Document* poignantly begins with a quote from Jeremiah 6:14, challenging the superficial discourse on peace in the Middle East: "They say: 'Peace, peace,' when there is no peace."[54] The document critiques the gap between rhetoric and reality, highlighting the ongoing Israeli occupation and its repercussions on Palestinian freedom and life.

The crisis of faith experienced by Palestinian Christians catalyzed the adoption of what Juan Luis Segundo termed "suspicion hermeneutics." This approach emerged as a response to a deep theological crisis: the discrepancy between the profound suffering of the Palestinian people, the global indifference to their plight, and the traditional understanding of a just and liberating God. Palestinian theologians found themselves at a critical juncture, where their lived realities clashed with the narratives employed to legitimize those realities, and their belief in a God of justice and liberation. Naim Ateek posits that PCT is a product of this critical intersection between faith and the harsh realities of occupation and injustice.[55] He argues that PCT evolves from the tension that arises when the belief in divine justice meets the stark

[51] Ateek, *Palestinian Theology of Liberation*, 26.

[52] Ateek, *Palestinian Theology of Liberation*, 27.

[53] See, for example, Raheb, *I Am a Palestinian Christian*, 55–58; Munther Isaac, *From Land to Lands, from Eden to the Renewed Earth* (Langham, 2015), 375–78; Naim Ateek, *A Palestinian Christian Cry for Reconciliation* (Orbis, 2008), 51–58.

[54] *Kairos*, para. 1.1.

[55] Ateek, *Palestinian Theology of Liberation*, 41.

reality of human injustice, particularly when such injustice is perpetrated by fellow humans and justified through theological arguments. Geries Khoury further articulates this theological conflict, rejecting any notion that God is complicit in the suffering of the Palestinian people at the hands of the Israeli government and its security forces. "If it is true that God is behind all our suffering . . . then we are the most wretched and God-forsaken of all people." He vehemently opposes the idea that such oppression could be considered part of the "good news" of the gospel.[56]

Applying Suspicion

The suspicion engendered by the stark realities faced by Palestinian Christians propels them into the second phase of Segundo's hermeneutical circle—the application of suspicion to uncover the underlying mechanisms of ideology.[57] Segundo elucidates that ideology shapes worldviews, including theological perspectives, by embedding certain presuppositions and biases into the fabric of thought. In this context, Palestinian Christian theologians employ suspicion as a tool to dissect and analyze the ideologies that justify and perpetuate their oppression. This critical examination aims to reveal how certain theological narratives and interpretations have been co-opted to support political agendas, thereby obscuring or distorting the essence of faith that calls for justice, peace, and liberation. By scrutinizing ideology, these theologians seek to reclaim and reinterpret theological concepts in a way that reflects the reality of their suffering and aligns with their understanding of God as a deity of justice and love.

Palestinian theologians, while not directly engaging with broader ideological discourses, focus on the intersection where ideology becomes enmeshed with theology. Their critique often centers on the use or, more accurately, the misuse of biblical texts within the context of the IPC. A core accusation implicit in their analysis is that the stance of Western Churches toward this conflict is deeply imbued with a Eurocentric perspective, one invariably shaped by prevailing power structures. This perspective is critiqued for often favoring narratives that align with geopolitical interests or theolog-

[56] Geries Khoury, "Olive Tree Theology: Rooted in the Palestinian Soul," *Al-Liqa' Journal* 26 (2006): 63.

[57] Segundo, *Liberation of Theology*, 9.

ical positions that inadvertently support the status quo of occupation and injustice.[58]

The claims of Palestinian theologians correspond to previous criticisms of biblical study, and especially the historical-critical method, focusing on the dominance of Western thought in biblical interpretation.[59] The main argument against the historical-critical approach is the question of whether it is really possible to read the text objectively or to uncover any definitive historical truths.[60] This critique is the central claim of postmodernism against the modernist understanding of science. In historical studies, postmodernism challenges the certainty that one can relate to facts, objectivity, or truth.[61] Instead, it argues that there could never be one perspective of the past, and that history is always complex and relative.[62] From the 1970s onwards, the perception of history underwent a significant transformation, influenced by the rise of hermeneutic studies. While the past had been seen as a series of events to be described and explained objectively by historians, the new approach emphasized the role of historians not merely as explainers but as interpreters or representers of the past. This shift acknowledges that the act of recounting history involves interpretation, bringing to light the subjectivity inherent in historical narratives. Historians, therefore, are recognized not just as objective observers but as active participants in shaping how the past is understood, highlighting the interplay between the historian's perspective and the

[58] See, for example, Mitri Raheb, *Faith in the Face of Empire: The Bible Through Palestinian Eyes* (Orbis, 2014), 30–33; Rafiq Khoury, "The Conflict of Narratives from Memory to Prophecy," in *The Invention of History: A Century of Interplay Between Theology and Politics in Palestine*, ed. Mitri Raheb (Diyar, 2012), 260–62; Jamal Khader, "Towards a New Theological Understanding vis-à-vis Palestine in the Twenty-First Century," in Raheb, *Invention of History*, 212–13.

[59] John Barton, "The Historical Critical Approaches," in *The Cambridge Companion to Biblical Interpretation*, ed. John Barton (Cambridge University Press, 1998), 9–12; Mark Brett, *Biblical Criticism in Crisis? The Impact of the Canonical Approach on Old Testament Studies* (Cambridge University Press, 1991), 1–6.

[60] Barton, "Historical Critical Approaches," 13.

[61] Beverley Southgate, *History, What and Why? Ancient, Modern, and Postmodern Perspectives* (Routledge, 1996), 8.

[62] See Bernard Lategan, "History and Reality in the Interpretation of Biblical Texts," in *Konstruktion von Wirklichkeit: Beiträge aus geschichtstheoretischer, philosophischer und theologischer Perspektive*, ed. Jens Schröter and Antje Eddelbüttel (de Gruyter, 2013), 135–52.

historical phenomena being studied.[63] Thus, some prefer to talk about a "remembered past," or to study history under the category of "collective memory."[64] This shift toward recognizing the interpretive role of historians must also be contextualized within the broader postmodern emphasis on suspicion and the critical examination of ideological biases.[65] Suspicion could be the response to any claim of objectivity. In historical studies this suspicion partly stems from the diversification of the scholarly community beyond its traditional makeup of predominantly European Protestant white men.[66] This shift prompted a reorientation of scholarly focus from solely recounting past events to engaging with the present's implications. Consequently, the previously unchallenged concept of the biblical text as a universal history came under scrutiny. Postmodern biblical scholars began to question and critique the notion of a singular, universal historical narrative. As the editors of the famous book *The Postmodern Bible* (1995) explain, there could not be any innocent reading of the Bible, as any reading is inherently ideological; thus traditional readings of the biblical text are assumed to be biased.[67]

Several Palestinian theologians have adopted and expanded on the critique of ideological biases, particularly with regard to the Zionist movement, viewing it through the lens of Western colonialism. Mitri Raheb, for instance, pointedly characterizes the expansion of Israeli settlements as a continuation of colonial endeavors, using colonial logic to assert control.[68] Such perspectives echo and are significantly informed by Edward Said's postcolonial critiques, which argue that the Zionist movement is an extension of nineteenth-century European colonial

63 Frank Ankersmit, "Historical Representation," *History and Theory* 27 (1988): 207, 209.

64 Robert Carroll, "Poststructuralist Approaches," in Barton, *Cambridge Companion to Biblical Interpretation*, 55–56. See, for example, Jan Assmann, *Moses the Egyptian: The Memory of Egypt in Western Monotheism* (Harvard University Press, 1997).

65 James Barr, *History and Ideology in the Old Testament: Biblical Statement at the End of a Millennium* (Oxford University Press, 2000), 28–32.

66 John Collins, *The Bible After Babel: Historical Criticism in a Postmodern Age* (Eerdmans, 2005), 9.

67 George Aichele et al., *The Postmodern Bible: The Bible and Culture Collective* (Yale University Press, 1995), 4.

68 Mitri Raheb, "Towards a New Hermeneutics of Liberation: A Palestinian Christian Perspective," in *The Biblical Text in the Context of Occupation: Towards a New Hermeneutics of Liberation*, ed. Mitri Raheb (Diyar, 2012), 25.

ambitions.[69] Said, a prominent Palestinian Christian intellectual, likened Israel's actions to those of historical empires, positioning Palestinians within the postcolonial discourse as resistance fighters against colonial oppression.[70] Naim Ateek further emphasizes this interpretation by framing the Israeli state's actions within the broader context of imperial injustice, suggesting that Israel is supported by modern-day empires that perpetuate its existence and expansion. From this viewpoint, the quest for justice—and, by extension, peace—is seen as inherently incompatible with the imperialist endeavors of colonization.[71]

Before clarifying how these perceptions are expressed in Christian theology in the context of the IPC, it is appropriate first to define the reference group that Palestinian theologians accuse of being partially responsible for their destiny: namely, Christian Zionists. In his introduction to *Challenging Christian Zionism*, Naim Ateek identifies Christian Zionists as Christians who support the gathering of all Jews to Israel and their claim to the entire land of Palestine based on a specific biblical interpretation, thus negating Palestinian rights.[72] Palestinian theologians often differentiate between two main groups of Christian Zionists.[73] The first group comprises evangelical churches in the United States, which endorse the state of Israel's establishment as part of their eschatological beliefs.[74] This group adheres to dispensationalism, a hermeneutical framework advocating for a literal interpretation of Old Testament promises. According to dispensationalist theology, the church and Israel are distinct entities, with the promises made to Israel in the Old Testament meant to be fulfilled explicitly by national Israel, not by the church.[75] This belief system gained momentum with

69 See, for example, Edward Said, *The Question of Palestine* (Vintage Books, 1979); Ateek, *Justice and Only Justice*, 22; Raheb, *Faith in the Face of Empire*, 33; Khoury, "Conflict of Narratives," 263.

70 Munther Isaac, "Challenging the Empire: Theology of Justice in Palestine," in Khoury and Zimmer-Winkel, *Christian Theology in the Palestinian Context*, 257–61.

71 Ateek, *Palestinian Christian Cry for Reconciliation*, 20.

72 Naim Ateek, introduction to *Challenging Christian Zionism: Theology, Politics and the Israel-Palestine Conflict*, ed. Naim Ateek, Ceder Duaybis, and Maurin Tobin (Melisende, 2005), 13.

73 See, for example, Ateek, *Justice and Only Justice*, 61–67; Katanacho, *Land of Christ*, 11–13; Raheb, *Faith in the Face of Empire*, 30–33.

74 See Katanacho, *Land of Christ*, 11–12.

75 Craig Blaising, "Dispensationalism: The Search for Definition," in *Dispensationalism, Israel and the Church: The Search for Definition*, ed. Craig Blaising and Darrell Bock (Zondervan, 1992), 13–36.

the establishment of the state of Israel, and was further energized by the events of the 1967 war, leading members of these evangelical groups to perceive these political developments as the manifestation of biblical prophecy, thereby reinforcing their support for Israel from a theological standpoint. While those evangelical groups go back to the nineteenth or even seventeenth centuries, the establishment of the state of Israel and the 1967 war prompted them to feel that, according to Raheb, "they were experiencing divine history unfolding before them."[76]

The second group consists of different mainstream churches, including Roman Catholic and various Protestant churches, that support the state of Israel because of either "ignorance" (as Ateek claims) or "confusion" (as Raheb puts it).[77] This second group is directly affected by two key events: the Holocaust and the establishment of the state of Israel.[78] These events led various circles in Christianity to link the biblical land of Israel and the modern state of Israel. Raheb argued that many Western Christians understand Judaism and the contemporary state of Israel only through the lens of the Holocaust.[79] As a result, post-Holocaust theology and Jewish-Christian dialogue caused many Western Christians to identify the biblical land of Israel with the modern state of Israel. Munther Isaac argued that Palestinian theologians are being asked to construct their theology in a way that will fit the paradigm of Western theology, in order to solve the Western problem of antisemitism.[80] According to this view, this sense of guilt brought the West to search for a solution for the Jewish people and thus to support the establishment of the state of Israel, and later to support its policies.[81]

PCT perceives the connection between the Jewish people and the land as another example of the domination of Western discourse and the mechanism of ideology. Mitri Raheb's commentary reflects on the European Christian perspective, suggesting a historical displacement of the Jewish people to a "distant country called Pales-

76 Raheb, *Faith in the Face of Empire*, 30; see also Ateek, *Palestinian Theology of Liberation*, 35.

77 Ateek, *Challenging Christian Zionism*, 16; Raheb, "Displacement Theopolitics," 18–19.

78 See previous chapter.

79 Raheb, "Displacement Theopolitics," 20.

80 Isaac, "Challenging the Empire," 259.

81 Ateek, *Justice and Only Justice*, 178; *Kairos*, para. 2.3.2.

tine."[82] This viewpoint implies a theological and historical distancing, reinforcing a narrative that aligns with the dispossession and relocation of Jewish identity away from European memory and toward a biblical homeland. But the connection of the Jewish people to the land led to the suppression of the Palestinian people and their history in the land. Raheb described this act as "displacement theology," as Western Christianity had "theologically replaced" the Palestinian people as the land's original people and suppressed the Palestinian narrative.[83] The link that was made by Zionist Christianity between the modern Jewish people and the land of Israel and, more so, the disregard for the native people of the land—as in the famous Zionist saying *a land without people for a people without land*—was seen by the Palestinian theologians as an ideological act.[84] As Raheb says, "What in a normal context could be seen as Orientalism, neocolonialism and racism, was baptized in a theological discourse and became divine intervention."[85]

Rafik Khoury's assertion parallels Mitri Raheb's critique, delving deeper into the colonial dynamics at play within the IPC.[86] Khoury suggests that the ideological framework of colonialism often involves the conquerors denying the conquered their history, subsequently crafting and imposing an alternative narrative that justifies the colonial project. This perspective sheds light on the contentious issue of historical narrative and memory in the conflict, where the imposition of a single narrative erases the rich tapestry of histories and identities inherent to the land and its peoples. It becomes clear according to this interpretation of the Palestinian theologians that the "invention" of history is what enabled the Zionist movements and those who support them—Christian Zionists—to link the state of Israel to biblical Israel. One of the mechanisms that helps forge this attitude is the literal reading of the Bible that interprets it as a historical book, without concern

82 Raheb, *Faith in the Face of Empire*, 21.

83 Raheb, "Displacement Theopolitics," 11.

84 Rafik Khoury, "The Effects of Christian Zionism on Palestinian Christians," in Ateek, Duaybis, and Tobin, *Challenging Christian Zionism*, 147; Raheb, "Displacement Theopolitics," 11. This saying, though widely associated with the Zionist movement, actually has roots in Christian Protestant writing from the mid-nineteenth century. See Diana Muir, "A Land Without a People for a People Without a Land," *Middle East Quarterly* 15 (2008): 55–62.

85 Raheb, "Towards a New Hermeneutics," 23.

86 Khoury, "Conflict of Narratives," 262.

for its underlying message.[87] In this vein, the Palestinian *Kairos Document* states: "It is unacceptable to transform the Word of God into 'letters of stone' [2 Cor 3:7]."[88] It stresses that the error lies in fundamentalist biblical interpretation, where the word of God becomes stagnant and is passed down as a lifeless text from one generation to the next. This lifeless text is wielded as a weapon in contemporary history, used to strip the Palestinian people of their rights in their own homeland.[89] The use of Paul's phrase "letter of stones" (2 Cor 3:7) in the passage above is emblematic of the central allegation of the Palestinian theologians. The claim is that Western readings of the Old Testament lack the new spirit that Christ revealed and that is known to Christians through the New Testament. This is seen as not only wrong, but also dangerous, as Paul says: "The letter kills, but the Spirit gives life" (2 Cor 3:6).

While it seems that the Palestinian *Kairos Document* refers to a literal reading of Evangelical Christian Zionism, the connection between the modern state of Israel and biblical Israel is also made by the other groups PCT refers to, who are not fundamentalists. Ateek's critique of Paul van Buren's work "Discerning the Way" highlights the complex interplay between biblical interpretation, historical injustices, and contemporary geopolitical realities.[90] Ateek contends that Van Buren, representing a post-Holocaust theological perspective, offers a reading of the biblical text that, while not literalist, inadvertently supports the ongoing marginalization of Palestinians by uncritically legitimizing Israel's actions and framing them within a divine approval. This critique underscores the broader challenge faced by Palestinian theologians of reconciling the rejection of antisemitism within Western Christian discourse with the need to address the consequences of such theological perspectives on the Palestinian people.

The emphasis on respecting the historical and religious narratives of Jewish individuals and Holocaust survivors is an acknowledgment of their suffering and the role faith plays in their understanding of the

[87] On the use of literalism in Biblical studies and its link to conservative Protestantism, see Aaron Franzen and Jenna Griebel, "Understanding a Cultural Identity: The Confluence of Education, Politics, and Religion Within the American Concept of Biblical Literalism," *Sociology of Religion* 74 (2013): 522–25.

[88] *Kairos*, para. 2.2.2.

[89] *Kairos*, para. 2.2.2.

[90] Paul van Buren, *Discerning the Way: A Theology of the Jewish-Christian Reality* (Seabury, 1980); Ateek, *Justice and Only Justice*, 62–63.

promise of land. However, Ateek and other Palestinian theologians like Mitri Raheb argue that the ongoing invocation of these promises by certain groups to justify expansion and occupation necessitates a reevaluation of these theological claims in light of current injustices.[91]

A New Way of Experiencing Theological Reality

In the third phase, following the discernment of a novel theological understanding, scripture is interpreted to expose and dismantle ideological influences within theology.[92] This process doesn't discard theological answers but focuses on addressing the theological questions that emerge from experiencing a transformed reality. This method aligns with James Cone's third step in the cycle of Black liberation theology, as detailed by Segundo.[93] Cone characterizes Black theology as a quest for fresh approaches to discussing God that enrich self-understanding. This is achieved by redefining the perception of God, particularly by severing the association between God and the oppressor. John Parratt's description of third world theology complements this by depicting it as an active search for self-identity that deeply engages with its traditions and cultural contexts while also addressing the social realities of contemporary Christian existence.[94]

Palestinian theologians engage in a process of recontextualizing their faith and identity by reinterpreting the biblical text outside of its association with the political reality of the IPC. A critical concern for them, as articulated by Ateek, is the challenge of how the church can convey the essence of the biblical message and its depiction of God in a way that is meaningful to Palestinians without negating any part of the Bible. The issue arises because the link between the biblical narrative and the modern state of Israel positions the text, and by extension, the God within, as excluding Palestinians.[95] Thus they seek to develop a hermeneutic that interprets the Bible from a distinctly Palestinian viewpoint. For PCT, the Bible represents a dynamic Word that illuminates each era differently, revealing to Christian believers what God

[91] Raheb, *I Am a Palestinian Christian*, 57–58; Ateek, introduction to *Challenging Christian Zionism*, 16–17.

[92] Segundo, *Liberation of Theology*, 29.

[93] Cone, *Black Theology of Liberation*, 40.

[94] John Parratt, introduction to *An Introduction to Third World Theologies*, ed. John Parratt (Cambridge University Press, 2004), 9.

[95] Ateek, *Justice and Only Justice*, 77.

communicates to us in our own time.[96] Historical occurrences are seen as part of a broader "salvation history" relevant to all humanity, showcasing how God reveals himself and his will to each generation. Raheb emphasizes that the scriptures are not mere records of past events but are intended to engage believers across all times, inviting them to partake in and identify with these foundational experiences.[97]

A contextual approach to reading the Bible, which is a hallmark of liberation theology, offers a framework for theologians to connect biblical narratives directly to their lived experiences. This method becomes especially pertinent in the story of the Exodus, frequently cited as a metaphor for liberation from oppression. Yet PCT necessitates a nuanced interpretation of the scriptures due to the unique historical and spiritual claims both Palestinians and Israelis make on the text. Unlike many liberation theologians who may use the Exodus as a straightforward allegory for sociopolitical emancipation, Palestinian theologians often grapple with more complex biblical narratives. For instance, the accounts of conquest under Joshua and Caleb, which some Christian Zionist narratives laud as divine precedent for claiming land, pose ethical and theological dilemmas for Palestinian Christians, highlighting troubling questions about divine justice and the inclusivity of God's promises.[98] This intricacy underscores the challenge Palestinian theologians face: engaging with the Bible in a way that respects its historical significance to their identity and faith, while also critically examining the implications of its narratives in the context of contemporary struggles for justice and peace.

Mitri Raheb stands out for his distinct approach to biblical interpretation, particularly with regard to the exodus narrative. Unlike others who might avoid contentious stories, Raheb chooses not to forsake the Exodus account.[99] Instead, he emphasizes a critical reading that focuses on "God's attitude to oppression." His approach underscores a belief in the transformative power of scripture when read with an emphasis on God's overarching condemnation of oppression, aiming to reclaim and reinterpret the exodus story in a way that resonates with the Palestinian experience of seeking liberation and justice. Raheb, however, like other Palestinian contextual theologians, also engaged

96 *Kairos*, para 2.2.2.

97 Raheb, *I Am a Palestinian Christian*, 60.

98 Younan, *Witnessing for Peace*, 58.

99 Raheb, *I Am a Palestinian Christian*, 89.

other biblical narratives in order to explain the true nature of God. Toward this end, both Ateek and Raheb look at the story of Naboth's vineyard (1 Kgs 21:1–16) and the story of the prophet Jonah.[100] These stories are meant to demonstrate the two main characteristics of God—namely, his universality, as seen in the story of Jonah, and his devotion to justice, as seen in the story of Naboth and King Ahab. Both stories are used to teach about the way in which biblical revelation should be understood, and, at the same time, how to oppose the standard Christian Zionist reading. Ateek captures the essence of his interpretative choice by drawing a parallel between the biblical story of Naboth's death and dispossession and the Palestinian experience since the establishment of the state of Israel.[101] He sees in Naboth's story a reflection of the broader tragedy of Palestine and the ongoing violation of individual rights. For Ateek, the importance of the story is found not only in its similarity to the Palestinian reality, but also in its biblical message. God in the story of Naboth did not ignore injustice; rather, he made sure that those responsible for it would be punished, even if there was a time lag between the sinful action and its punishment. Ateek employs the story as a caution to the state of Israel and its allies, emphasizing that God, as a deity of justice, who oversees history with a long memory, will not permit injustice to persist indefinitely. Through this interpretation, Ateek conveys a strong message that the divine principle of justice will ultimately address and rectify the wrongs experienced, signaling a hopeful yet stern reminder of accountability and the inevitability of divine intervention in the course of human affairs, especially in the context of sustained injustices.[102] While the story of Naboth serves Ateek for demonstrating the injustices facing the Palestinian people and God's anger in the future, Jonah's story is used in the context of the IPC as proof that God is a universal deity working for the benefit of the whole world. Therefore, unlike with the Zionist reading of the Bible, God cannot choose one nation over another. Ateek derives three main theological notions from the story of Naboth's vineyard: God is the God of justice; Israel's sin is parallel to Ahab's sin;

[100] The story of Naboth is mentioned in Ateek, *Justice and Only Justice*, 87–89, and Raheb, *I Am a Palestinian Christian*, 49–50. The story of Jonah is mentioned in Ateek, *Palestinian Christian Cry for Reconciliation*, 67–78, and Raheb, *I Am a Palestinian Christian*, 92–97.

[101] Ateek, *Justice and Only Justice*, 87.

[102] Ateek, *Justice and Only Justice*, 87.

God will respond to injustice, sooner or later.[103] The story of Naboth's vineyard, in Ateek's view, allows Palestinians to learn about the reality of their lives and gives them hope for the future. Moreover, it teaches God's true nature as an advocate of justice and protector of the weak.

Raheb draws a parallel between the biblical story of Naboth's vineyard and the contemporary situation in which Israeli forces confiscate Palestinian land, interpreting the state of Israel's use of power against Palestinians as analogous to the sin of Ahab and Jezebel.[104] He contends that the current policies of the state of Israel, particularly regarding the displacement of Palestinians and the establishment of settlements, reflect a departure from the values and principles traditionally associated with the God of Israel. This analogy underscores a profound critique of these policies as being fundamentally at odds with biblical standards of justice and righteousness, positioning them as modern manifestations of the injustices condemned in the biblical narrative. Similarly, Ateek and Rahab both marshal the story of the prophet Jonah to show the universal nature of God. For Ateek, Jonah was the first Palestinian liberation theologian, who learned in his flesh the existence of God as the universal God of all peoples, even the bitter enemies of Israel.[105] Both Rahab and Ateek emphasize the historical context in which the Jonah story was written. These two Palestinian theologians perceive Jonah as a nationalist, or even a Zionist nationalist, who was influenced by misconceptions of Judaism after the exile. According to historical researchers, the story was written after the city of Nineveh was destroyed. Ateek and Raheb, however, stress that it is not the historical record that is important to the biblical writer, but the message: God is a universal God, caring for all humankind, not just Israel. Ateek stresses that the core theological challenges addressed in the book of Jonah in the late fourth century BCE mirror those that Palestinians currently confront in their conflict.[106] For Ateek, under the banner of an outdated tribal theology that continues to assert the existence of a distinct Jewish god, the privileges of a chosen people of God, and an exclusive Jewish entitlement to the entirety of Palestinian land, the Palestinians endure oppression and dehumanization.[107]

103 Ateek, *Justice and Only Justice*, 88–89.

104 Raheb, *I Am a Palestinian Christian*, 50.

105 Ateek, *Palestinian Christian Cry for Reconciliation*, 67.

106 Ateek, *Palestinian Christian Cry for Reconciliation*, 75.

107 Ateek, *Palestinian Christian Cry for Reconciliation*, 75.

This comprehensive approach to biblical hermeneutics by Palestinian contextual theologians seeks to harmonize the biblical narrative with contemporary realities, particularly in the face of the IPC.[108] These theologians extend beyond merely contextual interpretations to posit a more encompassing framework that critically examines the continuity between biblical history and the present. They aim to counteract the readings offered by Zionist Christianity, which directly links biblical events to modern Jewish history, thereby challenging the convergence of biblical Israel with the modern state of Israel. Such a linkage, they argue, reveals contradictions between the biblical message of liberation and certain Old Testament narratives.

Sabbah and Ateek delve into these contradictions, especially regarding the theme of violence, questioning how these narratives align with the beatitude, "Blessed are the peacemakers, for they will be called children of God" (Matt 5:9).[109] They propose a solution in recognizing the Bible as a document that chronicles the gradual unfolding of divine revelation, reaching its fulfillment in Jesus Christ.[110] According to this perspective, God's revelation adapts over time, reflecting humanity's growing moral and spiritual understanding, which Vatican II echoes.[111] Thus, the Old Testament represents an earlier stage in this revelatory process, preparing humanity to fully grasp God's word incarnated in Christ.

Ateek suggests a radical approach of using the knowledge of Christ to discern which Old Testament passages remain authoritative for Christians today, indicating an advanced stage of divine revelation.[112] This stance, however, raises concerns among other Palestinian theologians about potentially slipping into a form of Marcionism, a second-century heresy that rejects the Old Testament.[113]

[108] Jamal Khader, "Biblical Hermeneutics in the Kairos Palestine Document," in Raheb, *Biblical Text in the Context of Occupation*, 268. Khoury, "Conflict of Narratives from Memory to Prophecy," 265.

[109] Sabbah, *Fourth Pastoral Letter*, para. 7.b; Ateek, *Justice and Only Justice*, 81.

[110] Sabbah, *Fourth Pastoral Letter*, paras. 13, 16; Isaac, *From Land to Lands*, 2–3; Ateek, *Justice and Only Justice*, 83.

[111] *Dei Verbum*, para. 32, https://vatican.va.

[112] Ateek, *Justice and Only Justice*, 82.

[113] Samuel Kuruvilla, *Radical Christianity in the Holy Land: A Comparative Study of Liberation and Contextual Theology in Palestine-Israel* (University of Exeter, 2009), 63; Khader, "Biblical Hermeneutics in the Kairos Palestine Document," 278.

The debate centers around the nature of the Bible: whether it is viewed as God's word mediated through human authors or a human document recording divine revelation. For Sabbah, aligned with Vatican II's declaration, the Bible stands as the unalterable word of God, asserting that neither the Old nor the New Testament should be excluded or partitioned for any motives, including political considerations.[114] This perspective contrasts with both Ateek's Anglican viewpoint and Raheb's interpretation of the Scriptures as purely testimonies of faith.[115] Regardless of these differences, both approaches converge on a critical theological principle: the evolution of divine revelation, culminating in the message of liberation as proclaimed through Jesus Christ. This principle serves as the foundational lens through which the biblical narrative is interpreted, emphasizing the universal and liberating essence of God's revelation that transcends historical and denominational distinctions.

This hermeneutic principle is crucial for addressing central themes in PCT, such as the divine election of Israel and the Promises regarding the land of Canaan. Palestinian theologians argue that any interpretation that portrays God as favoring one nation over others contradicts the universal revelation of God in Christ.[116] Ateek's reflection on historical shifts in Jewish understanding of God's promises underscores the evolving nature of religious identity and interpretation, highlighting the need for a theology that embraces God's universal love and justice as revealed in the life and teachings of Jesus Christ.[117]

For PCT, any interpretation of scripture must inherently grasp the universality of God's justice. Consequently, interpretations that conflate biblical Israel with the contemporary state of Israel overlook the broadening of God's message through Christ's teachings, challenging the depiction of God as just. From this perspective, theological justifications for the occupation diverge starkly from Christian doctrines, endorsing violence and holy war under the guise of divine sanction. Such theologies, according to the *Kairos Document*, not only misuse divine authority for temporal ends but also mar the divine likeness

114 Sabbah, *Fourth Pastoral Letter*, para. 9.
115 Raheb, *I Am a Palestinian Christian*, 59.
116 *Kairos*, para. 2.5.
117 Ateek, *Justice and Only Justice*, 102.

in those subjected to both political and theological oppression.[118] Regarding the concept of divine election, Raheb holds that the biblical narratives of promise and election were originally directed at a people who were marginalized and without sovereignty.[119] Asserting a claim of chosenness from a stance of dominance contradicts this foundational biblical ethos. Sabbah articulates divine election as God's call to live by his statutes and to share this guidance broadly.[120] He perceives the election of the Israelites primarily as an opportunity to disseminate God's teachings. In Sabbah's interpretation, the old covenant forms the bedrock for the new covenant, retaining its validity post-Christ. Hence, with Christ, the promises of the old covenant found their fulfillment, and the election of Israel took on a global dimension. The covenantal promises were intended to advance God's universal mission, with the Promised Land serving as a base for the Jews to construct the Temple and propagate monotheism globally. That is, after Christ, the Promises of the old covenant were fulfilled with Him, and the election of Israel was universalized.[121]

Mitri Raheb and Naim Ateek advocate for a reinterpretation of divine election and divine history by emphasizing the importance of reading the Bible through the perspective of the weak and oppressed.[122] This approach reflects a critical shift in understanding biblical narratives, advocating for an empathetic and justice-oriented engagement with scripture. By aligning the interpretation of divine actions and promises with the experiences and struggles of marginalized communities, Raheb and Ateek propose a theological framework that seeks to embody God's preferential option for the oppressed. This method underscores the transformative potential of biblical texts when applied to contemporary issues of injustice and conflict, offering a lens through which the ongoing struggle of the Palestinian people can be understood within the broader narrative of God's redemptive work in history.[123]

118 *Kairos*, para. 2.5.

119 Raheb, *I Am a Palestinian Christian*, 57–58.

120 Raheb, *I Am a Palestinian Christian*, 57–58.

121 See also *Kairos*, para 2.2.2; Elias Chacour, "Reconciliation and Justice: Living with the Memory," in *Holy Land, Hollow Jubilee: God, Justice and the Palestinians*, ed. Naim Ateek and Michael Prior (Melisende, 1999), 112.

122 Ateek, *Justice and Only Justice*, 130; Raheb, *I Am a Palestinian Christian*, 65.

123 Raheb, *Faith in the Face of Empire*, 72–73.

Palestinian theologians navigate the complex terrain of interpreting the divine covenant with Judaism with acute awareness of the sensitive historical and theological context, particularly in light of the Holocaust and subsequent Judeo-Christian dialogue. Their emphasis on the universal message of liberation in the biblical text has led to accusations of harboring antisemitic views and endorsing supersessionism. Critics like religion scholar Atelia Omer have categorized PCT as supersessionist for positing Christianity as overcoming the alleged ethnocentricity of Judaism.[124] Similarly, the International Council of Christians and Jews (ICCJ) has questioned whether PCT's emphasis on universality undermines the particularity of Jewish religion.[125]

Scholar Adam Gregerman further critiques Naim Ateek's theology as a return to the antisemitic roots of Christianity, suggesting it displaces Jews from their own narrative, akin to historic Christian supersessionism.[126] Gregerman warns that minimizing interpretations of the Bible that emphasize the original covenant with the Jewish people could veer into "anti-Jewish Universalism," perceiving the universal God of PCT as fundamentally opposed to Judaism. This critique highlights the tension between PCT's pursuit of a theology that addresses Palestinian suffering and seeks justice, and the necessity of navigating the historical and ongoing relationship between Christianity and Judaism with sensitivity and respect for the particularities of each faith's covenantal understandings.

Munther Isaac, a Lutheran Palestinian theologian, addresses the critical issue of supersessionism within PCT by advocating for a nuanced understanding of the term.[127] He differentiates between punitive replacement theology—which posits Judaism's replacement by the church coupled with the rejection of Jews—and his own approach of incorporation and continuity with biblical Israel rather than its

[124] Atelia Omer, "The Cry of the Forgotten Stones: The Promise and Limits of a Palestinian Liberation Theology as a Method for Peacebuilding," *Journal of Religious Ethics* 43 (2015): 372.

[125] "'Let Us Have Mercy Upon Words': A Plea from the International Council of Christians and Jews to All Who Seek Interreligious Understanding," Heppenheim, 2010, para. 3, https://iccj.org.

[126] Adam Gregerman, "Old Wine in New Bottles: Liberation Theology and the Israeli Palestinian Conflict," *Journal of Ecumenical Studies* 41 (2004): 315.

[127] Isaac, *From Land to Lands*, 377.

supersession.[128] This distinction is crucial in a landscape where definitions and interpretations of supersessionism vary widely and theological discourse remains in flux. Both the Community of Protestant Churches in Europe and the Roman Catholic Church have both engaged with the concept of supersessionism, reflecting an ongoing theological evolution.[129] The Catholic Church's 2015 document, "The Gifts and the Calling of God Are Irrevocable," narrows the definition of supersessionism to what is often termed punitive supersessionism, recognizing the enduring covenant God holds with Israel.[130] Palestinian theologians, while affirming the divine covenant with the Jewish people and rejecting antisemitism, also interrogate the political ramifications of these theological positions within the context of their lived reality. This balanced yet bold approach underscores an acute awareness of the delicacy surrounding Jewish-Christian relations while also pressing for a theology that addresses the pressing concerns of Palestinian Christians.[131]

A New Hermeneutics

In the final phase of the hermeneutic circle, as outlined by Juan Luis Segundo, the emphasis shifts to reinterpreting the Bible in a manner that resonates with and empowers the oppressed.[132] This stage is marked by a shift away from traditional interpretations of the biblical text toward an understanding shaped by the current sociopolitical and historical context of the community in focus. For Black theology, as Segundo notes and as James Cone exemplifies, this reinterpretation begins not with the biblical text itself but with the lived experience, history, and culture of African Americans.[133]

Similarly, PCT adapts this approach but anchors its reinterpretation in the unique historical continuity of Palestinian Christians with

[128] Isaac, *From Land to Lands*, 377; Kendall Soulen, *The God of Israel and Christian Theology* (Fortress, 1996), 30.

[129] Leuenberg Church Fellowship, "Church and Israel: A Contribution from the Reformation Churches in Europe to the Relationship Between Christians and Jews," 2001, para. 2:1.5, https://jcrelations.net.

[130] Commission for Religious Relations with the Jews, "'The Gifts and the Calling of God Are Irrevocable' (Rom 11:29): A Reflection on Theological Questions Pertaining to Catholic-Jewish Relations," 2015, para. 17, https://vatican.va.

[131] See, for example, Sabbah, *Fourth Pastoral Letter*, para. 55.

[132] Segundo, *Liberation of Theology*, 30.

[133] Segundo, *Liberation of Theology*, 30.

the biblical narrative. Jamal Khader, reflecting this perspective, positions Palestinian Christians within the biblical saga, asserting their direct lineage and spiritual heritage from Abraham, Isaac, Jacob, and through to Jesus Christ.[134] This viewpoint not only asserts a physical and spiritual connection to the land but also seeks to reclaim a narrative lost in the aftermath of the 1948 Nakba. According to Khader, Palestinian Christians are not just inheritors of a spiritual tradition but are also descendants of the biblical people of God, with their history intertwined with the biblical events. Mitri Raheb further emphasizes the necessity of developing a hermeneutic that acknowledges the Palestinian Christians' longstanding history in the land.[135] He laments the loss of narrative that positioned Palestinian history as starting in the nineteenth century, advocating instead for a theology that integrates biblical history as part of their collective identity and experience. This approach seeks not only to reclaim a narrative but to propose a theological interpretation that resonates with the contemporary realities and struggles of Palestinian Christians. In essence, this stage of the hermeneutic circle for PCT is about reasserting the connection between the Palestinian Christian community and the biblical story, offering a new theological lens through which to view their history, struggles, and aspirations. It is a call for a theology that acknowledges their identity as both the people of the land and the people of the book, seeking to bridge the gap between ancient promises and present realities.

The anchoring of the Palestinian Christian narrative within the biblical story is a central tenet of PCT, highlighting both the historical presence of Palestinians in the Holy Land and the uninterrupted continuity of the Christian church in this region. Unlike James Cone's Black theology, which situates the experiences and struggles of African Americans outside traditional church history, PCT firmly places Palestinian Christians within the flow of biblical and ecclesiastical history. This distinction underlines a profound connection to both the land and the biblical narrative, challenging the notion that Palestinian history commenced only with the events of 1948. Instead, PCT posits that Palestinian history is interwoven with the biblical saga, thereby bridging a significant historical and theological gap.

134 Jamal Khader, "Biblical Hermeneutics in the Kairos Palestine Document," 278.

135 Raheb, "Towards a New Hermeneutics," 26–28.

Central to PCT are the dual themes of Jesus and the land, which serve as pivotal concepts around which Palestinian theologians construct their theological discourse. Jesus is portrayed not merely as a spiritual figure to be venerated but as a model for action and engagement with the world, offering guidance on how to navigate the complexities of life and faith in the context of occupation and conflict. The land, meanwhile, is seen not just as a geographical entity but as a theological paradigm that reveals God's will and intentions for humanity.

The land, as a pivotal theme in both the Bible and PCT, is imbued with profound theological significance. Influenced by Walter Brueggemann's scholarship, PCT interprets the land not merely as a physical space but as a theological and missional paradigm.[136] Brueggemann posits that biblical faith deeply intertwines with the quest for a historical place and destiny, asserting that the longing for land and the portrayal of Israel as landless are more crucial to understanding biblical theology than periods of settlement and sovereignty. This perspective casts the biblical narrative as one of journey and pilgrimage, portraying Israel primarily as "people on the way" rather than settled inhabitants.[137] Such a characterization suggests that the biblical emphasis shifts from the land's promises to the people of Israel's worthiness of it during their times of dominion. For PCT, the story of divine revelation about the land serves as a key hermeneutic tool for interpreting the Bible, proposing that the Holy Land is emblematic of all lands.[138] It is seen as embodying a missional theology where the land is a witness to the possibility of resurrection and renewal following suffering.[139]

In this view, the land is not only a crucial element of faith but also a metaphor for spiritual and communal destiny. It emphasizes the concept that the land is given by God not just for possession but as part of a broader divine mission. This theology asserts that the land's true significance lies in its ability to bear witness to God's ongoing work in the world, highlighting themes of justice, stewardship, and hope for every community and nation.

[136] Walter Brueggemann, *The Land: Place as Gift, Promise and Challenge in Biblical Faith. Overtures to Biblical Theology* (Fortress, 1977), 3.

[137] Raheb, *I Am a Palestinian Christian*, 76.

[138] *Kairos*, para. 2.3; Isaac, *From Land to Lands*, 364.

[139] Younan, *Witnessing for Peace*, 61–61.

The notion of land universality represents a pivotal shift in PCT, transitioning from an exclusive view of God as merely the deity of Israel to a more inclusive understanding revealed through Christ. Isaac clarifies that this broadening perspective does not negate or undermine the land's importance in the New Testament. Instead, it reframes the land as a theological symbol that extends beyond specific geographical boundaries to embody God's universal promise of redemption and belonging. This perspective echoes the overarching message of the New Testament, where the coming of Christ heralds a new covenant that embraces all of humanity, offering a reinterpreted vision of the land not as a parcel of territory limited to one people but as a gift and promise available to all who follow Christ.[140] Ateek articulates that the particular land, once divinely selected for a specific people at a certain historical juncture, now serves as a universal model showcasing God's care and consideration for all nations and territories.[141] This perspective allows Palestinian theologians to interpret the biblical text historically, acknowledging their deep-rooted connection to their land, while also embracing a universal interpretation that contrasts with Christian Zionism. Younan emphasizes the intertwining of history and geography in the divine plan of salvation, stating, "As there is a history of salvation, there is also a geography of salvation."[142] Through this lens, the land is not only seen as a specific location with a historical claim but also as a symbolic space where the universal story of salvation unfolds, underscoring the inclusive nature of God's love and promise to humanity. This approach navigates the delicate balance between affirming a historical connection to the land and advocating for a theology that transcends particularistic interpretations, and offers a vision of the land as a place of universal significance and divine encounter for all peoples.[143] In this regard, liberation will come from breaking the connection between the Bible and the Zionist movement and embracing God's love for all.

Not all Palestinian theologians embrace a focus on the land as a paradigm. Ateek has highlighted that his emphasis on the land stems not from a preoccupation with territorial claims, but rather as a response to the misuse of biblical texts for political ends. He indicates that his

140 Isaac, *From Land to Lands*, 9–10.

141 Ateek, *Justice and Only Justice*, 108.

142 Younan, *Witnessing for Peace*, 61.

143 Younan, *Witnessing for Peace*, 61.

interest in discussing the land arises out of the necessity to address "the religious and political exploitation of Scripture."[144] This emphasis on the land emerges in response to its pivotal role within Zionist Christianity, which heavily leans on Old Testament narratives. Unlike the Old Testament, the New Testament does not prioritize the land as a central theme. However, the concept of the land as a paradigm is applicable in the context of Christ's teachings as well. Walter Brueggemann says that faith in Christ encapsulates the lessons Israel learned regarding the land: the state of being landless facilitates reliance on the promise of the land, whereas the act of seizing the land invariably leads to its loss. This perspective aligns with the broader Christian understanding that true faith and trust in God transcend physical possessions and territorial claims, emphasizing a spiritual journey and reliance on divine promises over earthly dominion.[145] Younan notes that the theology of crucifixion and resurrection is particularly relevant to Palestinians at this juncture in their history, as it illuminates their connection to the land.[146]

For the Palestinian community, Jesus transcends his role as a spiritual figure to become a deeply ingrained part of their historical and contextual identity. Unlike broader claims that culturally situate Jesus within various ethnicities or regions, for Palestinians the assertion "Jesus was a Palestinian" is rooted in the undeniable historical fact of Jesus's life and ministry within the geographical bounds of what is now considered Palestine. This perspective fosters a profound connection with Jesus, not only as a guide for faith and practice but as a seminal figure within their own narrative and cultural heritage. Geries Khoury's designation of Jesus as "our first Christian theologian in Palestine" encapsulates this sentiment, emphasizing a familial bond with Jesus as an "older brother" whose life, struggle, and unjust crucifixion resonate deeply with the Palestinian experience of suffering and resistance.[147] Thus, according to PCT, one must read the Bible and understand its meaning for today through the image of Christ and by following Jesus's acts. Ateek developed this analogy a step further. He argued

[144] Naim Ateek, "Biblical Perspective of the Land," in *Faith and the Intifada: Palestinian Christian Voices*, ed. Naim S. Ateek, Marc H. Ellis, and Rosemary Radford Ruether (Orbis, 1989), 108.

[145] Brueggemann, *The Land*, 169.

[146] Younan, *Witnessing for Peace*, 60.

[147] Younan, *Witnessing for Peace*, 63.

that Jesus was born and lived under occupation.[148] Ateek suggests that by examining the Gospels through this perspective, one can uncover a theology of liberation that is genuinely applicable to Palestinian Christians currently living under Israeli occupation. From the experience of Jesus's life under Roman occupation, as with their own experience under Israeli occupation, PCT thinkers developed their theology that pursues justice and liberation and following it, their theology of resistance.[149] As the *Kairos Document* emphasized, "resistance is a right and a duty for the Christian."[150] Resistance is a way to change reality and bring justice, and is therefore a leading issue in liberation theology, as evidenced in Segundo's hermeneutical circle. The only way to promote liberation is through resistance, as only by resistance can one change one's reality. The right to resist contains within it the right to construct one's own theology, a theology that leads to praxis. Thus, the emphasis on resistance is extremely important in liberation theology.[151]

Resistance is also a central axis in postcolonial theology and was theorized by Edward Said as a way to rediscover and repatriate what had been suppressed in the natives' past by the processes of imperialism. The *Kairos Document* states that the Israeli occupation, as an aggression against the Palestinian people, is an evil that must be resisted.[152] PCT's concept of resistance must also be understood in the context of the resistance movement in Palestinian society. It allows Palestinian Christians to be part of the Muslim Palestinian resistance against the occupation in a way that concurs with their religious beliefs, namely, in a nonviolent way.[153] The *Kairos Document* emphasizes resistance through

148 Ateek, *Palestinian Christian Cry for Reconciliation*, 11.

149 See, for examples, Katanacho, *Land of Christ*, 58–60; Raheb, *I Am a Palestinian Christian*, 102–4; Ateek, *Justice and Only Justice*, 134–37; *Kairos*, para. 4.

150 *Kairos*, para. 4.2.3. On resistance as a Christian duty, see Jürgen Moltmann, *The Experiment Hope* (Augsburg, 1977), 145–63; "European Political Theology," 11.

151 See Werner Jeanrond, "From Resistance to Liberation Theology: German Theologians and the Non/Resistance to the National Socialist Regime," in *Resistance Against the Third Reich, 1933–1990*, ed. Michael Geyer and John Boyer (University of Chicago Press, 1994), 187–203. On resistance theology in other postcolonial theologies see, for example, Selaelo Kgatla, "Forced Removals and Migration: A Theology of Resistance and Liberation in South Africa," *Missionalia* 41 (2013): 120–32.

152 *Kairos*, para. 4.2.1.

153 On PCT participants in Palestinian resistance, see Nicole Patierno, "Palestinian Liberation Theology: Creative Resistance to Occupation," *Islam and Christian-Muslim Relations* 26 (2015): 443–64.

civil disobedience, prioritizing the respect for life over death. It pays homage to those who have sacrificed their lives for the nation, advocating for the readiness of every citizen to defend their life, freedom, and land.[154] Jesus's teachings guide Palestinians toward seeking justice, and through Christ, they shape their eschatological hopes. This eschatological perspective, coupled with the anticipation of a liberated future, is vital in forming a new theology aimed at transforming their present and future. The focus on God's universal message and Jesus's teachings against oppression underlines an eschatological faith in a brighter future. Leveraging Jürgen Moltmann's theology of hope, Palestinian theologians strive to develop a theology rooted in hope for an end to oppression and a vision for their liberation. This hope is centered not just on religious concerns but on aspirations for peaceful coexistence and equality among all peoples. It necessitates both a remembrance of past injustices and a rectification of current conditions. Sabbah and Ateek advocate for moving beyond discourses of religious legitimacy to achieve this vision.[155] Sabbah clarifies that both peoples have political rights in the land, while three religions hold religious rights there. Consequently, should one of these religions assert a political right to the land on religious grounds, then the other two would justifiably have the right to make similar claims for the same reasons.[156] As Sabbah declares, everyone has a right to pray in Jerusalem. Only in this way will it be possible to truly reach Jerusalem, a Jerusalem where everyone lives together. Isaac concludes that a shared land is not just an option—it is the only viable path forward. This vision aligns with biblical teachings and, therefore, should also represent the prophetic vision of the church in both Palestine and Israel.[157]

Palestinian theologians often mention Jerusalem when they discuss the eschatological future. They dream of a holy city that will represent all three religions and a state with equality and rights for all.[158] There is no independent claim here to gain the land, its place,

[154] *Kairos*, para. 4.2.5.

[155] Naim Ateek, "Jerusalem in Islam and for Palestinian Christians," in *Jerusalem Past and Present in the Purposes of God*, ed. Peter Walker (Tyndale House, 1992), 140; Sabbah, *Fourth Pastoral Letter*, para. 53.

[156] Sabbah, *Fourth Pastoral Letter*, para. 53.

[157] Isaac, *From Land to Lands*, 380.

[158] Ateek, *Justice and Only Justice*, 173; Yunnan, *Witnessing for Peace*, 73; Sabbah, *Fourth Pastoral Letter*, para. 63.

or even the truth of the Christian message across Judaism and Islam. The argument focuses on religious pluralism, which accepts the differences between religions.

The new hermeneutic crafted by Palestinian theologians, culminating in the hermeneutical circle, emphasizes justice and universality. It positions the concept of land as a bridge from the local narrative to a universal discourse, highlighting the imperative of justice in biblical narratives. Jesus is portrayed as the conduit facilitating this shift, embodying the quest for liberation and symbolizing future hope. This dual focus enables a transition from the Palestinian context to embracing the Bible as a text with universal implications, allowing for advocacy on behalf of universal justice without contesting proximity to the divine. The local dimension anchors Palestinians within their own historical and biblical narrative, offering them a platform to critique Zionism's territorial claims.

This approach underpins Palestinian theologians' efforts to transform their lived reality and envisage a new future, opposing the Israeli occupation as a means to realize promises of liberation. By weaving together their people's history with biblical narratives and aligning the biblical message with their contemporary experience, they seek to redefine their position both locally and universally. Yet this endeavor also surfaces inherent tensions within PCT between the particularities of the Holy Land and the universal sanctity of all lands, reflecting an ongoing debate within Christianity about the significance of the Holy Land. This nuanced stance of PCT might not be entirely new but extends a longstanding theological discussion regarding the sacredness and centrality of the Holy Land in Christian theology.[159]

PCT AND COMPETING NARRATIVES

The intersection of biblical Israel and the modern state of Israel forms a pivotal concern for Palestinian theologians, encapsulating the complex interplay between historical connections and their contemporary implications on Palestinian lives, faith, and aspirations. This conundrum is situated within broader Christian theological discourse, grappling with the relationship between the historical narrative of a specific people and the universal claims of Christian faith across the

[159] Robert Wilken, *The Land Called Holy: Palestine in Christian History and Thought* (Yale University Press, 1992).

globe. Recent shifts in biblical studies and hermeneutics have oscillated between prioritizing faith or historical accuracy, placing Palestinian Christians in a particularly challenging position. On one hand, a historical interpretation affirms their connection to the land through the lineage of the early Christian church, setting them in direct contention with Judaism. On the other hand, a faith-centric approach allows for the dismissal of Zionist interpretations of the Bible but at the cost of their unique historical identity in the region.

Thus Palestinian theologians endeavor to navigate a balanced path. They employ liberation theology, prioritizing lived experiences and current realities as interpretative foundations, while also acknowledging the significance of biblical narratives as both universal and distinctly their own historical account. This dual approach enables them to claim their identity as an oppressed people within the biblical tradition without forsaking their specific historical and geographical ties to the land. However, their quest for a Christian identity also confronts the perceptions and attitudes of Western Christianity toward Judaism, further complicating their theological and existential journey. Through this intricate navigation, Palestinian Christian theologians seek to articulate a theology that resonates with their unique context, bridging the gap between the local and the universal, the historical and the faith-based, amid the backdrop of a contested land and divergent religious narratives.

The Jewish Return to History

The right of Jews to read biblical history as their own history expands in parallel with the readings of other postcolonial groups of the biblical text from their own context.[160] The tension between viewing the Bible as the historical narrative of the Jewish people and interpreting it as a universal text applicable to all humanity underscores a fundamental challenge within Christian theology, particularly in the context of the IPC. The primacy of Jewish interpretation, grounded in the Old Testament's depiction as the history of the Jewish people, poses a significant question: How can the Bible simultaneously serve as the history of humanity at large? This question becomes even more complex when considering concepts like divine election and prophetic promises, which traditionally denote a special relationship between God

160 See chapter 2.

and a specific people in a particular place. Yet, how can these concepts hold universal significance for Christians worldwide? This dilemma between particularism and universalism is not new to Christianity. Many theologians have sought to navigate these waters, especially within the discourse between Judaism and Christianity. At the core of this debate is the concept of divine election: is it an exclusive covenant between God and the Jewish people, as Judaism maintains, or has it been universalized through the advent of Jesus Christ, as Christianity contends? This pivotal question is emblematic of the broader theological disputes that shape Jewish-Christian relations and, by extension, the contemporary IPC. The ambiguity of the biblical text on this matter leaves much room for interpretation, making the exegesis of scripture a central battleground in these theological and political conflicts. The challenge lies in reconciling the biblical narrative's particularity with the Christian faith's universal claims, a task that necessitates a nuanced approach to scriptural interpretation. The IPC, with its deep-rooted historical and religious dimensions, brings this theological tension into sharp relief, highlighting the critical role of hermeneutics in navigating the intricate relationship between faith, history, and contemporary geopolitical realities.[161]

While the thorny issue of particularism versus universalism continued into the twentieth century, attempts to promote Jewish-Christian dialogue suggested different ways to bridge the apparent gaps.[162] In any case, the topic itself has become a highly sensitive one, as it reverberates with suppressed perceptions and sentiments of antisemitism in Christian theology. It is for this reason that many have criticized the use of the terms *universalism* and *particularism*. These terms are frequently used in biblical as well as religious studies. However, they are not theological in origin, but rather derivative from the Enlightenment, carrying its zeitgeist along with their Christian roots.[163] This means that these concepts often have an evaluative connotation—of deciding right versus wrong. Anders Runesson has argued that in many cases such terms are biased: there is often an (almost unconscious) tendency

161 See, for instance, Joseph Blenkinsopp, "Old Testament Theology and the Jewish-Christian Connection," *Journal for the Study of the Old Testament* 28 (1984): 3–15.

162 See, for example, Paul van Buren, *A Christian Theology of the People of Israel* (Seabury, 1983).

163 Joseph Blenkinsopp, "YHWH and Other Deities: Conflict and Accommodation in the Religion of Israel," *Interpretation* 40 (1986): 360.

for contemporary historians and theologians to mark universalism as positive and particularism as negative.[164] While Runesson was referring to the study of ancient Judaism and Christianity, his arguments are pertinent to our own times, in which universalism is elevated in philosophical, ideological, and political deliberations, especially those embedded in humanistic and liberal thought.

For many in the Christian world, the Zionist movement, the establishment of the state of Israel, and the 1967 war are steeped in drama. It has been claimed that with these events, Judaism is returning to history. But when did it leave history? And to what kind of history is it returning? Amnon Raz-Krakotzkin has suggested that the only way to understand the familiar Christian Zionist expression is in relation to the history of salvation, the same history that, according to Christianity, the Jews departed from with the coming of Jesus.[165] Over the last two thousand years the Jews never regarded themselves as having disappeared from history. The Christian narrative regarding a return of the Jews to "history" seems to create a launching point between political reality and a redemptive apocalyptic. Moreover, Judaism is largely perceived as a religion through which one can bridge between then and now, namely, between realpolitik and salvation history. Judaism is perceived as having frozen in time, a historical remnant of something that once existed and was supposed to pass from the world. Like the Old Testament, Jews preserve "letters of stone" that do not change, as if they too are like the salvation history, ahistorical. If so, the return of the Jews to the land of Israel and the establishment of the state of Israel are seen as having double significance: both as biblical history repeating itself as a paradigm, and as a prophetic continuation of redemptive history, as if the path of redemption had merged again with human history. Ateek contends that Christian Zionists, by positioning the Jewish people at the heart of God's historical plan, have inadvertently contributed to a skewed theological perspective. This viewpoint diverges from traditional Christian theology, which places Christ at the core of

[164] Andres Runesson, "Particularistic Judaism and Universalistic Christianity? Some Critical Remarks on Terminology and Theology," *Studia Theologica—Nordic Journal of Theology* 54 (2000): 55–58.

[165] Amnon Raz-Krakotzkin, "The Return to the History of Redemption (Or, What Is the 'History' to Which the 'Return' in the Phrase 'The Jewish Return to History' Refers?)," in *Zionism and the Return to History: A Reappraisal*, ed. Shmuel Eisenstadt and Moshe Lissak (Yad Izhak Ben-Zvi, 1990), 249–79.

divine history. According to Ateek, this shift prioritizes national and geopolitical interests over the central Christian tenet of Christ's primacy in God's salvific narrative, leading to theological and political implications that affect the IPC.[166]

The concept that the establishment of the state of Israel could bear theological significance remains a contentious topic within the Christian world. This perspective gains traction especially when Judaism is seen as a link to a storied past, as if history had been paused, awaiting the fulfillment of divine prophecy. Raheb's metaphor of history being "put on hold and frozen" encapsulates this view, suggesting that Judaism holds a unique position in bridging the chasm between the religious past, the political present, and the eschatological future.[167] This interpretation implies a deep intertwining of religious narratives with contemporary geopolitical events, underscoring the complexities of integrating faith with the unfolding of history in a manner that acknowledges the potential prophetic implications of modern statehood for the Jewish people.

Exodus: Between a Paradigm and a Monopoly

Let us briefly return to the story of Exodus, which is so central to liberation theology, as well as to the Zionist movement. The choice of liberation theologians in South America and elsewhere to use the exodus tradition as a paradigm for their liberation was part of an attempt to define the identity of Christian communities in South America at the close of the colonial age.[168] The exodus narrative is fundamental to the formation of the Israelite identity, establishing them as God's chosen people. Historian Adrian Hastings posits that the biblical account played a pivotal role in the evolution of nationalism by providing a comprehensive model of nationhood within Israel itself.[169] This model encompasses a unified people, language, religion, territory, and governance, offering a framework for understanding the complex interplay between divine selection and national identity. According to Hastings, it is not just the concept of the union of people that can be found in

166 Ateek, *Palestinian Christian Cry for Reconciliation*, 76.

167 Raheb, "Displacement Theopolitics," 9.

168 Robert Schreiter, *New Catholicity: Theology Between the Global and the Local* (Orbis, 2004), chap. 1.

169 Adrian Hastings, *The Construction of Nationhood: Ethnicity, Religion and Nationalism* (Cambridge University Press, 1997), 18.

the Bible, but more importantly, it is the notion of a close relationship between God and his people, and the understanding that public misfortune is a consequence of God's displeasure. This theology of history grew out of a sense of covenantal relationship of a particular people with God, and, soon enough, generated what Hastings described as the concept of a multitude of chosen peoples as standing in contrast to the singular notion of the Christian church as the chosen entity.[170]

Anthony Smith, in his book *Chosen People*, explored the idea of a divine covenant among peoples and ethnic groups.[171] Smith's analysis of the biblical Exodus underscores its significance in the development of nationalism, emphasizing the notion of chosenness as being earmarked for special purposes by the divine. This concept implies a distinctive relationship between a group or nation and a higher power, suggesting that such a group is destined for a particular role or mission within a broader historical or cosmic narrative. According to Smith, the various nations are built on cultural resources and foundations of holiness, including the myth of chosenness. The stronger these elements are, the stronger the survival of the given group. In our days as well, the members of those nations that can boast a rich heritage of such cultural resources as community, territory, history, and destiny are more likely to retain their sense of national identity and ensure the survival of their national community, despite increasing pressures for radical change and cosmopolitan assimilation.[172]

Hastings's and Smith's views of the evolution of nationalism signal its roots in a biblical reading. While there are differences of opinion about the importance of religion in the nationalist movement, there is no doubt that the biblical story is taken by Christian groups, among them liberation theologians, as a paradigm for their national story. Therefore, the exodus narrative also played an important role in the development of nationalism. Hence, different liberation theologies around the world can use the very same paradigm for their political struggle; the liberation of one does not contradict that of any other. So, for instance, Blacks' struggle for equality in South Africa does not contradict or diminish the struggle of the poor in South America. The message is the same universal Christian message throughout the

170 Adrian Hastings, "Christianity and Nationhood: Congruity and Antipathy," *Journal of Religious History* 25 (2001): 250–51.

171 Anthony Smith, *Chosen People* (Oxford University Press, 2003), 48.

172 Smith, *Chosen People*, 260.

world—a message of divine justice. As such, different people in different contexts can read the Exodus story as their own story.

The problem for Christian Palestinian theologians is that the Jewish Zionist movement also uses this paradigm. But when Jewish Zionism enlists the story of the exodus, the ability of Christian Palestinian theologians to make use of the story in their own theological and political narratives is limited, as it may be seen as co-opted by Jewish Zionism.[173] Ateek acknowledges the significance of the journey to Palestine and the founding of the state of Israel for Jews as a link between their ancient past and the current era. However, he argues that the uncritical adoption of this historical narrative imposes a heavy burden on the Palestinians. By invoking the motif of the Promised Land there arises an inevitable expectation of liberation and settlement that, historically, necessitates the subjugation, assimilation, dominance, or displacement of the indigenous inhabitants. Therefore, the reading of the Bible by the Zionist movement is no longer a particular or optional reading of the biblical text but a national reading, as it mobilizes divinity for the benefit of one, monopolistic side of the conflict. Particularity in the context of the divine can exist only as long as it does not come at the expense of others or falsify the universal message. And in a territorial clash such as the IPC, any reading of the biblical text that prefers one side automatically excludes the other.

Zionist reading of the Bible does not necessarily object to the view that the biblical story is a paradigm for all nations, but it is unwilling to forsake the claim that the text represents the Jewish—and only the Jewish—historic reality. Liberal-left Christian circles' support for the establishment of a Jewish homeland in the Holy Land—following the horrors of WWII, and especially the Holocaust—represents an apparent legitimization of the Jewish people's right to read the scriptures through Jewish eyes.

The story of the exodus emblematizes the complexity of the Zionist connection—Christian and Jewish—between biblical Israel and modern Israel. Compared to other groups, Christian Zionists' reading of the Exodus is complex and layered. First and foremost, it is a historical reading that proves the connection of the Jewish people to the land of Israel—the land of their ancestors.[174] But the story of the exodus is

173 Ateek, *Justice and Only Justice*, 87.

174 As mentioned in the Israeli Declaration of Independence.

also read contextually, similar to other postcolonial theologies, emphasizing God's special relationship with the oppressed and persecuted. Since the biblical story was written as a particular story of the Jewish people, the paradigmatic repetition takes on additional meaning, affirming God's choice of his people. Thus it leads to a deeper layer of reading—the eschatological one. According to this view, if indeed the establishment of the state of Israel fulfills God's promises to his people, it presents a sign for the coming future.

The Historical Jesus as a Point of Contention

The tension between interpreting the Bible as a historical document and as a source of religious faith is not limited to the Old Testament but is also evident in the study of the New Testament.[175] Palestinian theologians underscore their link to Jesus, a connection that is both historical and spiritual, highlighting the significance of the historical Jesus to their theological framework. This emphasis arises first from their desire to root their identity in the Holy Land and its sacred narrative. Jesus represents a pivotal figure in Christian hermeneutics, altering the interpretative lens through which scriptures are viewed. The Old Testament gains full clarity only when seen through the prism of Christ's mission, making his life and teachings crucial for interpreting themes such as divine promises and election. This approach to scripture, grounded in the historical and lived reality of Jesus, sets PCT apart from Zionist-Christian interpretations. Ateek emphasizes that the theological perspective, which is foundational for evaluating the relevance and authority of the Scriptures in the lives of Christians, is rooted in the profound understanding and love of God as manifested through the life, death, and resurrection of Jesus Christ.[176]

Second, Palestinian theologians' focus on the historical Jesus is also motivated by a desire to challenge the concept of Jesus's Judaism that developed in Western Christianity, which often negates or nullifies his Palestinian identity. However, as Michael Sandford points out, Palestinian theologians tend to refrain from openly referring to "Jesus the Palestinian" in public discourse, as they do not wish to be seen as using Jesus for political purposes.[177] Sandford references Isaac's remarks on

[175] See Vanhoozer, "Scripture and Tradition," 149–51.

[176] Ateek, *Justice and Only Justice*, 1.

[177] Michael Sandford, "Is Jesus Palestinian? Palestinian Christian Perspectives on Judaism, Ethnicity and the New Testament," *Holy Land Studies* 13 (2014): 127–30.

the phrase "Jesus was a Palestinian," acknowledging that, historically, Jesus was indeed from the region known today as Palestine, and by that account could be described as a Jewish Palestinian.[178] Isaac, however, expresses a personal reservation about the phrase's usage, suggesting that it is often employed for political purposes rather than historical accuracy or religious reverence.

Palestinian theologians are not the first to use the historical Jesus in order to construct their identity, and by doing so they are responding to a well-known discourse on the "quest for the historical Jesus" in modern Christianity.[179] This trend, which emerged at the end of the nineteenth century as an attempt to distill from the Christian sources an authentic picture of the historical figure of Jesus of Nazareth, quickly developed into a fruitful discussion of the possibility and necessity of this very quest. The debate led to critical questions about the relationship between theology and the study of history, and vice versa. Despite the many challenges posed by the quests for the historical Jesus, increasing numbers of scholars and theologians have joined these quests over the years, each hoping to find the "real Jesus."[180] It seems that the search for the authentic Jesus was equally a search by various scholars or groups looking for a way to create a link between themselves and Jesus. However, it was no less a quest for a way to frame their own identity or worldview in a manner which correlates with their image of Jesus.

The quest for the historical Jesus has evolved over time. In research today, it is customary to name a few different stages of the quests for the historical Jesus: the first, or "old quest"; the "no quest"; the "new" or "second quest"; and finally the "third quest."[181] Clive Marsh offers a more complex reading of the various quests that aims to account for

178 Sandford, "Is Jesus Palestinian?" 127.

179 This usage of the word *quest* was first coined by Albert Schweitzer in his landmark book, *The Quest of the Historical Jesus: A Critical Study of Its Progress from Reimarus to Wrede*, trans. W. Montgomery (A&C Black, 1910).

180 Michael Wolter, "Which Jesus Is the Real Jesus?" in *The Quest for the Real Jesus*, ed. Jan van der Watt (Brill, 2013), 1–18.

181 On the history of the quests see, for example, Gregory Dawes, *The Historical Jesus Quest: Landmarks in the Search for the Jesus of History* (Deo, 1999); William Thompson, *The Jesus Debate: A Survey and Synthesis* (Paulist, 1985), 90–114; James Dunn, *Jesus Remembered* (Eerdmans, 2003); Paul Eddy and James Beilby, "The Quest for the Historical Jesus: An Introduction," in *The Historical Jesus: Five Views*, ed. Paul Eddy and James Beilby (InterVarsity Press, 2009), 10–54.

the methodology and ideology of the questers. He proposes defining "nine interlocking Quests of the Historical Jesus": the positivist quest (forms 1 and 2), the romantic quest, the form-critical quest, the quest of the non-Jewish Jesus, the traditio-historical quest, the existentialist quest, the Jewish-Christian quest, and the postmodern quest.[182] I will focus on the last two, the Jewish-Christian quest and the postmodern quest, both of which emerged around 1970 and are critical for the understanding of PCT.

The Jewish-Christian quest, also referred to as the "third quest," or the "new quest," began in the late 1970s and is characterized by a different methodological approach from the previous quests.[183] This quest is influenced by postmodern conceptions of history, which recognize that history is influenced by those who recount it, and seeks to understand Jesus's activity and teachings within his social and religious context.[184] The publication of the Dead Sea Scrolls marked a crucial juncture in the advancement of the third quest, as they allowed for a fresh perspective on the society of Second Temple Judaism and its religious factions.[185] The Jewish-Christian quest also emphasizes the importance of Jesus's Judaism and the need to place Jesus in his proper historical context as a Galilean Jew. Jesus's Judaism became a major subject of scholarly research as well.[186] These studies, born from the post-Holocaust discourse on Judaism, assume that understanding the Judaism of Jesus's time can shed light on the gospel.[187] Understanding Judaism would help the church understand Jesus, who was himself a Jew, and enable it to more fully grasp the historical, cultural, and theological context in which he lived and taught. Recognizing Jesus as a Jew, rooted in the religious life and traditions of Second Tem-

[182] Clive Marsh, "Quests of the Historical Jesus in New Historicist Perspective," *Biblical Interpretation* 5 (1997): 415–16.

[183] N. T. Wright, *Jesus and the Victory of God* (Fortress, 1996), 83–124. According to Wright, the two quests continued stimulatingly. Others argue that the distinction between the second and the third quest is only diachronic; see Eddy and Beilby, "Quest for the Historical Jesus," 28.

[184] Wright, *Jesus and the Victory of God*, 5.

[185] Craig Evans, "Assessing Progress in the Third Quest of the Historical Jesus," *Journal for the Study of the Historical Jesus* 4 (2006): 35; Dunn, *Jesus Remembered*, 89.

[186] Ben Witherington III, *The Jesus Quest: The Third Search for the Jew of Nazareth* (IVP Academic, 1995), 9–13.

[187] Stefan Reif, preface to Géza Vermes, *Jesus the Jew* (SCM, 2001).

ple Judaism, challenges long-standing tendencies within Christian theology to separate him from his Jewish identity. As with the first two quests, here as well allegations have been made that the quest for the historical Jesus—or, even more so, its outcomes, such as the widespread recognition that the historical Jesus was first and foremost a Jew—would teach us less about Jesus himself and more about his image in the eyes of the modern or postmodern scholars who search for him.[188] Despite this, the focus of these movements, whether grounded in postmodern research or Jewish-Christian dialogue, highlights important topics in contemporary theology and has theological implications.[189]

The postmodern quest, which could also be referred to as the post-colonial quest, began in the 1960s and 1970s in another part of the world, mainly the global South. This quest was part of an identity search on the part of various marginal groups which, in a postmodern world, declared that the image of Jesus as presented in the pastoral tradition of the West did not represent them.[190] They aimed to affirm the historical Jesus as a pivotal component of their own identity, understanding that inquiries into who Jesus was inherently intertwine with reflections on their personal and collective identities. Therefore, they sought the historical Jesus to whom they could relate from their own context. Essentially, they were trying to understand Jesus and his teachings in a way that was meaningful and relevant to their own experiences and contexts. The theologies that developed in the global South, even if strongly influenced by the European theological discourse, were not bound by the shackles of the Enlightenment. As Gonzalez Faus argued, in Europe the figure of the historical Jesus is subject to scholarly analysis and research, while in Latin America Jesus serves as a model and guide for following and living out the principles

[188] See Marsh, "Quests of the Historical Jesus," 415–16; Wolter, "Which Jesus Is the Real Jesus?" 1–18.

[189] See, for example, Paula Fredriksen, "What You See Is What You Get: Context and Content in Current Research on the Historical Jesus," *Theology Today* 52 (1995): 76.

[190] Halvor Moxnes, *Jesus and the Rise of Nationalism: A New Quest for the Nineteenth Century Historical Jesus* (I. B. Tauris, 2012), 1. See also Victor Ezigbo, *Re-imagining African Christologies: Conversing with the Interpretations and Appropriations of Jesus Christ in African Theology* (Pickwick, 2010), 1; Sturla Stålsett, *Discovering Jesus in Our Place: Contextual Christologies in a Globalized World* (ISPCK, 2003), viii.

of discipleship.[191] Therefore, when in their quests history and theology collide, their resolution of the conflict will be different. As Cone explained, without historical knowledge about the specific Galilean from the first century, it becomes impossible to understand the nature of his existence in the present.[192]

The pursuit of the historical Jesus within postmodern and postcolonial theology aligns with Bultmann's emphasis on religious experience as central.[193] This search isn't for a Jesus detached from the post-Easter Christ, but reflects how Jesus is envisioned in the lives of contemporary believers.[194] Just as historical perceptions of Jesus have often mirrored the image of modern European man, there's a compelling argument that Jesus's image can and should equally resonate with the experiences of Black people in South Africa, the impoverished in Latin America, and other marginalized groups, particularly given the significant role of ethnicity and race in theological discussions.[195]

The shift from a "flight from dogma," which motivated early quests for understanding Jesus, to a "flight from history" evident in later and postcolonial quests, underscores how attempts to bridge the past and present frequently project current realities onto a reconstructed past.[196] This evolution reveals the changing priorities and contexts in theological exploration, where initial efforts aimed to escape rigid doctrinal interpretations evolve into efforts to reinterpret historical narratives through the lens of contemporary experiences and struggles. When religious identity is crafted in the image of Jesus, the search for an authentic Jesus is inevitably influenced by one's worldview, or what Kahr termed "the fifth gospel." Jeffery Siker points out that the

[191] González Faus, "Hacer teología y hacerse teología," in *Vida y reflexión: Aportes de la teología de la reflexión al pensamiento teológico actual* (Centro de Estudios y Publicaciones, 1983), 79; quoted in Jon Sobrino, *Jesus the Liberator: A Historical Theological Reading of Jesus of Nazareth*, trans. Paul Burns and Francis McDonagh (Orbis, 1993), 50.

[192] Cone, *Black Theology of Liberation*, 112–13.

[193] Rudolf Bultmann, *Jesus and the Word*, trans. Louise Smith and Erminie Huntress (Nicholson & Watson, 1935). See also Wright, *Jesus and the Victory of God*, 22.

[194] John Ottuh, "Biblical Research in Africa: Historical Jesus Quest in Inculturation Perspective," *Academic Journal of Interdisciplinary Studies* 2 (2015): 188.

[195] Jeffry Siker, "Historicizing a Racialized Jesus: Case Studies in the 'Black Christ,' the 'Mestizo Christ,' and White Critique," *Biblical Interpretation* 15 (2007): 27–28.

[196] James Dunn titled the chapters of his book that dealt with this period "The Flight from Dogma" and "The Flight from History." Dunn, *Jesus Remembered*, 25, 74.

Christian belief in the incarnation of God as a specific individual at a particular moment in history naturally leads diverse groups to find connections between their unique characteristics and the particularity of Jesus.[197] It suggests not merely a resemblance to Jesus but an understanding of Jesus as embodying characteristics of their group identity.

The pursuit of the historical Jesus is crucial for shaping the discourses of post-Holocaust and postcolonial theology, both of which begin with acknowledging that previous dominant discourses in Western theology were shaped by the Western theologian's identity, thus limiting discussions on history and faith. As Marsh noted, the figure of Jesus is invariably used toward specific ends, underscoring the subjective nature of historical interpretation, despite attempts to maintain objectivity.[198] The exploration of the historical Jesus navigates the intricate tensions between modern and postmodern paradigms, alongside the biblical narrative. This journey underscores a transition from a stringent historical analysis, detached from dogma, toward a focus on the post-Easter Jesus, emphasizing message over historicity. This shift corresponds with the postmodern critique of a singular historical narrative, highlighting skepticism toward narrative construction and the impact of power dynamics on historical portrayal. The postmodern reevaluation of history and religious thought occurs as theological discourse transitions from prioritizing historical accuracy to theological interpretation. This is evident in the evolution of post-Holocaust and postcolonial theological movements. Originating from a critique within Christianity of its perceived universality and the Western-centric historical perspective, these movements challenge the exclusion of non-European perspectives from the salvation narrative. Consequently, the recognition of Jesus's Jewish heritage and the significance of Jewish tradition in his life seemed to fade from the Christian narrative. Similarly, the portrayal of Jesus with Western or liberal traits alienated those who could not identify with these characteristics, thus marginalizing non-Western Christians from connecting with the historical Jesus. This dilemma prompts a more inclusive understanding of history, acknowledging its complexity and the multiplicity of narratives that coexist without negating each other. Such a perspective encourages diverse studies on Jesus, exploring his various portrayals

[197] Siker, "Historicizing a Racialized Jesus," 27.

[198] Marsh, "Quests of the Historical Jesus," 425.

as cynical, apocalyptic, revolutionary, or deeply rooted in Judaism. This approach also allows postcolonial Christian theology to examine the ties between the historical Jesus and its core ideas, broadening the scope of theological exploration and offering a richer tapestry of interpretations that reflect the diverse global Christian community. This intersection introduces a pivotal challenge for PCT, which emerges from the intersection of post-Holocaust and postcolonial theological movements. Within these dynamics, a tension exists between historical and faith-based interpretations of Jesus, namely, the contrast between the pre-Easter and post-Easter Jesus. These movements diverge in their focus, with one emphasizing the historical Jesus to understand his Jewish context and the other highlighting the universal message and teachings of the post-Easter Jesus to foster a connection across diverse Christian groups globally.

This dichotomy complicates PCT. Specifically, PCT navigates a delicate balance: while appearing to prioritize a universal interpretation over historical specificity to counteract Christian Zionism, this approach does not entirely apply to their perception of Jesus. Rather than eschewing the historical context of the biblical text, Palestinian theologians seek to engage with Jesus's historical heritage in their land while also establishing a faith-based connection that transcends mere historical ties. This dual approach aims not only to contest the special relationship Christian Zionism claims with Judaism but also to forge a connection with the historical Jesus that is both historical and faith driven.

4
Witness in the Holy Land
The Formation of the Palestinian Christian Narrative

INTRODUCTION

Chapter 3 explored the way Palestinian theologians engage Western audiences by underscoring the friction between post-Holocaust and postcolonial theological discourses and their consequences for the Palestinian populace. As discussed in chapter 1, the objective of Palestinian theology extends beyond merely contesting Christian Zionism. It aims to carve out a distinct national and religious identity for Palestinians. In pursuit of this goal, Palestinian theologians have crafted their unique Christian narrative. This narrative competes with that of Christian Zionism, employing the theological concept of "witness" to articulate their position and identity within the broader Christian and geopolitical context.

In this chapter I will attempt to outline the main issues Palestinian theologians address through the lens of "witness." Using this lens, I will present the narrative of Palestinian Christian theologians. This narrative portrays the Palestinian struggle as part of a larger fight for universal justice and equality and emphasizes the idea that Palestinians are a unique and specific group with a distinct territory.[1]

1 See Elie Kedourie, *Nationalism* (Blackwell, 1993).

Palestinian theologians face an inherent tension when interpreting the Bible. On the one hand, they want to connect the text to their own history in Palestine by reading it historically. On the other hand, they want to reject Zionist Christian interpretations of this very text. This tension is evident in their conception of the Promised Land, as well as in their relation to the historical Jesus. This tension represents the intersection or conflict between two theological movements that Palestinian theologians are grappling with: post-Holocaust theology and postcolonial theology.

Palestinian theologians find themselves in a quandary, caught between the hammer and the anvil: their close connection to Judaism through their shared sacred history of the land, and their status as marginalized figures within the Christian world. In order to turn this difficult position into a strength, it is necessary to find a way to bridge the gap between post-Holocaust and postcolonial theology and use elements from both to create a collective identity. They attempt to do it by using the past as a source of collective memory rather than as purely historical facts. Palestinian theologians seek to establish the authority of their teaching by claiming the role of witness with a special knowledge of the past, which they can access due to their status as both historical and politically persecuted figures. In this way they are able to use the past to shape their future, by reclaiming and reinterpreting the past in ways that help to build and justify their theological authority and collective identity.

The transformative dimension of witnessing in the context of divergent narratives about historical events cannot be overstated. Within the framework of Christianity, the act of bearing witness is endowed with profound theological significance, as a privilege bestowed by divine selection (Acts 10:41). Those chosen to bear witness draw upon the Holy Spirit for the authority and power to testify (Acts 1:8). This spiritual empowerment imbues their testimonies with a weight that goes beyond mere recounting of events; it carries an inherent authority to shape perception and understanding among the audience.

The act of witnessing extends beyond the passive recollection of events. It involves an active, interpretive process that not only reconstructs past events but also imbues them with meaning aimed at illuminating future paths.[2] This interpretative act is dynamic, with the nature of the testi-

[2] Gunter Thomas, "Witness as a Cultural Form of Communication," in *Media Witnessing: Testimony in the Age of Mass Communication*, ed. Paul Frosh and Amit Pinchevski (Palgrave Macmillan, 2009), 96.

mony and the message it conveys being inherently malleable, shaped by the specificities of context and audience. The necessity of an audience in the act of witnessing underscores its fundamentally public character, emphasizing the communal aspect of memory and interpretation. The role of the witness in Christian theology—and, indeed, in any historical or contemporary analysis—serves not just as a conduit of facts but as an interpreter of truth.[3] The witness's testimony can thus transform the audience's perception, potentially altering their understanding of the event and its implications. This transformation underscores the power of narrative in shaping historical memory and communal identity.

In order to understand how the Palestinian theologians comprehend the notion and function of witness, I will provide a short survey that examines how it is applied in Christianity in general and how its role and meaning has shifted over the course of the twentieth century in Christian discourse. A brief examination of the notion of witness in early Christianity, including the function of the holy places in Jerusalem and the Jews as witnesses, will serve as a background for and shed light on its role in contemporary Christianity in general, and in PCT in particular. Then I will present the development of the notion of witnessing in modern Christianity, focusing on its use in postcolonial and post-Holocaust theologies.

"BE MY WITNESS": WITNESSING IN EARLY CHRISTIANITY

Although the theological category of witness has been almost entirely neglected in modern scholarship, the notion of "Christian witnessing" and its function has become increasingly pervasive in the past fifty years. The notion gains discussions in the context of Christian mission and public theology, and in official statements of different churches or of specific theological strands. A simple search for the phrase "bearing witness" on the Vatican website indicates this progression: the phrase appears in 87 statements of Pope Paul VI, in 1,441 statements of Pope John Paul II, and in 1,696 statements of Pope Francis—all over a period of less than seven years.[4] Today, in the Roman Catholic and Protestant worlds as well, the terms *mission*, *evangelism*, and *witnessing* are often used interchangeably.[5]

3 John Peters, "An Afterword: Torchlight Red on Sweaty Faces," in Frosh and Pinchevski, *Media Witnessing*, 46.

4 See https://vatican.va.

5 David Bosch, *Transforming Mission: Paradigm Shifts in Theology of Mission* (Orbis, 2011), 421.

In the New Testament the apostles are perceived as the ones who witnessed the story of Christ (John 15:27; Acts 1:22). They are identified as witnesses to the resurrection but were also required to witness Jesus's life story and teachings. Their witness is therefore expressed not only through their telling of what they saw, but also in their practice of Jesus's teachings and demonstrably following in his way. The apostles were supposedly present during the life, death, and resurrection of Jesus. We find this in Acts, in the search for a replacement for Judas, when Peter states that an apostle should be: "One of the men who have accompanied us during all the time that the Lord Jesus went in and out among us" (Acts 1:21). The apostles were not the only witnesses to the gospel: God, the Old Testament, and Jesus himself are also considered witnesses. Yet it was the mission of the apostles to spread the official narrative of what happened, namely, the witness (John 5:31–40).[6] As outlined in 1 John 1:2: "His life was revealed, and we have seen it and testify to it, and declare to you the eternal life that was with the Father and was revealed to us."

The witness of the apostles is twofold. The first aspect was concerned with eyewitnessing the actual events; the second manifested itself in their practice of Jesus's gospel. It means that their mission as witnesses did not stop with providing proof of past events, but included interpretations of these events for the future.[7] By following Jesus and his teaching and through the presence of the Holy Spirit, the apostles spread the news that not only was there a man called Jesus who had died and was resurrected, but that in doing so he offered salvation to humanity. Here it is important to note that the emphasis on eyewitnesses can only be found in Luke—both Luke's Gospel and Acts—and John. It is possible that the nature of these texts, Luke as historical text and John as apologetic text, explain the need for eyewitnesses as a way to validate the Christian argument.[8]

[6] See Urban von Wahlde, "The Witnesses to Jesus in John 5:31–40 and Belief in the Fourth Gospel," *Catholic Biblical Quarterly* 43 (1981): 385–404.

[7] Suzanne de Dietrich, "'You Are My Witnesses': A Study of the Church's Witness," *Interpretation* 8 (1954): 273.

[8] See Dennis Nineham, "Eye-witness Testimony and the Gospel Tradition. III," *Journal of Theological Studies* 11 (1960): 253–64. Nonetheless, there is a claim that in the first century, witnessing was only understood as eyewitnessing, and that the idea of witness by deeds developed at the end of the first century—as represented in Luke and John.

In order to convince people of the authenticity of their message, the apostles were obliged to testify about what they had seen and learned, and it was important that their testimony be perceived as reliable. Their credibility derived from their presence at crucial events, but also from the fact that they lived the life they preached, by personal example, thus indicating their total commitment to the message.[9] This commitment often resulted in torment and persecution, or even death, but that only strengthened the credibility of the testimony. In the second century, as persecution increased, degrees of witnessing began to develop, as the martyrs who died for their faith were conferred a higher status of holiness than those who merely confessed their faith in their lives.[10] Such martyrs—"witnesses" in Greek—were sometimes also seen as eyewitnesses to Jesus because it was believed that he revealed himself to the martyrs upon their deaths.[11] For the most part, however, the credibility of their testimony was based on their faithful imitation of Jesus's sacrifice publicly. By drawing on and replicating elements of the past, Christians have been able to shape their collective memory and to continue to bear witness to the divine events that are central to their faith. This imitation of the past has played a role in the creation and preservation of the Christian collective memory. The memory of suffering serves as a resource for culture making and identity formation in various settings and contexts, highlighting a critical aspect of collective memory's role in shaping social and individual identities.[12]

The question of how the church can continue to testify about the story of Jesus after the time of the apostles, in the absence of direct eyewitnesses, is addressed through the paradigm provided by Paul, the first postresurrection apostle.[13] Paul's acceptance of his mission and status after receiving a revelation of Jesus marks a transition in the

[9] See Brian Wicker, *Witness to Faith? Martyrdom in Christian and Islam* (Ashgate, 2006), 34.

[10] Tripp York, "Early Church Martyrdom: Witnessing For or Against the Empire," in *Witness of the Body: The Past, Present, and Future of Christian Martyrdom*, ed. Michael L. Budde and Karen Scott (Eerdmans, 2011), 24–27.

[11] See William Frend, *Martyrdom and Persecution in the Early Church: Study of a Conflict from the Maccabees to Donatus* (Basil Blackwell, 1965), 15.

[12] Elizabeth Castelli, *Martyrdom and Memory: Early Christian Culture Making* (Columbia University Press, 2004), 31–32.

[13] Peter O'Brien, "Mission, Witness, and the Coming of the Spirit," *Bulletin for Biblical Research* 9 (1999): 214.

nature of witnessing. He positions himself not as an eyewitness in the traditional sense, but as one who bears witness through "the testimony of our conscience" (2 Cor 1:12), advocating for a form of testimony rooted in one's actions in the world, characterized by "frankness and godly sincerity." This approach suggests that witnessing is not confined to firsthand observation of Christ's resurrection but extends to living a life that reflects the teachings and essence of Jesus. The Holy Spirit plays a crucial role in this process, empowering individuals and the church as a whole to bear witness to Christ through their lives and actions.[14] This transformation of the concept of witnessing from a direct recounting of events to a lived expression of faith allows for the continuation of testimony about Jesus across generations.

Despite the passage of time beyond the era of the apostles, the firsthand accounts of those who directly witnessed the life and teachings of Christ have not vanished. Their testimonies continue to be preserved and revered within the practices of liturgy, the canonical texts of the Scriptures, and the sanctity of holy places. New Testament scholar Richard Bauckham provides a compelling argument that the New Testament serves as a testament to eyewitness accounts.[15] By narrating the story of Christ as observed by the apostles, the text effectively continues the apostolic mission of bearing witness to Christ's life. One also finds this notion in the introduction to Luke: "Just as they were handed on to us by those who from the beginning were eyewitnesses and servants of the word. . . . So that you may know the truth concerning the things about which you have been instructed" (Luke 1:2–4). By combining the authenticity of the apostles as eyewitnesses with their interpretations of the events to which they were witness, the New Testament preserves the apostles' testimony. In Bauckham's words, their testimony is "where history and theology meet."[16]

We can see another example of this process in the institutionalization of this testimony in the holy places. Church historian Robert Markus argues that the notion of holy places developed in Christianity as a continuation of martyrdom and the worship of the martyrs cult, that is, after the establishment of Christianity as the imperial reli-

14 de Dietrich, "'You Are My Witnesses,'" 278.

15 Richard Bauckham, *Jesus and the Eyewitness: The Gospel as Eyewitness Testimony* (Eerdmans, 2006). Here I refer only to Bauckham's discussion of the theological model of the Gospel as eyewitness.

16 Bauckham, *Jesus and the Eyewitness*, 6.

gion, there was a need to preserve the church heritage as the testimony of heroic, persecuted people, and thereby commemorate the martyr witness.[17] Markus highlights that the development of sacred sites in Christianity was significantly influenced by a growing reverence for the past and a desire to experience it as if it were present.[18]

The function of the geography and the holy places in Jerusalem as witness to the story of Christ is clearly evident in the writings of the fourth-century bishop Cyril of Jerusalem.[19] Cyril highlighted the significance of holy sites as testimonials to the veracity of Christianity. He pointed to the natural world and specific locations as bearers of divine testimony. The heavens, through the Father's voice, the Jordan River among rivers, and the Sea of Tiberias among seas, all serve as witnesses to Christ's presence and actions. Additionally, Golgotha, with its commanding presence, and the Holy Sepulcher, alongside the enduring stone, provide tangible evidence to the faithful. These sites, imbued with historical and spiritual importance, affirm the foundational events of Christianity, offering believers physical connections to the narratives that shape their faith. As the theologian Peter Walker has argued, Cyril formulates his theology as part of his struggle to elevate Jerusalem's position in Christianity and to promote its new statues, mainly in contrast to Eusebius's support of Caesarea.[20] For Cyril, the holy places of Jerusalem act as witnesses to the story of Christ because they provide believers with concrete proof of the Christian story, and allow them to better visualize events that they were not able to witness directly themselves.[21] Cyril described the significance of the witness of the holy places and the privilege of the pilgrims in Jerusalem: "Others merely hear, but we see and touch."[22] Thus, the holy

[17] Robert Markus, "How on Earth Could Places Become Holy? Origins of the Christian Idea of Holy Places," *Journal of Early Christian Studies* 2 (1994): 257–71.

[18] Markus, "How on Earth Could Places Become Holy?" 271.

[19] Cyril of Jerusalem, *Catechetical Lecture* 10. Cyril repeats the list of witnesses to Christ—with some changes, twice in his lecture (13.38–40 and 14.22–23). See Peter Walker, *Holy City, Holy Places?* (Clarendon, 1990). On Cyril's promotion of Jerusalem see also Brouria Bitton-Ashkelony, *Encountering the Sacred: The Debate on Christian Pilgrimage in Late Antiquity* (University of California Press, 2005), 57–62.

[20] See Walker, *Holy City, Holy Places?* On Cyril's promotion of Jerusalem see also Bitton-Ashkelony, *Encountering the Sacred*, 57–62.

[21] Maurice Halbwachs makes a similar point in *On Collective Memory* (University of Chicago Press, 1992), 199–201.

[22] Cyril of Jerusalem, *Catechetical Lecture* 13.39.

places, like the text of the New Testament, partially compensate for the fact that no later Christian believers witnessed the resurrection. Walker elucidates that for Cyril, despite Christ's physical absence from the earthly realm, Jerusalem serves as a repository of unique, tangible, and visible artifacts that reinforce a Christian's faith.[23] This perspective is further supported by historian Lorenzo Perrone, who suggests that Cyril's writings sometimes elevate the holy places of Jerusalem to the status of a "fifth gospel."[24] In terms of role, the witness of the holy places differs from the witness of the apostles. The former is understood as a tool for believers to grasp the story of Jesus, while the latter involves the mission of spreading his gospel. One might suggest that the witness of the holy places is analogous to the witness of John the Baptist, or the Old Testament as mentioned in John (John 5:31–40). This is a more passive witnessing than that of the apostles, but it is attainable for later believers and enables them to learn and affirm the Christian message.

Jews as Witnesses

The perception that Jews served as witnesses to the truth of Christianity can be traced to the early Christian period.[25] The most influential figure in the development of this idea in Western Christianity was Augustine, at the end of the fourth century and at the beginning of the fifth.[26] Augustine's concept of Judaism as a witness stems from the ambivalent attitude of Christianity and the New Testament toward Judaism.[27] On one hand, Jews were seen as deserving of punishment for their disbelief and their role in the death of Christ; on the other hand, the existence of the Jews after the events of the New Testament—alongside Paul's view that they retained their status as chosen in the eyes of God (Rom 11:26–31)—was perceived by Augustine as contradictory and

[23] Walker, *Holy City, Holy Places?* 331.

[24] Lorenzo Perrone, "'The Mystery of Judaea' (Jerome, *Ep.* 46): The Holy City of Jerusalem Between History and Symbol in Early Christian Thought," in *Jerusalem: Its Sanctity and Centrality to Judaism, Christianity, and Islam*, ed. Lee Levine (Continuum, 1991), 223.

[25] See Stephen Haynes, *Jews and the Christian Imagination: Reluctant Witnesses* (Macmillan, 1995), 6–7. In recent decades, various churches have indirectly acknowledged the existence of this doctrine by releasing official documents condemning it.

[26] See Jeremy Cohen, *Living Letters of the Law: Ideas of the Jew in Medieval Christianity* (University of California Press, 1999), 26–27; Haynes, *Jews and the Christian Imagination*, 27–33.

[27] Cohen, *Living Letters*, 29.

unreasonable. So Augustine developed a theology that saw the Jews as witnesses to the Christian message and thus gave meaning to their existence and their special status.[28] Jews were punished by God for their disbelief and were thus expelled from their land and dispersed among the nations. But their very existence as a people scattered around the world was designed to promote the Christian message—to show what happens to those who do not believe, and by their devotion to their religion, to testify to God's involvement in history, and so also to the role of Christ and his sacrifice.[29] Thus the testimony of the Jews is dual: their punishment and humiliation in the Christian world is indicative of the consequences of their disbelief, and of the triumph of the Christian faith, and their observance of Jewish traditions, the commandments, and the Old Treatment preserve the biblical prophecies that authorize the truths of Christianity.

Augustine highlights the widespread presence of Jews across the globe, underscoring their role as unwitting witnesses to the Christian faith.[30] He posits that the dispersion of Jews and the universal presence of their Scriptures serve as validation for Christian claims about Christ, particularly the prophecies concerning him found in Jewish texts. According to Augustine, this wide distribution of Jews and their sacred writings provides tangible evidence supporting the Christian interpretation of biblical prophecies about the Messiah. This ambivalence, which led Augustine to develop his theory about the Jews as witness, is similar to the challenges which Cyril, bishop of Jerusalem, faced in relation to the city of Jerusalem (not to Jews by themselves). Cyril needed to find a way to speak about the religious significance of Jerusalem despite Jesus's prophecy of its destruction (Matt 24:2; Mark 13:2, Luke 21:5–6), and despite its reputation as the city that murdered Christ. In the case of the holy places, as well as in the case of Judaism, the role bestowed on the witnesses allowed them to preserve the perception that they were of religious significance or uniqueness, albeit it changed their purpose. They no longer testified to the divine covenant with Judaism but took on a new role as witnesses to the triumph of Christianity and to the Christian history of salvation.

[28] See Paula Fredriksen, *Augustine and the Jews: A Christian Defense of Jews and Judaism* (Yale University Press, 2010), 327–30.

[29] Cohen, *Living Letters*, 35–41.

[30] Augustine, *City of God* 18.46; cited in Haynes, *Jews and the Christian Imagination*, 30.

Comparing the doctrine of witnesses developed by Augustine to that of the apostles as witnesses, it seems that the dual testimony of the Jewish people is a kind of reflection of the apostles' testimony. The apostles witnessed the life of Jesus and his teaching, and the Jews witnessed the religious history that preceded Him—thus confirming what followed. The apostles witnessed Christ in their faith, while the Jews witnessed him with the consequences of their disbelief. However, the question arises as to why the Jews' "collective memory" is seen as sufficient for maintaining their role as witnesses, while the Christians who followed the apostles were not seen in the same light. The testimony of the apostles ended with their death and was replaced by the testimony of the martyrs and the eyewitness accounts of the Gospels. The testimony of the Jews regarding the old covenant, and their role in the death of Christ, was perceived as having been passed down from generation to generation.

The Italian philosopher Giorgio Agamben's observation on a dual notion of witness may be helpful here.[31] Agamben noted that in Latin there are two different words for "witness": *testis*, which refers to the testimony of the person testifying at the trial (namely, a third party to the event who tells what happened), and *superstes*, which refers to the testimony of a person who took an active part in the event (either the perpetrator or the victim). One might say, then, that while the apostles were witnesses to the events—the life of Jesus, the crucifixion, and the resurrection—the Jews were considered to have played an active role as perpetrators in the persecution of Jesus. As Augustine stressed: "Those who killed the Lord when proudly empowered have merited subjection."[32] So the Jews bear their sin, as well as their testimony, as a sign—just as Cain carried a sign for the murder of Abel and was punished by exile.[33] Therefore, as part of the history of salvation, they retain their role as witnesses, and their testimony—as well as their guilt—carries on from generation to generation.

WITNESSING IN MODERN CHRISTIANITY

To fully grasp the significance of the concept of witness in Palestinian theology, it is important to first understand its usage in modern

[31] Giorgio Agamben, *Remnants of Auschwitz: The Witness and the Archive* (Zone Books, 1999), 17.

[32] Augustine, *Contra Faustum* 12.12; cited in Cohen, *Living Letters*, 29.

[33] Cohen, *Living Letters*, 27–28.

Christianity, particularly in the two main streams of thought that inform Palestinian theology: postcolonial theologies and post-Holocaust theology. These have shaped the way the term is understood and used by Palestinian theologians.

The turn of the twentieth century saw a shift from performing mission to witnessing. Although Acts describes the Christian mission as "witnessing," the term *mission* seems to have been far more common. This assumption is based on the need for early twentieth-century theologians to explain the transition from *mission* to *witness*, suggesting that the use of the term *witness* was not common before. This shift stemmed from a state of "crisis of mission."[34] As one of the consequences of the Enlightenment, which undermined the status of religion and God in society, along with the development of the natural sciences, as well as the French and American Revolution, many thinkers shared the idea of the end of the era of Christendom.[35] Therefore, the Christian mission had to adapt to a new reality in which the role of Christianity, its power, and its social place were questioned and eventually eroded. In addition, the Western world was no longer the center of Christianity, with the number of Christians rising worldwide, thanks mainly to centers of faith in South America and Africa. This raised questions about how to carry out a mission that is not Eurocentric.[36] The crisis in relation to the mission during the twentieth century eventually led to dramatic changes in the Western church's mission and its understanding of its role as a witness to Christ. The first major change, evident in the conference of the International Mission Council (IMC), a Protestant ecumenical organization, that took place in Tambaram, India (1938), concerned the assumption that the Christian mission should target not only the non-Christian world but also the Christians in the West.[37] The trauma of WWI and the rise of fascist and Nazi regimes led to the realization that the church must also operate within the Christian world. That means that a mission to the church itself was required.

The first buds of the notion of "mission as witnessing" were evident at a meeting of the IMC in Canada in 1947, titled "The Christian

[34] David Bosch, *Witness to the World: The Christian Mission in Theological Perspective* (Wipf and Stock, 2006), 2–3.

[35] Bosch, *Witness to the World*, 3–5.

[36] Bosch, *Witness to the World*, 6.

[37] Bosch, *Transforming Mission*, 378.

Witness in a Revolutionary World."[38] It was the theologian Karl Barth in 1956 who called for the transformation of "the church mission" into "the church role as a witness to God."[39] In light of this view a mission should be undertaken only in the form of a proclamation of faith, demonstrated through one's words and deeds. The notion of mission as witness followed first of all the realization in the Christian world that the church no longer held the position of power that it had in the past. Consequently, churches today can offer only their witnessing of the Christian message by persuasion, rather than coercion.[40] The approaches diverge mainly on their point of departure. Witnessing is done modestly and humbly, as Jesus himself delivered his message, as opposed to missionizing or evangelizing, which became understood in the twentieth century as forceful actions.[41] In other words, witnessing is not an aggressive action intended to convert, but rather a conversation in which one shares one's faith as a witness, without the intention of imposing it on others. Hence the Christian mission reverted to its role as described in Acts 1:8 as "witness." But the crisis of faith in the Christian world following the Enlightenment, which further deepened in the West after the two world wars, raised the question: What is the essence of Christian witnessing?

In the aftermath of WWII, Western Churches sought to reconsider the role of the church in the broader world and the significance of its testimony or witness. Since the Christian mission was no longer considered merely a mission external to the church, both the Roman Catholic and the Protestant churches began to examine their place in the world and their responsibility for the evil or suffering in it.[42] If in the past Western Churches had held themselves apart from mundane affairs, after WWII they began to develop political or public theologies that dealt with Christian responsibility and the church's

[38] See Ans Joachim van der Bent, *Historical Dictionary of Ecumenical Christianity* (Scarecrow, 1994), xv.

[39] Karl Barth, *The Doctrine of Reconciliation*, vol. 4 of *Church Dogmatics*, trans. G. W. Bromiley (T&T Clark, 1956). See Joseph Mangina, *Karl Barth: Theologian of Christian Witness* (Routledge, 2004).

[40] See Andrew Suderman, "'Who'll Be a Witness for My Lord?': Witnessing as an Ecclesiological and Missiological Paradigm," *Missionalia* 44 (2016): 72; Bosch, *Transforming Mission*, 410.

[41] Bryan Stone, *Evangelism After Christendom: The Theology and Practice of Christian Witness* (Brazos, 2007), 10.

[42] Bosch, *Transforming Mission*, 385.

role in society.[43] The meaning of Christian witness changed from broadcasting the message of salvation through Christ to encouraging social justice, reconciliation, and peace. The use of the phrase "Christian witnessing" post-WWII is a continuation of the trend of understanding mission as witnessing. While the notion of mission expanded to include the churches' actions within Christian society, so did the understanding of the role of Christian witnessing. But this is not enough to explain how the concept of Christian witnessing has become so prevalent in Western Churches—and not only in relation to mission.[44] While in the first years after WWII, different uses of the phrase "Christian witness" can be found, especially in the context of mission, within a few decades this phrase became commonly applied to the way in which churches in the West—and soon, in developing regions as well—defined their role in the world.

In the current era, the terms *witness* or *testimony* appear frequently in literature, politics, and public discourse in the Western world.[45] In order to understand the important place that the notion of witnessing has occupied in current Christian theology, whether in missionary theology, in public theology, or in general, one must first understand the discourse on witnessing and especially on "moral witnessing," which has developed simultaneously in the West.

The Israeli philosopher Avishai Margalit has proposed a definition of "moral witness" in modern times. According to Margalit, the role of moral witnesses is to preserve our collective memory of radical evil.[46] Margalit highlights the profound connection between the moral witness and the religious martyr, emphasizing that the essence of moral witnessing transcends mere observation to embody a deeper, existential engagement with suffering and evil. This engagement requires the witness to be personally vulnerable, placing themselves at risk, which

43 On the differences between political theology and public theology see Max Stackhouse, "Civil Religion, Political Theology and Public Theology: What's the Difference?" *Political Theology* 5 (2004): 275–93.

44 See Karl Barth, *The Word of God and the Word of Man*, trans. Douglas Horton (Hodder and Stoughton, 1978), 186; cited in Mangina, *Karl Barth: Theologian of Christian Witness*, 16. See also Christoph Schwobel, "Theology," in *The Cambridge Companion to Karl Barth*, ed. John Webster (Cambridge University Press, 2000), 23.

45 Bradford Vivian, *Commonplace Witnessing: Rhetorical Invention, Historical Remembrance, and Public Culture* (Oxford University Press, 2007), 2.

46 Avishai Margalit, *The Ethics of Memory* (Harvard University Press, 2004), 147–52.

imbues their testimony with authenticity and moral weight. Just as a martyr's ultimate sacrifice serves as a testament to their unwavering faith in a higher moral order and divine justice, the moral witness, through their proximity to and direct experience of suffering and injustice, bears testimony to these truths. Their hope lies in the belief that their testimony will not only be acknowledged but will resonate within a moral community, either presently existing or yet to emerge, thereby fostering a collective consciousness and response to the witnessed injustices. The category of moral witness, as Margalit defines it, is most recognizable in the post-WWII discourse, as the witness of the war is considered to have a moral responsibility to share what he or she has witnessed.[47] Witnessing thus becomes an act of taking responsibility for the past for the sake of the future.[48]

WWII, and especially the Holocaust, sharpened the discourse on the role of witnessing to injustice and atrocities. The need to testify about what happened in the Holocaust led to a discourse on the "crisis of witnessing."[49] The author and Holocaust survivor Primo Levi claimed that only those who remained speechless, the *Muselmanner*, could attest to the events of the Holocaust. Accordingly, the survivors who can speak, can only witness them by proxy.[50] Some have gone so far to argue that the Holocaust was an "event without witnesses."[51] Agamben posits that the power of Primo Levi's testimony lies in its engagement with the paradox of testifying to the untestifiable.[52] This paradox underscores the profound responsibility of the witness, who must speak not only for themselves but also for those who cannot bear witness—those whose experiences defy articulation. This principle of testifying on behalf of those who cannot do so takes on new meaning in the age of mass media, as "second-level testimony" is created. Those who are exposed to human suffering through media become themselves "distant witnesses" or "media witnesses," and assume responsi-

47 Jay Winter, "The Moral Witness and the Two World Wars," *Ethnologie française* 37 (2007): 468.

48 Andreas Huyssen, *Present Pasts: Urban Palimpsests and the Politics of Memory* (Stanford University Press, 2003), 16.

49 See Shoshana Felman and Dori Laub, *Testimony: Crises of Witnessing in Literature, Psychoanalysis and History* (Routledge, 1992).

50 See Agamben, *Remnants of Auschwitz*, 34, and Primo Levi, *The Drowned and the Saved*, trans. Raymond Rosenthal (Random House, 1989), 83–84.

51 See Felman and Laub, *Testimony*; Agamben, *Remnants of Auschwitz*, 35.

52 Agamben, *Remnants of Auschwitz*, 34.

bility for continuing to testify on others' behalf.[53] While these people were not directly exposed to the events, they assume the moral role of the witness.[54] Hence, testimony becomes almost imperative in postwar Western society. Since the evidence of injustice in the world cannot be escaped, people cannot shirk the duty to preserve this testimony, to maintain the memory in order to "remember and not to forget."

This discourse on "moral witness" and the conception of Western society's role in bearing witness by proxy to the injustices of the world is crucial to the understanding of Christian witness since the second half of the twentieth century. As noted above, the link between Christian witnessing and social justice can be found in Barth's writings prior to WWII, and references to the subject of social justice were also made at the 1939 International Mission Council conference in Tambaram, India.[55] However, Christian witnessing differs from secular moral witnessing. While the moral witness testifies to a hope for worldly change, Christian testimony brings with it a faith in this hope—for God acts in the world of reconciliation. South African theologian David Bosch's perspective emphasizes that Christian hope is nurtured by the collective memory and experience of God's faithfulness throughout history. This foundational belief shapes the church's mission and witness in the world, suggesting that every act of kindness, justice, peace, and support in times of distress is not only a reflection of God's love but also an invitation to explore the deeper joy and hope that underpin such actions. The church, through its witness to past divine interventions and its ongoing commitment to embodying Christ's teachings, offers a vision of hope that transcends present difficulties.[56] The role of the apostles as witnesses of early Christianity was to testify to a specific event, namely, the life of Jesus, and to its significance. They testified to the truths of the event, as well as to the truths of the Christian message of salvation. But Christian moral

53 Paul Frosh and Amit Pinchevski, "Introduction: Why Media Witnessing? Why Now?" in Frosh and Pinchevski, *Media Witnessing*, 5–7.

54 Vivian, *Commonplace Witnessing*, 2–3.

55 International Mission Council, *The Place of the Church in Evangelism*, 1939, 46; cited in Filho, *Twentieth Century Mission Theology*, 33. It was certainly not the prevalent view at that time. Elias Filho, "Twentieth Century Mission Theology: Conciliar and Evangelical Streams in Conversation" (PhD diss., Fuller Theological Seminary, 2005), 33.

56 Stanley Hauerwas and Samuel Wells, "The Gift of the Church and the Gifts God Gives It," in *The Blackwell Companion to Christian Ethics*, ed. Stanley Hauerwas and Samuel Wells (Blackwell, 2004), 19.

witnessing today does not only indicate man's possibility of salvation, but also God's involvement in the world and the recognition of a God of justice and love.[57] To a large extent, this transition from "witness to salvation" to "witness to justice" is related to a renewed understanding of eschatological thinking in modern times, when, according to Moltmann "the present becomes the frontier where the future is gained or lost"[58]—the hope of the fulfillment of God's promises related to a world of justice and the need for Christianity to act in recognition of such a world and to condemn evil.[59] Since the message of the different Christian churches is that of reconciliation and justice, it also allows the Christian world to speak in one voice, and to bear "common witnessing" as part of the ecumenical movement.[60]

Witnessing in Postcolonial Theologies

After WWII the concept of Christian witness changed drastically. Christian witnessing in the Western world could no longer refer solely to the resurrection of Christ and its implications but had to respond to the war and to its consequences, particularly the Holocaust, as well as prewar phenomena like colonialism and racism. Thus the churches took on the responsibility to bear witness to these evils and to respond to them. So, for instance, the World Council of Churches was founded in 1947 to "participate in the struggle of a new just world."[61] In this regard, the Cameroonian theologian Mbengu Nyiawung articulates a compelling vision for the church's role in society, emphasizing the urgent need for engagement in social justice issues.[62] By framing this endeavor as a core responsibility of the church, Nyiawung underscores the importance of active, vocal advocacy for the oppressed and marginalized.

57 On the tension between justice and love see Bosch, *Transforming Mission*, 412.

58 Jürgen Moltmann, "Hope and History," *Theology Today* 25 (1968): 371. See Wolfhart Pannenberg, "Constructive and Critical Functions of Christian Eschatology," *Harvard Theological Review* 77 (1984): 119–39.

59 Jürgen Moltmann, *Theology of Hope: On the Ground and the Implications of a Christian Eschatology*, trans. James Leitch (SCM, 1967), 299.

60 Neil Arner, "Ecumenical Ethics: Challenges to and Sources for a Common Moral Witness," *Journal of the Society of Christian Ethics* 36 (2016): 101–19.

61 World Council of Churches, *Costly Commitment*, 1997, https://oikoumene.org.

62 Mbengu Nyiawung, "The Prophetic Witness of the Church as an Appropriate Mode of Public Discourse in African Societies," *HTS Theological Studies* 66 (2010): 1–8.

The development of liberation theology in South America and similar postcolonial movements in the global South had an important impact on the discourse of witnessing.[63] While Western churches were "second" witnesses to injustice—as they did not suffer from that injustice but only witnessed it, liberation theologians saw themselves as true moral witnesses and even as martyrs, as they not only witnessed suffering, but also endured it themselves.[64] In suffering they drew near to Jesus and likewise attested to their loyalty to God. Because God gives a special place to those who are suffering (the poor, the oppressed), poverty and oppression are not just a social issue but are imbued with theological significance. Gutiérrez emphasizes the crucial link between the church's witness and its response to poverty and injustice, particularly in contexts marked by widespread suffering.[65] He posits that the credibility of the gospel's proclamation hinges on the church's commitment to addressing these social issues. This perspective suggests that the church's engagement with the poor and marginalized isn't just a moral or ethical choice but a theological imperative that directly impacts the authenticity of its message. The importance of the poor derives from their witnessing through suffering, imitating the testimony of the first witness, Jesus Christ.[66] Jesus's suffering serves as an instrument for God's mission, as it connects with the tradition of the prophets and takes on the role of the suffering servant (Isa 53).[67] So does Paul's suffering and the Christian witnesses that follow him, which are instruments for spreading God's gospel. Through suffering, they imitate Jesus and are likewise a representation of the suffering servant.[68] Moltmann highlights the

[63] Bosch, *Transforming Mission*, 442–50.

[64] Gustavo Gutiérrez, *A Theology of Liberation: History, Politics, and Salvation*, trans. John Eagleson (Orbis, 1973), 70.

[65] Gutiérrez, *Theology of Liberation*, 162.

[66] The idea that Jesus was the first witness is developed by Karl Barth, *Doctrine of Reconciliation*, 126–34.

[67] Deborah Schiffrin and Young Kee Lee, "God's Mission in Suffering and Martyrdom," in *Suffering, Persecution and Martyrdom: Theological Reflections*, ed. Christof Sauer and Richard Howell (AcadSA, VKW, 2010), 215–16.

[68] Schiffrin and Lee, "God's Mission," 215–16. See Christoph Markschies, "Jesus Christ as a Man Before God: Two Interpretive Models for Isaiah 53 in the Patristic Literature and Their Development," in *The Suffering Servant: Isaiah 53 in Jewish and Christian Sources*, ed. Bernd Janowski and Peter Stuhlmacher (Eerdmans, 2004), 225–324. In the twentieth century, as Jesus is understood to be the first witness/martyr

collective dimension of Christian suffering and solidarity, emphasizing that participation in "the fellowship of Christ's sufferings" (Phil 3:10) is not limited to the apostle Paul or individual experiences but extends to the entire community of believers.[69]

The idea of moral witness is translated—especially in the African context—into "prophetic witness," defined as a testimony made in the name of God for justice, and acting against the forces of power, including risk-taking that can lead to death.[70] That is, the moral or prophetic witness—like Jesus and the martyrs of early Christianity—is willing to sacrifice his or her life for the sake of the testimony. But while in early Christianity the use of the word *martyr* soon narrowed to describe mainly those who died for their faith, postmodern theology, and particularly liberation theology, uses *martyr* in a broader sense to include all those who suffer for their testimony. Gutiérrez elucidated this evolution and clarified that discussing a spirituality of martyrdom extends beyond the realm of bloody and violent loss of life.[71] It encompasses everyday dedication, selfless acts undertaken at significant personal expense, characterized by joy and peace, amid profound threats and rewards, suspicions (even within the church), and fraternal support.

Following Margalit's insights, scholars view moral witness as a testimony that must stem from self-risk and revolt against the centers of power that lead to this suffering.[72] Thus this kind of witnessing in Christianity can only emerge in the post-Christendom era, when the church has abandoned its commitment to empire.[73]

The Jewish Witness in Post-Holocaust Theology

The understanding of the use of the term *witness* in relation to Jews after the Holocaust is crucial for comprehending Palestinian theology,

---

and Christian communities are considered to follow him in their witnessing, they also have inherited his role as suffering servant.

69 Jürgen Moltmann, *The Way of Jesus Christ: Christology in Messianic Dimensions*, trans. Margaret Kohl (SCM, 1990), 156.

70 See Nyiawung, "The Prophetic Witness"; Wessel Bentley, "Defining Christianity's 'Prophetic Witness' in the Post-Apartheid South African Democracy," *Studia Historiae Ecclesiasticae* 39 (2013): 275–93.

71 Gustavo Gutiérrez, "The Task and Content of Liberation Theology," trans. Judith Condor, in *The Cambridge Companion to Liberation Theology*, ed. Christopher Rowland (Cambridge University Press, 1999), 35.

72 See Margalit, *Ethics of Memory*, 148.

73 Gutiérrez, *Theology of Liberation*, 63.

as Palestinian theologians attempt to define their own identity in relation to Judaism as it is perceived within Christianity.

The emphasis on the role of Jews as witnesses preserved the notion of Judaism as representing a definite group and heritage, but at the same time promoted the Christian conception of Judaism as being opposed to Christianity. In the post-Holocaust period, as part of the attempt to rid Christianity of antisemitic notions, there is also a great deal of concern about "Jewish witnessing." Some Christian theologians have argued that after the Holocaust, the concept of "Jewish witnessing" cannot be preserved, as it is one of the foundations of Christian antisemitism.[74] But these theologians still seek, like Augustine, to preserve the unique status of Judaism, this time as a positive element. They do not entirely dismiss the concept of "Jewish witnessing," but change its tone: the Jews are not the blind witnesses who cannot see the truth of their message anymore; they are rather the only ones who can attest to the history of divine connection with the world.[75] The American theologian Clark Williamson underscores the fundamental connection between Christianity and Judaism, claiming that severing ties with Judaism means disconnecting from the vibrant lineage and testimony of biblical faith.[76] He emphasizes that Judaism is not merely a historical or theological precursor to Christianity but a living tradition where biblical faith continues to thrive and evolve. Thus, for example, Pope Benedict XVI declared: "The Fathers say that the Jews, to whom Holy Scripture was first entrusted, must remain alongside us as a witness to the world. But what does this witness say?"[77] He then explained that this witness means faith, hope, and love. Pope Benedict XVI articulates the complex relationship between Israel and the church through the figure of Christ, suggesting that Christ acts as both a bridge and a boundary. This dual role underscores the intrinsic connection and the distinct paths of Israel and the church within the broader context of faith and salvation history.[78] The need to change the meaning of Jewish witnessing was felt as a result of the transformation

[74] Haynes, *Jews and the Christian Imagination*, 123–25.

[75] Haynes, *Jews and the Christian Imagination*, 7–8.

[76] Clark Williamson, *Has God Rejected His People? Anti-Judaism in the Christian Church* (Wipf and Stock, 1982).

[77] Joseph Ratzinger, *Many Religions—One Covenant: Israel, the Church, and the World* (Ignatius, 1999), 104–6.

[78] Ratzinger, *Many Religions—One Covenant*, 104–6.

of the witness concept in Christianity. If the Christian mission no longer forces the truth but testifies to it, and this testimony is made with a focus on reconciliation and justice, then Christianity must recognize that there are other ways to see and understand God. Thus, the Synod of the Evangelical Church of the Rhineland declared in 1980: "We believe that in their respective calling Jews and Christians are witnesses of God before the world and before each other."[79]

In accordance with the general view of Christianity in the twentieth century, Jewish suffering also conferred on Jews the status of moral witnesses.[80] The suffering and mass murder of the Jews in the Holocaust, and the mere fact of the preservation of their faith, led Christian theologians to even speak of "Jewish martyrdom." Since martyrdom is perceived as an imitation of Jesus, after the Holocaust one can even come across statements, albeit clearly provocative, such as "the crucifixion of the Jews."[81]

As was clarified in the last document of the Commission for Religious Relations with the Jews (2015), the Jewish witnessing is not meant to replace Christianity, but to complement it: "Church and Judaism cannot be represented as 'two parallel ways to salvation,' but . . . the Church must 'witness to Christ as the Redeemer for all.'"[82] While the Jewish testimony is important in understanding the divine history and its connection to humanity, it does not create an independent path to salvation, and therefore Christianity is obliged to continue sharing its testimony of Jesus as the divine Savior.[83] In what follows, we shall see the merging of the various theological aspects of witnessing in the

[79] Synod of the Protestant Church of the Rhineland and of Some Key Theologians, "Towards Renovation of the Relationship of Christians and Jews," trans. Franklin H. Littell, *Journal of Ecumenical Studies* 17 (1980).

[80] See the Commission for Religious Relations with the Jews, "We Remember: A Reflection on the Shoah," 1998, https://vatican.va.

[81] See, for example, the title of Franklin Littell's book, *The Crucifixion of the Jews: The Failure of Christians to Understand the Jewish Experience* (Harper & Row, 1975).

[82] Commission for Religious Relations with the Jews, "'The Gifts and the Calling of God Are Irrevocable' (Rom 11:29): A Reflection on Theological Questions Pertaining to Catholic-Jewish Relations," 2015, para. 12, https://vatican.va.

[83] For an analysis of the document "Gifts and the Calling of God" see Gavin D'Costa "'Supersessionism': Harsh, Mild or Gone for Good?" *European Judaism* 50 (2017): 99–107. The document's emphasis on Jewish witnessing arises from the inquiry about the necessity of a mission to Judaism.

Palestinian Christian discourse, and how it has affected the refinement of their markers of identity.

BEARING WITNESS IN THE HOLY LAND: PALESTINIAN WITNESS

The use of the concept of witness by Palestinian theologians combines the way this term is used in the Christian discourse on Judaism and in political postcolonial discourse as well. Following the notion of witnessing as it was developed in liberation theology and quickly among global South churches in general, Palestinian theologians understood their role as witnesses to injustices in the region stemming from the sociopolitical reality of occupation.[84] As far as Palestinian theologians are concerned, their very suffering, especially as a minority, gives their witness a theological significance and a martyrological status.[85] Ateek and Sabbah conceive of their witnessing as a testimony to Jesus's message of peace and reconciliation.[86] In this way, they ally themselves with the message for which Jesus struggled, that his apostles were asked to deliver, and that should be understood nowadays as an eschatological hope for a better world.[87] This understanding of Jesus, his message, and its eschatological meaning is derived primarily from the theological writing of Jürgen Moltmann. Moltmann's theological perspective emphasizes that Jesus's ministry was fundamentally about bringing the kingdom of God near to those on the margins of society—the poor, sinners, outcasts, and victims of discrimination.[88] Through acts of forgiveness, miraculous healings, and the sharing of hope, Jesus manifested God's kingdom as a present reality for these marginalized groups, challenging the social and religious norms of his time.

In a time and place in which the biblical text itself is at the center of the conflict, as in the Palestinian-Israeli case, one may ask: How is it possible to know the true message for testimony? The answer provided

84 *Kairos*, para. 1.

85 Yunnan, *Witnessing for Peace*, 41–45.

86 Naim Ateek, *Justice and Only Justice: A Palestinian Theology of Liberation* (Orbis, 1989), 115–16; Michel Sabbah, *Second Pastoral Letter of Patriarch Sabbah: Pray for Peace in Jerusalem*, 1990, https://lpj.org; Younan, *Witnessing for Peace*, 49–50.

87 Ateek, *Justice and Only Justice*, 6; Mitri Raheb, *I Am a Palestinian Christian* (Fortress, 1994), 62–64; Yohanna Katanacho, *The Land of Christ: A Palestinian Cry* (Pickwick, 2013), 117–19.

88 Moltmann, "The Crucified God," *Theology Today* 31 (1974): 6.

by Palestinian theologians, much like liberation theologians, is to read the text with a Christocentric perspective.[89] Ateek stressed the importance of distinguishing between the Bible as the written word of God and Jesus Christ as the living or incarnate Word of God.[90] The living Word assists in discerning and interpreting the written word. Rahab and Ateek hold that in order to appreciate the scriptures, one must first understand that these are books written from a minority perspective, that of a persecuted people, either Israel in the Old Testament, or the Christian communities and apostles in the New Testament.[91] Raheb explains that the Holy Scripture is a book about a minority.[92] Thus, the stand of being a minority allowed an authentic understanding of the scriptures. That is why, according to Raheb, the Bible appeals first of all to the persecuted and the oppressed. Persecutors comprehend the Bible differently from the persecuted. Raheb stresses that a right understanding of the Bible conceives that "the book of the persecuted has the crucified lord as its centerpiece."[93]

Palestinian theologians assert that witnessing is not solely a mission for Christians but also the essence of divine election, which embodies the opportunity to testify to God's presence and actions. Raheb specifically highlights that this notion of witnessing speaks most profoundly to those who perceive themselves as unworthy, weak, and powerless.[94] The election of Israel should be understood in the same manner. God's promises were meant to give hope to people who were weak and stateless, but one cannot claim to be elected from a position of power.

The idea of witnesses as God's chosen appears already in Acts 10:41. However, the Palestinian theologians' emphasis on this issue should be understood within its context, as a reaction to Zionist Christian writing. The conception of witnessing to God allows them a double maneuver: it retains the role of the Jews as elected—in line with the

[89] See Raheb, *I Am a Palestinian Christian*, 63; *Kairos*, para. 2.2.2; Michel Sabbah, *Fourth Pastoral Letter: Reading the Bible Today in the Land of the Bible* (Jerusalem, 1993), para. 1.4.

[90] Naim Ateek, "Reflections on Sabeel's Liberation Theology and Ecumenical Work (1992–2013)," in *Theologies of Liberation in Palestine-Israel: Indigenous, Contextual, and Postcolonial Perspectives*, ed. Nur Masalha and Lisa Isherwood (Lutterworth Press, 2014), 21–33.

[91] Raheb, *I Am a Palestinian Christian*, 62; Ateek, *Justice and Only Justice*, 130–31.

[92] Raheb, *I Am a Palestinian Christian*, 62.

[93] Raheb, *I Am a Palestinian Christian*, 62.

[94] Raheb, *I Am a Palestinian Christian*, 65.

Western Christian world after Vatican II—and allows the Palestinians to define themselves as God's elect. Thus, while the election of Judaism has not been abolished, its validity (or at least the implications of its validity) is no longer relevant. The very fact that the Palestinians are witnesses to God, especially as a persecuted minority, grants them special status. Yet this status is not exceptional, since there are others who serve the same role of moral witness.

In this context, Raheb and Yunnan emphasize that the difference between *witnessing* and *victimhood* must be noted as a victim, unlike a witness, is not responsible nor accountable to the situation.[95] Witnessing, then, is a humble position of bearing God's message of justice and peace, and a victim, with the powerful emotion of guilt, can easily become the oppressor.[96] Therefore, Raheb elucidates that the Palestinians should not enter into a competition with the Jews contesting the question, Who are the greater victims? Alternatively, they should understand their own place as witnesses.[97] This issue is precarious for Palestinian theologians, as in their eyes the status of the Jews as victims of the Holocaust led to the legitimization of the establishment of the state of Israel, based on biblical hermeneutics.

When Palestinian theologians take upon themselves the role of moral witnesses, it is as if they are illegitimately competing with those whose role of victimhood and witness is broadly acknowledged—the Jews. To overcome this predicament, Palestinian theologians use the notion of justice and power: Israel, as the one who holds power, must side with justice. If not, it becomes just another colonialist power or empire, as understood in postcolonial discourse.[98] If the state of Israel abuses its power, it can no longer speak on behalf of moral witnessing. This observation is also evident from God's terms of the promises: only a just society can be God's elected and witness to him.[99]

95 Mitri Raheb, *Faith in the Face of Empire: The Bible Through Palestinian Eyes* (Orbis, 2014), 115–16.

96 Yunnan, *Witnessing for Peace*, 49–50.

97 Raheb, *Faith in the Face of Empire*, 115.

98 Mitri Raheb, "Towards a New Hermeneutics of Liberation: A Palestinian Christian Perspective," in *The Biblical Text in the Context of Occupation: Towards a New Hermeneutics of Liberation*, ed. Mitri Raheb (Diyar, 2012), 16. The danger of human power is also emphasized in Sabbah's pastoral letters.

99 Ateek, *Justice and Only Justice*, 105–7; Katanacho, *Land of Christ*, 70–72.

To highlight the transformation of the state of Israel from a representative of moral witness to an oppressor, Raheb makes use of ecclesiastical history, arguing that the church also underwent a transformation from a persecuted people to a persecutor after the Constantinian shift and the establishment of Christian empire.[100] The Jews, too, according to this doctrine, went from being persecutors during Jesus's era to being persecuted under the Christian empires—culminating in the Holocaust. Finally, due to their status as victims, and the power that was given to them based on European guilt, Jews became once again the persecutors and oppressors, this time of the Palestinians.[101] Palestinian Christian theologians claim that the post-Holocaust victim status of Israel made it possible for some to use the Bible in order to legitimize the Israeli occupation.[102] Ateek expresses that before the establishment of the state of Israel, the Old Testament held a vital place in Christian scripture, serving as a guide and testimony to Jesus.[103] However, following the creation of the state, certain Jewish and Christian interpreters have predominantly viewed the Old Testament as a Zionist text. This perspective has become so prominent that it has almost become distasteful to Palestinian Christians. Therefore, Palestinian theologians emphasize the difference between witnessing and victimhood. Witnessing does not come with power, on the contrary, it is the role of the weak, and it derives from a divine mission. As witnesses, Palestinians fight against injustice, while Israel, in the name of victimhood, causes it. The writers of the *Kairos Document* proclaimed: "Do not repay evil for evil" (1 Pet 3:9).[104]

Palestinian theologians enrich the concept of witnessing by asserting themselves as the original inhabitants of the Holy Land and successors to the early church, thus positioning themselves as eyewitnesses to the resurrection. This extension of the term encompasses not only witnessing through suffering but also through historical continuity. Drawing parallels to the Christian perception of Judaism, which involves passing down witnessing through generations, Palestinian theologians argue for a similar continuity in their community. They emphasize that

[100] Raheb, *I Am a Palestinian Christian*, 63; Naim Ateek, *A Palestinian Christian Cry for Reconciliation* (Orbis, 2008), 100–101.

[101] Ateek, *Justice and Only Justice*, 179.

[102] *Kairos*, paras. 2.3–2.5.

[103] Ateek, *Justice and Only Justice*, 77.

[104] *Kairos*, para 4.1.

their witnessing is rooted in their historical presence in the Holy Land and their lineage from the early apostles, presenting their testimony as a direct continuation of the first apostles' accounts. Elias Chacour, a Palestinian Melkite theologian, highlights this connection, pointing to a two-thousand-year legacy where their ancestors were firsthand witnesses to Jesus Christ of Nazareth, a heritage intricately woven into their identity and narrative as Palestinian Christians.[105] Ateek also states that the Palestinian Christians see themselves as a continuation of the cloud of witnesses to Jesus who came before them.[106] The meaning of this heritage is that the Palestinians are not only witnesses to the message of Christ, but—in some way or another—witnesses to Christ's historical story too. Palestinian Christian theologians base this claim on the notion of localization of the collective memory (that is, the significance of the holy places to pilgrims all over the world) and on the notion that the holy places serve as a source of knowledge or as a way to get closer to Jesus.[107] It is remarkable that Palestinian Christian theologians (for example, Ateek and Younan) note Cyril of Jerusalem's recognition of Jerusalem's holy places as enduring witnesses to Christ. This perspective holds significance for countless pilgrims today, affirming that Palestine serves as a "fifth gospel" to them, enriching their spiritual experience with a tangible connection to biblical events.[108]

The idea of the "fifth gospel" is associated with Cyril of Jerusalem, yet the term itself was only claimed in the eighteenth century as an attempt to bring pilgrims to the Holy Land.[109] Conceptualizing the holy places in terms of the *fifth gospel*, much like the New Testament itself, provides the believer with a unique knowledge concerning the major events relating to Jesus, a sort of knowledge that is missing from those who were not there to witness Jesus's life themselves. In fact, Palestinian theologians continue to develop Cyril's theology of the holy places further and seek to give it a new and relevant meaning by shifting the

105 Elias Chacour, "Reconciliation and Justice: Living with the Memory," in *Holy Land, Hollow Jubilee: God, Justice and the Palestinians*, ed. Naim Ateek and Michael Prior (Melisende, 1999), 111.

106 Ateek, *Justice and Only Justice*, 113.

107 Halbwachs, *On Collective Memory*, 52–53; Castelli, *Martyrdom and Memory*, 14–15.

108 Ateek, *Justice and Only Justice*, 113; Yunnan, *Witnessing for Peace*, 142 (emphasis mine).

109 See, for example, Jennifer Stevens, *The Historical Jesus and the Literary Imagination 1860–1920* (Liverpool University Press, 2010).

focus from the function of the land as witness to the theological role of its inhabitants. Justifying their new theological approach, they claim that as the importance of the land was not obvious in the first century and the idea was developed with great efforts by Cyril of Jerusalem, so the Palestinian theologians hope to establish the new status of the Palestinian Christian community not just as the descendants of the first Christian communities, but as one with real theological significance, as a "true witness to Christ." Ateek contends that while visiting museums can provide individuals with a significant understanding and appreciation of the past, visiting the churches of the region, participating in worship with the local Christians, and personally meeting them can offer pilgrims not only an appreciation for the present but also a priceless experience and insight into the vibrant and enduring Christian communities of the land.[110] These communities, like their forebears, have steadfastly borne witness to Christ for the past two millennia. Elias Chacour, in his book *Blood Brothers* (1984), was the first to use the phrase "living stones" (1 Pet 2:4) in the context of the Christian community in the Holy Land.[111] That is, if the stones of the holy places hold testimony within them, why not the people themselves? Rahab took this observation a step further and suggested that local Christians be treated as the "sixth gospel."[112] Thus, in this hermeneutic discourse on the holy places, Palestinian Christians are given the role of eyewitness, equal to the four Gospels in the New Testament—a status similar to the holy places.

This is not simply a new emphasis and a minor shift from late antique discourse on sacred geography in Palestine but rather a renewed emphasis and a constructive reimagining. It reflects a vibrant new rhetoric of "living stones" that seeks to enrich and expand the paradigm of witness as it has developed throughout Christian history. Therefore, as the holy places in late antique Christianity are understood as the "fifth gospel," thus creating a further pillar of the New Testament apostles' testimony, the Palestinians identify themselves as the "sixth gospel," claiming for themselves a new theological role within the Christian witnessing tradition. In this claim they draw on two discourses discussed above: the Christian discourse on Judaism

110 Ateek, *Justice and Only Justice*, 114 (emphasis mine).

111 Elias Chacour, *Blood Brothers* (Chosen Books, 1984), 175.

112 Raheb, "Towards a New Hermeneutics of Liberation," 26.

and the postcolonial discourse. This dual usage as moral witnesses on the one hand and eyewitnesses on the other enables them to claim a kind of ultimate witnessing, a role that was previously reserved only for the apostles. This remarkable and innovative self-perception of those Palestinian Christian theologians—as "living stones" and a "sixth gospel"—marks a significant stance in their discourse regarding their unique identity and political positions, all the while relating an active role to the notion of witness.

In order to gain the role of witness, one needs to have knowledge of an event that others lack. Palestinian Christians' firsthand knowledge of Christ and the resurrection is derived from their historical connection to Jesus and his apostles, and from the fact that they are inhabitants of the same land.[113] Since, according to Palestinian theologians, Jesus was a Palestinian who lived in the Holy Land, today's Palestinian Christians have a special connection with him, living a parallel version of his life, thus weaving together the Christian past and Christian-Palestinian present. This argument is not self-evident. Acts emphasizes that the gospel of Jesus was spread to the whole world, and that after him, the differences between Jesus's people—the Jews—and the Gentiles are no longer of the same importance. However, as I demonstrated above, Jews were seen as having a special role as witnesses to Jesus and the Christian gospel, and more importantly, starting from the second half of the twentieth century, Jewish witnessing took on a renewed, positive meaning.

While Palestinians recognize the historical role of the Jews as witnesses to God manifested in their status as elected, they also see themselves as equally important. However, when it comes to their knowledge and understanding of Jesus, Palestinian theologians believe that their role as witnesses is larger than that of the Jews, for they, unlike the Jews, recognize his gospel. Ateek posits that Palestinian Christians find themselves paradoxically disadvantaged by Western Christians due to their acknowledgment of Jesus as the Messiah. Had they maintained a "Jewish" identity, they might now enjoy the support of the Western world and could lay claim to Palestine.[114] Ateek argues that if Judaism is

[113] See Walker, *Holy City, Holy Places?*. Since both Ateek and Younan refer directly to Cyril, it is clear that they based their argument on his writing. Ateek, *Justice and Only Justice*, 113; Yunnan, *Witnessing for Peace*, 142.

[114] Naim Ateek, "Jerusalem in Islam and for Palestinian Christians," in *Jerusalem Past and Present in the Purposes of God*, ed. Peter Walker (Tyndale House, 1992), 131.

accepted as evidence of Jesus's life, Palestinians should be able to claim the very same status. But unlike the Jews settling in the state of Israel today, the testimony of the Palestinians is twofold. First, they claim to testify to the suffering and injustice of the Arab-Jewish conflict. Thus they place themselves on a continuum along the developing discourse in postcolonial theology. Their suffering has meaning because through it they become moral witnesses, and even more so, living martyrs. The testimony of suffering allows them to promote a different discourse on divine election, not akin to the Zionist one of Jews as the chosen people but rather based on divine preference for the weak and oppressed. Thus Palestinian Christian theologians have built their own national narrative, one that both reflects and competes with the Jewish one. It is a narrative that provides them with a sense of being a select group and gives religious significance to their presence in the Holy Land. The theology of witnessing allows Palestinian Christian theologians to frame their national claims with religious significance, and through their connection to the land they provide a new meaning to the triad of Bible, land, and people.[115]

[115] For further reading see, among others, Gideon Aran, *Kookism: The Roots of Gush Emunim, Jewish Settlers' Sub-culture, Zionist Theology, Contemporary Messianism* (Carmel, 2013).

Conclusion

> I am from there. I am from here.
> I am not there, and I am not here.
> I have two names, which meet and part,
> and I have two languages.
> I forget which of them I dream in.
>
> **Mohamed Darwish**[1]

HISTORY, FAITH, AND IDENTITY IN PCT

This study is devoted to the methods by which Palestinian Christian theologians use biblical interpretation to shape and reshape their national-political identity. The study was conducted in relation to three dominant categories: the Palestinian people, the Christian world, and Judaism as it is perceived within Christianity today. I argued that PCT was developed mostly for a Western Christian audience. Palestinian theologians have taken an active part in the ongoing discourse on political theology that has developed since the second half of the twentieth century in Western Christianity.

As we saw in chapter 1, this theology was originally written by Palestinian theologians in a Palestinian context. The motivation to develop PCT was mainly a response to internal Palestinian affairs. The

1 Mahmoud Darwish, "Edward Said: A Contrapuntal Reading," *Cultural Critique* 67 (2007): 177.

possibility of producing a national-political Christian theology allowed Palestinian Christians to partake in the Palestinian national struggle. This should be understood in relation to two important facts. First, starting in the 1970s and continuing to a greater extent in the 1980s, the Palestinian national-political discourse was transformed into a Muslim discourse using Muslim religious terminology to describe the national struggle. Therefore, today the prominent role of Palestinian Christians in the development of Arab nationalism is widely perceived as not merely irrelevant but in fact threatening to Islam and thus to Palestinian identity. Moreover, prominent figures from the past, such as George Antonius or George Habash, formerly a source of Palestinian Christian pride, are now viewed in some Palestinian circles as symbols of dangerous attempts to implant Western concepts in the Arab world. For instance, although Khoury doesn't explicitly refer to Antonius or Habash by name, he generally discusses Arab Christian intellectuals who "resorted to the new thought of ideologies of the West."[2] The infrequent mention of these figures by Palestinian theologians suggests a deliberate effort to distance themselves from them. On the contrary, figures like Edward Said, a Palestinian Christian intellectual who openly criticized the West in his works, were not perceived as threats and are more openly acknowledged.

Second, there is suspicion among Muslims in the Arab world that, as Arab Christians are part of the Christian community, they have ties to the Western world. Thus during an ongoing "culture war" between the Arab world and the Western one, Palestinian Christians' loyalty is questionable. This suspicion is also directly connected to objections against Christian support for the state of Israel, as well as attempts within the state of Israel to create separation and sectarianism within Palestinian society in order to "divide and rule." So Palestinian Christians must prove that they are an integral part of the Palestinian struggle, as well as of the Palestinian people. Political or public theology allows them to do just that and still preserve Christian religious principles, such as nonviolent struggle. In the same way, postcolonial theology allows Palestinian Christians to participate in a critical discourse vis-à-vis the West, and thus to use their dual affiliation—both to the Arab world, and to the Christian religion—to establish a new

2 Rafiq Khoury, "The Role of the Arab Christian in the Arab National Movements," *Al-Liqa' Journal* 35 (2010): 54–55.

role for the Arab Christian tradition. By following the example of individuals like Edward Said and of various Christian groups around the world, they posit themselves and their religious beliefs as part of the critical and poignant discourse against the wrongdoings of the West and emphasize that they are not supporters of Western colonialism.

As we saw in chapter 2, Palestinian Christian theologians attempt to construct their national-political collective identity by establishing boundaries between themselves and the "other" conflicting groups they face. In this case, and in the context of the IPC, it is Jews and Christian Zionists who are perceived as conflicting groups. The Palestinian Christian identity, which defines itself through its political conflict with Jews and its theological differences with Judaism in general, also takes aim at Judaism, particularly Judaism as perceived in the eyes of Western Christianity. Thus the discourse of the formation of identity takes place first and foremost as an intra-Christian discourse and not an interreligious one. Obviously, this should be understood within the political context of the IPC. The conflictual relationship between Palestinian Christians and Western Christianity's perception of Judaism becomes even more significant because there are political implications, in the form of Western support for the state of Israel, which can directly affect the reality of the Palestinian people.

The attempt of the theologians to construct a Palestinian Christian collective identity is undertaken within a national-political conflict over the rights of each people to the same territory, the Holy Land. Therefore, as we saw in chapter 3, the Palestinian theologians first *deconstructed* the Christian Zionist narrative, which had its roots in biblical Judaism, and only then *reconstructed* the Palestinian Christian one. The basis for the construction of identity, as well as the connection to the territory, is created through a connection to the past, or to the "myth of origin" of both Christians and Jews—that is, to the common Old Testament. Palestinian theologians first disassemble the connection between biblical Israel and modern Israel and between the Jewish people and the Holy Land based on the biblical text. Especially in the post-WWII era, the intention is not to disconnect the Jewish people from the text itself or from their historical roots, but rather to refute the claim that the biblical narrative has contemporary national-political implications and that the concept of the divine election of the Jewish people implies that they have contemporary rights to the land of Israel.

Palestinian theologians are aware of the discourse in which they partake—namely, the theological and political discourse that developed in Western Christianity since WWII—and the sensitivity that exists around Jewish-Christian relations (chapter 2). According to Palestinian theologians, Western Christianity's guilty reaction to the horrors of the Holocaust and its roots in European antisemitism leads to discriminatory treatment in favor of the Jews. At the same time, Palestinian theologians cannot avoid the decision of the Roman Catholic Church, as well as the various Protestant churches, to utterly reject the notion of supersessionism. However, they are also aware that this rejection does not adequately address the significance of the Jewish people's chosen status in relation to Christianity, particularly in terms of its national and political implications. The discourse within Christian theology around the conception of Judaism, and about replacement theology or supersessionism, was never fully resolved. The Christian world's urgent need to expunge antisemitism from Christian theology after the Holocaust required hasty action that left many questions unresolved. This may be compared to a large, aching hole in a wisdom tooth which has not undergone a root canal, but only a temporary filling. A root canal is a laborious and delicate undertaking, yet without it, the malady cannot be truly healed.

Nevertheless, Palestinian theologians are part of the world churches and thus committed to the decision of rejecting supersessionism. Therefore, rejection of the common understanding will put them out of the bounds of the accepted discourse. If Palestinian theologians are to be heard, they must know the limits of the discourse in which they participate; but that does not mean that PCT cannot criticize Western Christianity for ignoring the implications of unresolved issues regarding divine election. Palestinian theologians argue that, as part of efforts to redress past wrongs, many Western theologians, particularly in Europe, have adopted a discourse that oscillates between condemning the Jewish people and unjustly praising them. In this discourse, Judaism is granted by some Christian theologians a new prestige due to its status as the older brother of Christianity, the faith whose roots precede those of the Christians. But this view preserves, in many cases, the image of the Jews as ahistorical. That is, they are not part of progressive history, but are frozen in time, as a kind of a node that connects the present, the past, and the future. That is why many Western theologians turn to Judaism to learn about the historical Jesus, as Judaism is seen as connected directly to Christian sacred time (chapter

2). Moreover, some evangelicals view the Jewish people as having the power to control history, because the return of the Jews to their land is seen as eschatologically significant, and as a move that drives divine history (chapter 3). Thus, when the Palestinian theologians construct their identity vis-à-vis Judaism, and especially vis-à-vis Christianity's perception of Judaism, they must find a way to break the metaphysical connection between the Jewish people and the Holy Land.

But, building on Smith's idea that a shared history is a fundamental construct in the definition of nationalism, I argued that this endeavor is more fundamental.[3] The stronger the connection to the past, the stronger the claim for ethnic or national identity.[4] As we have seen, Palestinian theologians argued that the connection between the Jewish people and the land of Israel has resulted in the Palestinians being erased from history, or at least relegated to a secondary and marginal position—as if the history of the Holy Land froze after the time of Jesus and continued only with the return of the Jewish people to the land as part of the Zionist project (chapter 3). This perception led Western thinkers to view the land of Israel as "a land without people." Likewise, Palestinians are often perceived by Zionist Christians as a people without history, or with a history as a nation which began only in 1948. Thus, to establish their identity in connection with both the Christian world and its view of the Jewish people, Palestinian theologians seek to challenge this particular reading of history: a universal reading that focuses on the West and its story as a triangulation point. According to Palestinian theologians, this reading deprives them of their own history and puts them in a position where they must prove that they are indeed a separate ethnopolitical group, a nation with rights over their land. On the contrary, their absence from the Christian history of the Holy Land invalidates their claim to nationality.

As we saw in chapter 3, the Palestinian theologians' argument against a reading of history that denies the Palestinian people their past is based on a suspicion of the way certain interpretations of the Bible are used to support this denial, presenting what they claim is a distorted, one-sided view of the past that does not reflect the true complexity and diversity of the region. Palestinian Christian theologians seek to recreate or

3 Anthony Smith, *Myths and Memories of the Nation* (Oxford University Press, 1999), 15.

4 Smith, *Myths and Memories*, 15.

reconstruct the connection between their national-political identity as Palestinians and what they regard as their land. This effort of the Palestinian theologians aims to strengthen the connection between the Palestinian people and their history, and to resist efforts to erase or deny their existence and their right to self-determination. To do so, they use a double argument. The first is the call for universality. According to Palestinian theologians, God as a universal deity cannot favor one group over another. Through this approach, Palestinian theologians seek to challenge dominant narratives that privilege certain groups and ignore the experiences and perspectives of others. Within this claim for universality, there is also a call to transform the meaning of the divine history into one that is not tied to a specific place and to a particular people. In parallel, they advocate for the idea that the cultural and historical contexts of different groups are an essential part of the Christian mission.

However, there is a paradox inherent here: Palestinian theologians attempt to dismantle the Zionist argument by advocating for a universal Christianity that does not favor any group over another, while at the same time seeking to create a distinct identity for themselves that sets them apart in the Christian world, in order to confer religious meaning on their connection to the Holy Land. This paradox arises from the separation that exists in Western Christianity between the Holy Land and the Christian communities living there. While the Holy Land is viewed by many in the Christian world as the center of Christian history, Palestinian Christians are often seen by Western Christianity as marginal to the Christian church. It is this paradox that lies at the heart of PCT (chapter 3). In contrast, various theological movements in the global South approach their writings from the margins in terms of both divine time and divine place. For these groups, it is necessary to engage with Christian history as being separated from time and place in order to grapple with the paradox of particularism—the difficulty of reconciling the fact that Christianity, which originated in a specific region and time with the incarnation, did not reach these groups until a thousand (or more) years later (chapter 2).[5]

The Palestinian theologians I examined did not face these challenges. They do not view themselves as new Christians, or as a group discon-

[5] On the "scandal of particularity" see Robin Le Poidevin, "Multiple Incarnation and Distributed Persons," in *The Metaphysics of the Incarnation*, ed. Anna Marmodoro and Jonathan Hill (Oxford University Press, 2011), 229.

nected from Christian history, but as a people who have always been at the hub of Christianity. However, the texts I examined seem to indicate that Palestinian theologians concur that in the eyes of Western Christianity they are perceived as a marginal group that must prove its connection to history. Therefore, Palestinian theologians construct their arguments to stand on the two dimensions that make up history—time and place. While time is linear and has a direction that cannot be reversed, place, as Michel de Certeau has argued, can be entered and exited.[6] In the case of historical narratives, while there may be a gap between the time of the story and the present moment, place can serve as a link between the two. Robert Markus concluded that places acquired sanctity as the past became anchored in the present. The significance of these places always rested on their historical relevance, and it was the enduring impact of past human actions that conferred sanctity upon them.[7] The concept of sacred space and a Christian topography with sacred sites developed relatively late in Christian history. This evolution was largely driven by a heightened awareness of the past and the human desire to connect with it in the present. Therefore, connecting themselves to the Holy Land allows Palestinian theologians to claim their place in history. However, their relationship to the Holy Land as a sacred space is complex because emphasizing the sanctity of the place also risks reinforcing the Christian-Zionist argument, which asserts that the return of the Jews to their land has eschatological significance, a significance which Palestinian theologians seek to undermine and deny by any means.

Similarly, their attitude toward the Holy Land and pilgrimage can reinforce the idea of universal history, which applies to Christians everywhere. This complex relationship between the perception of pilgrimage to holy places and the role of indigeneity in Christianity reinforces the tension between the universal and the particular.[8] Leaning

[6] On the definition of place in modern time and the debate about the differences between space and place see Michel de Certeau, *The Practice of Everyday Life*, trans. Steven Rendall (University of California Press, 1984); Marc Augé, *Non-Places: Introduction to an Anthropology of Supermodernity*, trans. John Howe (Verso, 1995).

[7] Robert Markus, "How on Earth Could Places Become Holy? Origins of the Christian Idea of Holy Places," *Journal of Early Christian Studies* 2 (1994): 271.

[8] Andrew Walls, *Missionary Movement in Christian History: Studies in the Transmission of Faith* (Orbis, 1996), 7–9; Brouria Bitton-Ashkelony, *Encountering the Sacred: The Debate on Christian Pilgrimage in Late Antiquity* (University of California Press, 2005).

too heavily toward either side can impede Palestinian argumentation.[9] To address this tension, Palestinian theologians, like other postcolonial thinkers, aim to shift the discourse from one of universal history to one that recognizes that the past can and should be understood from multiple perspectives. Postcolonial theology allows Palestinians to use their position as a marginalized group in the eyes of the West to strengthen their arguments (chapter 3). As a theology that prioritizes liberation and justice and therefore elevates the role of the oppressed to those chosen by God, postcolonial theology enables Palestinian theologians to use their status as marginalized individuals to make their voices heard. They use postcolonial discourse to restore the centrality of their land and their place in Christian history by adopting a different approach to interpreting history. Palestinian theologians relate to biblical history as a collective memory and narrative rather than a sequence of objectively verifiable events. This shift in perception, which is common to postcolonial theology, enables the perception of history from multiple perspectives and challenges the universality of the past.

In this new understanding of history, Palestinian theologians position and perceive themselves as *witnesses* (chapter 4). In this revised view of biblical history, presence during the events and oral traditions about the divine history, passed down from generation to generation, are crucial. By positioning themselves as witnesses, Palestinian theologians can provide "testimony" to the events of the past. This is the same concept that gives Judaism its place in Christianity—the idea that Jews were present at the time and place of historical Christian events and therefore possess authentic firsthand knowledge of that period of origin. Unlike the Jews, however, Palestinian theologians seek to establish their testimony from within the framework of Christian faith. They connect themselves to Jesus through their status on the margins, as those who struggle against empires and suffer under imperialists' boots. They connect themselves to Christian history through their continuous presence in the Holy Land. As Antony Smith has argued, they construct their national-political identity through recurrence, continuity, and reappropriation of the past.[10] Palestinian Christian theologians establish their connection to the past by asserting the authenticity of the myth of their unique origin. This allows them to turn their

9 Walls, *Missionary Movement in Christian History*, 7–9.

10 Anthony Smith, *Myths and Memories of the Nation* (Oxford University Press, 1999), 11–12.

testimony into a valid act of witnessing—to establish for themselves a status of possessing existential knowledge that connects them to sacred place and time. As Maurice Halbwachs explained, it is not paradoxical to assert that when a noteworthy event occurs, the presence of firsthand witnesses can actually raise the likelihood of alterations in its description. In such cases, it becomes challenging to establish the precise details of the event. This is particularly true when the event evokes strong emotions in various groups of people, leading to passionate debates and discussions about its nature and implications.[11] Palestinian theologians use their role as witnesses to claim their connection to Christian history and to give meaning to their relationship with the Holy Land. In a discourse centered on interpretation, the question is not what happened, but how we interpret the past and give meaning to the present and the future. A witness can assert the authenticity of his connection to the past and the knowledge that comes from experience rather than indirect study.

IDENTITY AND DISCOURSE: WHAT IS CONTEXTUAL IN PALESTINIAN CHRISTIAN "CONTEXTUAL THEOLOGY"

The attempt to construct a Palestinian Christian identity by theologians is based on participation in an existing discourse. This is done within a complex system of thought in which Palestinian theologians do not shape the discourse itself but only their place within it. As we saw in chapter 2, Palestinian theologians are confronted with two distinct but parallel theological trends in the broader discourse of Western Christianity post-WWII: the first is a theology that contracts with Christianity's conception of Judaism and assumes a divine alliance with Judaism; the second is a political theology that places emphasis on the role of the church in the world, and the involvement of the church in struggles against injustice around the globe. These two theological trends arose from a shared context and a common critique of the West and its treatment of "the other." Post-WWII Western Christianity embraced principles such as pluralism, a complex understanding of history, skepticism of power, and support for the oppressed. This last concept emphasizes the significance of the oppressed in society and the value of equality and human rights.

As Palestinian theology, like other postcolonial theologies, is written for a specific audience, it engages with a preexisting discourse that

11 Maurice Halbwachs, *On Collective Memory* (University of Chicago Press, 1992), 194.

has its own set of rules and assumed truths.[12] The discourse is a system of knowledge shaped by various powerful factors. The participants in the discourse can choose certain patterns that exist within the shared culture, but they do not create these patterns, which are imposed on them by culture, society, or social norms.[13] Those norms determine not only what can be said but also who can say it and under what circumstances—which also shift over time, following sociohistorical changes. Palestinian theologians participate in a discourse primarily directed at Western Christianity. Thus this discourse is most naturally shaped by Western norms and perspectives. Postcolonial theologians use this discourse to critique the West and its hegemony, but in order to be heard they are obliged to conform to Western social norms. This is one of the paradoxes of a dehegemonic discourse in Christianity: it very quickly becomes dehomogeneous as diverse, previously silenced voices emerge and contribute to the conversation. The Christian theologians who represent different groups have no choice but to sustain a common ground that allows for continued dialogue and progress.

Here we return to the idea of the *canon* as a shared collective memory (which comes from Jan Assmann).[14] The Bible forms a basis that allows general discourse since it is preserved as a common denominator for all groups concerned. But the interpretation of the Holy Scriptures also depends on social values and norms, and changes accordingly. Thus, the postmodern approach, which rejects the existence of objective historical truths and the construction of overarching narratives, produces new multiple truths that shape the political theological discourse. After WWII, it was the ethics of human rights, and the concern for the oppressed or the victim that set the boundaries of theological discourse, which sometimes translated into divine justice and liberation. In this discourse, those who are deemed to be occupying the position of the victim or the oppressed may relate to sensitive issues and point out problems or injustices that those who

[12] Michael Bamberg and Anna De Fina, "Discourse and Identity Construction," in *Handbook of Identity Theory and Research*, ed. Seth Schwartz, Koen Luyckx, and Vivian Vignoles (Springer, 2011), 178.

[13] Michel Foucault, "The Ethic of Care for the Self as a Practice of Freedom: An Interview with Michel Foucault," *Philosophy & Social Criticism* 12 (1984): 112–31.

[14] Jan Assmann, "Globalization, Universalism, and the Erosion of Cultural Memory," in *Memory in a Global Age: Discourses, Practices and Trajectories*, ed. Aleida Assmann and Sebastian Conrad (Palgrave Macmillan, 2010), 133.

are perceived as having power, privilege, or status cannot. This enables Palestinian theologians to speak out in ways that others, such as the Western Christians, are unable to. One of these voices is the call for return to the repressed issue of replacement theology, and its redefinition, in order to clarify its political implications. The avoidance of this issue amounts, according to PCT, to voicing only those claims that support the Jewish side of the story.

Two main problems arise from this mode of discourse. The first is the danger of the conversion of victims into oppressors.[15] As the hermeneutical circle clearly shows (chapter 3), the success of a struggle against oppression, which ends in the liberation of one group, can lead to the oppression of another group. What's more, being chosen and gaining liberation can result in oppression of others and the delegitimation of the status of the chosen by God. The Indian philosopher Aijaz Ahmad has said, "Everyone gets the privilege, sooner or later, of being colonizer, colonized and postcolonial—sometimes all at once."[16]

The second problem is the question of the contextualization of the discourse: If one promotes the emergence of discourse from different perspectives by different people around the globe and negates the concept of one universal truth or one grand narrative, how can it be that different theologies eventually become so similar? How is it possible that reading Palestinian theology sounds almost exactly like reading South African theology? As Israeli sociologist Shmuel Eisenstadt argued in another context, while such diversity has certainly undermined the old hegemonies, at the same time it has been closely connected—perhaps paradoxically—with the development of new multiple common reference points and networks, with a globalization of cultural networks and channels of communication far beyond what existed before.[17] In line with Eisenstadt's argument, it appears that postcolonial theologies operate within similar knowledge-systems and share the Western conception of truth, which posits that empowering the oppressed is necessary to bring about change in their situation. Moreover, it seems the duty of the powerful, the colonial oppressors of

[15] See Laura Jeffery and Matei Candea, "The Politics of Victimhood," *History and Anthropology* 17 (2006): 287–96.

[16] Aijaz Ahmad, "The Politics of Literary Postcoloniality," *Race & Class* 36 (1995): 9.

[17] Shmuel Eisenstadt, "The Transformations of the Religious Dimension in the Constitution of Contemporary Maternities," in *Religion and Politics: Culture Perspective*, ed. Bernhard Giesen and Daniel Suber (Brill, 2005), 33.

the past, is to help the victims in their struggle for liberation. The main values professed are justice and equality, and they are explained by way of a constant dialectic between oppressed and oppressor, victim, and victimizer. Thus a new universal ethical discourse has been developed.

THE ROLE OF THE THEOLOGIAN IN CONSTRUCTING IDENTITY

A topic that preoccupied me in my research was the role of Palestinian theologians in the current national-political discourse: namely, how theologians take part in that discourse and how they attempt to form a collective identity. I eventually concluded that the connection between contemporary reality, the holy past, and the eschatological future is central to theologians' attempt; it is essential to the role of the theologian as well as to his contribution to the discourse. Theology has the ability to give a group in times of crisis a forward-directed perspective imbued with deep meaning. The theologian can offer hope for the future based on the interpretation of the past. As Michel Sabbah puts it: "Throughout this process, the Word of God will be our best guide, even in the midst of doubts and denials. Therefore, we are invited to read the Bible, to study it and to live it."[18] Referring to the Arab Spring, Mitri Raheb presented this concept in a remarkable way. Raheb explained that the role of the theologian is not necessarily to lead the people out of Egypt but to guide them on their way through the desert; to be an arrow and thus give strength to the laborious movement toward the future, through conferring hope.[19] Thus, Raheb asks, "Can we imagine another Middle East? Can there be a different future?" He further explains that "prophetic imagination helps us see beyond the current realities, and Christian hope empowers us to move to a new vision into action."[20]

It is my hope that this study will shed light on the role of theology in the process of the formation of a group self-definition in a time of transformation and crisis, within the framework of encounter with other cultures. It may illuminate the rich cross-fertilization of ideas

[18] Michel Sabbah, *Fourth Pastoral Letter: Reading the Bible Today in the Land of the Bible* (Jerusalem, 1993), para. 2.

[19] Mitri Raheb, *Sailing Through Troubled Waters: Christianity in the Middle East* (Diyar, 2013), 105–16.

[20] Mitri Raheb, *Faith in the Face of Empire: The Bible Through Palestinian Eyes* (Orbis, 2014), 13.

that allows us to better understand, reflect, and reconsider key concepts in this intricate encounter.

I have examined here the effort made by major Palestinian Christian thinkers to form a discourse on their identity and their political claims that they addressed in English to Western Christianity. But PCT has evolved simultaneously in both English and Arabic. Most often, these different audiences were not presented with translations of the same writings but with two different types of writings authored by the very same theologians, one addressed to the Western Christian world and the other to the Arab Muslim one. Thus I offer here an analysis of one perspective of their discourse. I hope to conduct further research to compare Palestinian theology written in English to that written in Arabic. This can be particularly interesting because Palestinian Christians are situated on the periphery of two major civilizations: Western Christian and Eastern Arab. When Palestinian Christian theologians write in English, they adjust to the universal Western Christian premises formulated post-WWII and the Holocaust. When they write in Arabic, they adjust to the universal Eastern-Arab or Muslim premises shaped following external and internal trends within this civilization (Islamization, the Arab Spring, etc.). In theory as well as in practice, not one but two universalist discourses are conducted simultaneously. An examination of this fascinating phenomenon awaits future inquiry.

Bibliography

Abraham, Susan. "What Does Mumbai Have to Do with Rome? Postcolonial Perspective on Globalization and Theology." *Theological Studies* 69 (2008): 376–93.

Abu-Manneh Bashir. "Jerusalem in the Tanzimat Period." *Die Welt des Islam* 30 (1990): 1–44.

Adam, Andrew. "Docetism, Käsemann, and Christology: Why Historical Criticism Can't Protect Christological Orthodoxy." *Scottish Journal of Theology* 49 (1996): 392–99.

Agamben, Giorgio. *Remnants of Auschwitz: The Witness and the Archive*. Zone Books, 1999.

Ahmad, Aijaz. "The Politics of Literary Postcoloniality." *Race & Class* 36 (1995): 1–2.

Aichele, George, et al. *The Postmodern Bible: The Bible and Culture Collective*. Yale University Press, 1995.

Anderson, Gary. "Israel and the Land: Does the Promise Still Hold?" *Christian Century* 13 (2009): 22–24.

Andiñach, Pablo R., and Alejandro F. Botta, eds. *The Bible and the Hermeneutics of Liberation*. Society of Biblical Literature, 2009.

Ankersmit, Frank. "Historical Representation." *History and Theory* 27 (1988): 205–22.

Aran, Gideon. *Kookism: The Roots of Gush Emunim, Jewish Settlers' Subculture, Zionist Theology, Contemporary Messianism*. Carmel, 2013.

Arner, Neil. "Ecumenical Ethics: Challenges to and Sources for a Common Moral Witness." *Journal of the Society of Christian Ethics* 36 (2016): 101–19.

Ashkenazi, Jacob. *The Mother of All Churches: The Church of Palestine from Its Foundation to the Arab Conquest*. Yad Izhak Ben-Zvi, 2009.

Assmann, Jan. "Collective Memory and Cultural Identity." *New German Critique* 65 (1995): 125–33.

Assmann, Jan. "Globalization, Universalism, and the Erosion of Cultural Memory." In *Memory in a Global Age: Discourses, Practices and Trajectories*, edited by Aleida Assmann and Sebastian Conrad, 121–37. Palgrave Macmillan, 2010.

Assmann, Jan. "Monotheism and Its Political Consequences." In *Religion and Politics: Culture Perspective*, edited by Bernhard Giesen and Daniel Suber, 141–60. Brill, 2005.

Assmann, Jan. *Moses the Egyptian: The Memory of Egypt in Western Monotheism*. Harvard University Press, 1997.

Ateek, Naim. "Biblical Perspective of the Land." In *Faith and the Intifada: Palestinian Christian Voices*, edited by Naim S. Ateek, Marc H. Ellis, and Rosemary Radford Ruether, 108–18. Orbis, 1989.

Ateek, Naim. Introduction to *Challenging Christian Zionism: Theology, Politics and the Israel-Palestine Conflict*, edited by Naim Ateek, Ceder Duaybis, and Maurin Tobin, 13–19. Melisende, 2005.

Ateek, Naim. "Jerusalem in Islam and for Palestinian Christians." In *Jerusalem Past and Present in the Purposes of God*, edited by Peter Walker, 125–50. Tyndale House, 1992.

Ateek, Naim. *Justice and Only Justice: A Palestinian Theology of Liberation*. Orbis, 1989.

Ateek, Naim. *A Palestinian Christian Cry for Reconciliation*. Orbis, 2008.

Ateek, Naim. *A Palestinian Theology of Liberation*. Orbis, 2017.

Ateek, Naim. "Reflections on Sabeel's Liberation Theology and Ecumenical Work (1992–2013)." In *Theologies of Liberation in Palestine-Israel: Indigenous, Contextual, and Postcolonial Perspectives*, edited by Nur Masalha and Lisa Isherwood, 21–33. Pickwick, 2014.

Attridge, Derek, Geoff Bennington, and Robert Young. *Post-Structuralism and the Question of History*. Cambridge University Press, 1987.

Augé, Marc. *Non-Places: Introduction to an Anthropology of Supermodernity*. Translated by John Howe. Verso, 1995.

Azar, Michael. "Origen, Scripture, and the Imprecision of 'Supersessionism.'" *Journal of Theological Interpretation* 10 (2016): 157–72.

Bamberg, Michael, and Anna De Fina. "Discourse and Identity Construction." In *Handbook of Identity Theory and Research*, edited by Seth Schwartz, Koen Luyckx, and Vivian Vignoles, 177–99. Springer, 2011.

Barger, Lilian Calles. *The World Come of Age: An Intellectual History of Liberation Theology*. Oxford University Press, 2018.

Barr, James. *History and Ideology in the Old Testament: Biblical Statement at the End of a Millennium*. Oxford University Press, 2000.

Barr, James. "Story and History in Biblical Theology: The Third Nuveen Lecture." *Journal of Religion* 56 (1976): 1–17.

Barth, Karl. *The Doctrine of Reconciliation*. Vol. 4 of *Church Dogmatics*. Translated by G. W. Bromiley. T&T Clark, 1956.

Barth, Karl. *The Word of God and the Word of Man*. Translated by Douglas Horton. Hodder and Stoughton, 1978.

Barton, John. "The Historical Critical Approaches." In *The Cambridge Companion to Biblical Interpretation*, edited by John Barton, 9–20. Cambridge University Press, 1998.

Bauckham, Richard. *Jesus and the Eyewitness: The Gospel as Eyewitness Testimony*. Eerdmans, 2006.

Baum, Gregory. *Theology After Auschwitz*. Council of Christian and Jews, 1976.

Baumgart-Ochse, Claudia. "Claiming Justice for Israel/Palestine: The Boycott, Divestment, Sanctions (BDS) Campaign and Christian Organizations." *Globalizations* 14 (2017): 1172–87.

Baumgarten, Helga. "The Politicization of Muslim-Christian Relations in the Palestinian National Movement." In *Islam, Judaism, and the Political Role of Religions in the Middle East*, edited by John Bunzl, 75–97. Gainesville: University Press of Florida, 2004.

Baumgarten, Helga. "The Three Faces/Phases of Palestinian Nationalism, 1948–2005." *Journal of Palestine Studies* 34 (2005): 25–48.

Beker, Christiaan. "The New Testament View of Judaism." In *Jews and Christians: Exploring the Past, Present, and Future*, edited by James Charlesworth, 60–69. Crossroad, 1990.

Bentley, Wessel. "Defining Christianity's 'Prophetic Witness' in the Post-Apartheid South African Democracy." *Studia Historiae Ecclesiasticae* 39 (2013): 275–93.

Benton, Matthew. "The Modal Gap: The Objective Problem of Lessing's Ditch(es) and Kierkegaard's Subjective Reply." *Religious Studies* 42 (2006): 27–44.

Berger, Peter, and Luckmann, Thomas. *The Social Construction of Reality*. Anchor, 1967.

Bevans, Stephen. "The Church in Mission." In *The Cambridge Companion to Vatican II*, edited by Richard Gaillardetz, 136–54. Cambridge University Press, 2020.

Bevans, Stephen. *Models of Contextual Theology*. Orbis, 1992.

Bitton-Ashkelony, Brouria. *Encountering the Sacred: The Debate on Christian Pilgrimage in Late Antiquity*. University of California Press, 2005.

Bitton-Ashkelony, Brouria. "Territory, Anti-Intellectual Attitude, and Identity Formation in Late Antique Palestinian Monastic Communities." *Religion & Theology* 17 (2010): 244–67.

Blaising, Craig. "Dispensationalism: The Search for Definition." In *Dispensationalism, Israel and the Church: The Search for Definition*, edited by Craig Blaising and Darrell Bock, 13–36. Zondervan, 1992.

Blau, Yehoshua. *A Grammar of Christian Arabic: Based Mainly on South-Palestinian Texts from the First Millennium*. Secrétariat du Corpus SCO, 1967.

Blenkinsopp, Joseph. "Old Testament Theology and the Jewish-Christian Connection." *Journal for the Study of the Old Testament* 28 (1984): 3–15.

Blenkinsopp, Joseph. "YHWH and Other Deities: Conflict and Accommodation in the Religion of Israel." *Interpretation* 40 (1986): 354–66.

Boas, Adrian. *Jerusalem in the Time of the Crusades: Society, Landscape and Art in the Holy City Under Frankish Rule*. Routledge, 2001.

Boff, Leonardo. *Church, Charism and Power: Liberation Theology and the Institutional Church*. Translated by John Diercksmeier. Wipf and Stock, 1985.

Boff, Leonardo, and Clodovis Boff. *Introducing Liberation Theology*. Translated by Paul Burns. Orbis, 1989.

Borgehammar, Stephan. *How the Holy Cross Was Found: From Event to Medieval Legend*. Almquist & Wiksell, 1991.

Bosch, David. *Transforming Mission: Paradigm Shifts in Theology of Mission*. Orbis, 2011.

Bosch, David. *Witness to the World: The Christian Mission in Theological Perspective*. Wipf and Stock, 2006.

Braaten, Carl. *History and Hermeneutic*. Wipf and Stock, 1966.

Brett, Mark. *Biblical Criticism in Crisis? The Impact of the Canonical Approach on Old Testament Studies*. Cambridge University Press, 1991.

Brooks, Susan, and Mary Engel. *Lift Every Voice: Constructing Christian Theologies from the Underside*. Harper & Row, 1990.

Brueggemann, Walter. *The Land: Place as Gift, Promise and Challenge in Biblical Faith. Overtures to Biblical Theology*. Fortress, 1977.

Brueggemann, Walter. "Three Responses to Gary Anderson / 'Israel and the Land': Does the Promise Still Hold?" *Christian Century* 13 (2009): 25–26.

Bultmann, Rudolf. *Jesus and the Word*. Translated by Louise Smith and Erminie Huntress. Nicholson & Watson, 1935.

Burge, Gary. *Jesus and the Land*. Baker Academic, 2010.

Buttelli, Felipe. "Public Theology as Theology on Kairos: The South African Kairos Document as a Model of Public Theology." *Journal of Theology for Southern Africa* 143 (2012): 90–105.

Campos, Michelle. "From the 'Ottoman Nation' to 'Hyphenated Ottomans': Reflections on the Multicultural Imperial Citizenship at the End of Empire." *Ab Imperio* 1 (2017): 163–81.

Carmel, Alex. "Activities of the European Powers in Palestine." *Asian and African Studies* 19 (1985): 43–91.

Carroll, Robert. "Poststructuralist Approaches." In *The Cambridge Companion to Biblical Interpretation*, edited by John Barton, 50–66. Cambridge University Press, 1998.

Castelli, Elizabeth. *Martyrdom and Memory: Early Christian Culture Making.* Columbia University Press, 2004.

Cerulo, Karen. "Identity Construction: New Issues, New Directions." *Annual Review of Sociology* 23 (1997): 385–409.

Chacour, Elias. *Blood Brothers.* Chosen Books, 1984.

Chacour, Elias. "Reconciliation and Justice: Living with the Memory." In *Holy Land, Hollow Jubilee: God, Justice and the Palestinians*, edited by Naim Ateek and Michael Prior, 111–15. Melisende, 1999.

Chaillot, Christine. *The Dialogue Between the Eastern Orthodox and Oriental Orthodox Churches.* Volos Academy Publication, 2016.

Chopp, Rebecca, and Ethna Regan. "Latin American Liberation Theology." In *The Modern Theologians: An Introduction to Christian Theology Since 1918*, edited by David Ford and Rachel Muers. Blackwell, 2005.

Clarno, Andy. *Neoliberal Apartheid: Palestine/Israel and South Africa After 1994.* University of Chicago Press, 2017.

Clement of Alexandria. *The Instructor.* Translated by William Wilson. In *Ante-Nicene Fathers*, edited by Alexander Roberts, James Donaldson, and A. Cleveland Coxe. Christian Literature, 1885.

Coe, Shoki. "Contextualizing Theology." In *Mission Trend* 3 (1976): 19–22.

Coe, Shoki. *Recollections and Reflections.* 2nd ed. Dr. Shoki Coe Memorial Fund, 1993.

Cohen, Jeremy. *Living Letters of the Law: Ideas of the Jew in Medieval Christianity.* University of California Press, 1999.

Colbi, Saul. *A History of the Christian Presence in the Holy Land.* University Press of America, 1988.

Collins, John. *The Bible After Babel: Historical Criticism in a Postmodern Age.* Eerdmans, 2005.

Cone, James. *A Black Theology of Liberation.* Lippincott, 1970.

Cone, James. *My Soul Looks Back.* Abingdon, 1982.

Connelly, John. *From Enemy to Brother: The Revolution in Catholic Teaching on the Jews, 1933–1965.* Harvard University Press, 2012.

Cornelison, Robert. "The Development and Influence of Moltmann's Theology." *The Asbury Theological Journal* 55 (2000): 15–28.

Cox, Harvey. *The Silencing of Leonard Buff: The Vatican and the Future of World Christianity.* Collins, 1988.

Crane, George. "Collective Identity, Symbolic Mobilization, and Student Protest in Nanjing, China, 1988–1989." *Comparative Politics* 26 (1994): 395–413.

D'Costa, Gavin. "'Supersessionism': Harsh, Mild or Gone for Good?" *European Judaism* 50 (2017): 99–107.

Darwish, Mahmoud. "Edward Said: A Contrapuntal Reading." *Cultural Critique* 67 (2007): 177.

Davies, William. *Gospel and the Land: Early Christianity and Jewish Territorial Doctrine.* University of California Press, 1974.

Dawes, Gregory. *The Historical Jesus Quest: Landmarks in the Search for the Jesus of History*. Leiderdorp: Deo, 1999.

Day, Katie, and Sebastian Kim. Introduction to *A Companion to Public Theology*, edited by Tom Greggs, 1–24. Brill, 2017.

de Certeau, Michel. *The Practice of Everyday Life*. Translated by Steven Rendall. University of California Press, 1984.

de Dietrich, Suzanne. "'You Are My Witnesses': A Study of the Church's Witness." *Interpretation* 8 (1954): 273–79.

De La Torre, Miguel. "Liberation Theology." In *The Cambridge Companion to Christian Political Theology*, edited by Craig Hovey and Elizabeth Philip, 23–43. Cambridge University Press, 2015.

Della Porta, Donatella and Diani Mario. *Social Movements: An Introduction*. Blackwell, 1999.

Di Segni, Leah, and Yoram Tsafrir. "The Ethnic Composition of Jerusalem's Population in the Byzantine Period (312–638 CE):" *Liber Annuus* 62 (2012): 405–54.

Donaldson, Terence. "Supersessionism and Early Christian Self-Definition." *Journal of the Jesus Movement in Its Jewish Setting* 3 (2016): 1–32.

Dowty, Alan. "Prelude to the Arab–Israel Conflict: European Penetration of Nineteenth Century Ottoman Palestine." *Contemporary Review of the Middle East* 1 (2014): 3–24.

Doyle, Dennis. "The Concept of Inculturation in Roman Catholicism: A Theological Consideration." *U.S. Catholic Historian* 30 (2012): 1–13.

Drummond, Dorothy. *Holy Land, Whose Land? Modern Dilemma, Ancient Roots*. Fairhurst, 2004.

du Toit, Andre. "Puritans in Africa? Afrikaner 'Calvinism' and Kuyperian Neo-Calvinism in Late Nineteenth-Century South Africa." *Comparative Studies in Society and History* 27 (1985): 209–40.

Dunn, James. *Jesus Remembered*. Eerdmans, 2003.

Dussel, Enrique. *Beyond Philosophy: Ethics, History, Marxism, and Liberation Theology*. Rowman & Littlefield, 2003.

Dussel, Enrique. "Exodus as a Paradigm in Liberation Theology." In *Exodus: A Lasting Paradigm*, edited by Bas van Israel and Anton Weiler, 83–92. T&T Clark, 1987.

Dworkin, Donald. *Justice for Hedgehogs*. Harvard University Press, 2011.

Eckardt, Alice. "Post-Holocaust Theology: A Journey Out of the Kingdom of Night." *Holocaust and Genocide Studies* 1 (1986): 169–92.

Eckardt, Roy, and Alice Eckardt. *Your People, My People*. Quadrangle, 1974.

Eddy, Paul, and James Beilby. "The Quest for the Historical Jesus: An Introduction." In *The Historical Jesus: Five Views*, edited by Paul Eddy and James Beilby, 10–54. InterVarsity Press, 2009.

Eisenstadt, Shmuel. "The Transformations of the Religious Dimension in the Constitution of Contemporary Maternities." In *Religion and Politics:*

Culture Perspective, edited by Bernhard Giessen and Daniel Sober, 17–38. Brill, 2005.

Egeria. *Egeria's Travels to the Holy Land*. Translated by John Wilkinson. Ariel, 1981.

Escobar, Samuel. "Liberation Theology." In *The Blackwell Encyclopedia of Modern Christian Thought*, edited by Alister E. McGrath, 333–36. Blackwell, 1993.

Eusebius. *The Life of Constantine*. Translated by Ernest Cushing Richardson. In *Nicene and Post-Nicene Fathers*, edited by Philip Schaff and Henry Wace. Christian Literature, 1890.

Evans, Craig. "Assessing Progress in the Third Quest of the Historical Jesus." *Journal for the Study of the Historical Jesus* 4 (2006): 35–54.

Evans, Craig. "The Two-Source Hypothesis." In *The Synoptic Problem: Four Views*, edited by Stanley Porter and Bryan Dyer, 27–46. Baker Academic, 2016.

Ezigbo, Victor. *Re-imagining African Christologies: Conversing with the Interpretations and Appropriations of Jesus Christ in African Theology*. Pickwick, 2010.

Fairclough, Norman. *Critical Discourse Analysis: The Critical Study of Language*. Longman, 1995.

Farah, Rima. "The Rise of a Christian Aramaic Nationality in Modern Israel." *Israel Studies* 26 (2021): 1–28.

Faus, González. "Hacer teología y hacerse teología." In *Vida y reflexión: Aportes de la teología de la reflexión al pensamiento teológico actual*. Centro de Estudios y Publicaciones, 1983.

Felman, Shoshana, and Dori Laub. *Testimony: Crises of Witnessing in Literature, Psychoanalysis and History*. Routledge, 1992.

Filho, Elias. "Twentieth Century Mission Theology: Conciliar and Evangelical Streams in Conversation." PhD diss., Fuller Theological Seminary, 2005.

Forrester, Duncan. "The Scope of Public Theology." *Studies in Christian Ethics* 17 (2004): 5–19.

Foucault, Michel. "The Ethic of Care for the Self as a Practice of Freedom: An Interview with Michel Foucault." *Philosophy & Social Criticism* 12 (1984): 112–31.

Foucault, Michel. *Power/Knowledge: Selected Interviews and Other Writings 1972–1977*. Pantheon, 1980.

Franke, John. "Reforming Theology: Toward a Postmodern Reformed Dogmatics." *Westminster Theological Journal* 65 (2003): 1–26.

Franzen, Aaron, and Jenna Griebel. "Understanding a Cultural Identity: The Confluence of Education, Politics, and Religion Within the American Concept of Biblical Literalism." *Sociology of Religion* 74 (2013): 521–43.

Fredriksen, Paula. *Augustine and the Jews: A Christian Defense of Jews and Judaism*. Yale University Press, 2010.

Fredriksen, Paula. "What You See Is What You Get: Context and Content in Current Research on the Historical Jesus." *Theology Today* 52 (1995): 75–97.

Frei, Hans. *The Eclipse of Biblical Narrative*. Yale University Press, 1974.

Frend, William. *Martyrdom and Persecution in the Early Church: Study of a Conflict from the Maccabees to Donatus*. Basil Blackwell, 1965.

Friedman, Jonathan. "The Past in the Future: History and the Politic of Identity." *American Anthropologist* 94 (1992): 837–59.

Frosh, Paul, and Amit Pinchevski. "Introduction: Why Media Witnessing? Why Now?" in Frosh and Pinchevski, *Media Witnessing*, 1–22.

Frosh, Paul, and Amit Pinchevski, eds. *Media Witnessing: Testimony in the Age of Mass Communication*. Palgrave Macmillan, 2009.

Galadza, Daniel. *Liturgy and Byzantinization in Jerusalem*. Oxford University Press, 2018.

Galadza, Peter. "Eastern Catholic Christianity." In *The Blackwell Companion to Eastern Christianity*, edited by Ken Parry, 291–318. Blackwell, 2007.

Gallagher, Paul. "Salvation from the Jews? Israel in Liberation Theology." *Asia Journal of Theology* 23 (2009): 281–96.

Gerber, Haim. "A New Look at the Tanzimat: The Case of the Province of Jerusalem." In *Palestine in the Late Ottoman Period: Political, Social, and Economic Transformation*, edited by David Kushner, 30–45. Yad Izhak Ben-Zvi, 1986.

Giddens, Antony. *A Contemporary Critique of Historical Materialism*. University of California Press, 1981.

Giddens, Antony. *Modernity and Self-Identity*. Polity, 1991.

Gilbert, Felix. "Intellectual History: Its Aims and Methods." *Historical Studies Today* 100 (1971): 80–97.

Goldingay, John. "The 'Salvation History' Perspective and the 'Wisdom' Perspective Within the Context of Biblical Theology." *Evangelical Quarterly* 51 (1979): 194–207.

Goren, Haim. "Nineteenth Century Jerusalem as a Test Case of European Involvement in the Near East: A Reappraisal." In *The History of Jerusalem: The Late Ottoman Period (1800–1917)*, edited by Israel Bartal and Haim Goren, 19–32. Yad Izhak Ben-Zvi, 2010.

Graham, Elaine. *Between a Rock and a Hard Place: Public Theology in a Post-Secular Age*. SCM, 2013.

Gregerman, Adam. "Comparative Christian Hermeneutical Approaches to the Land Promised to Abraham." *CrossCurrents* 64 (2014): 409–24.

Gregerman, Adam. "Old Wine in New Bottles: Liberation Theology and the Israeli Palestinian Conflict." *Journal of Ecumenical Studies* 41 (2004): 313–40.

Griffith, Sidney. "The Church of Jerusalem and the 'Melkites': The Making of an 'Arab Orthodox' Christian Identity in the World of Islam." In *Christians and Christianity in the Holy Land: From the Origins to the Latin Kingdoms*, edited by Ora Limor and Guy Stroumsa, 175–204. Yad Izhak Ben-Zvi, 2006.

Griffith, Sidney. *The Church in the Shadow of the Mosque: Christians and Muslims in the World of Islam*. Princeton University Press, 2007.

Griffith, Sidney. "From Aramaic to Arabic: The Language of the Monasteries of Palestine in the Byzantine and Early Islamic Period." *Dumbarton Oaks* 51 (1997): 11–31.

Griffith, Sidney. "The Monks of Palestine and the Growth of Christian Literature in Arabic." *The Muslim World* 78 (1988): 1–28.

Gruber, Judith. "Doing Theology with Cultural Studies Rewriting History—Reimagining Salvation—Decolonizing Theology." *Louvain Studies* 42 (2019): 103–23.

Gutiérrez, Gustavo. *The Power of the Poor in History*. Translated by Robert Barr. SCM, 1983.

Gutiérrez, Gustavo. "The Task and Content of Liberation Theology." Translated by Judith Condor. In Rowland, *Cambridge Companion to Liberation Theology*, 19–38.

Gutiérrez, Gustavo. *A Theology of Liberation: History, Politics, and Salvation*. Translated by John Eagleson. Orbis, 1973.

Habermas, Jürgen. *The Structural Transformation of the Public Sphere: An Inquiry into a Category of Bourgeois Society*. Translated by Thomas Burger. Polity, 1989.

Haiduc-Dale, Noah. "Rejecting Sectarianism: Palestinian Christians' Role in Muslim-Christian Relations." *Islam and Christian-Muslim Relations* 26 (2015): 75–88.

Halbwachs, Maurice. *On Collective Memory*. Translated by Lewis Coser. University of Chicago Press, 1992.

Harris, Jonathan. *Byzantium and the Crusades*. Bloomsbury, 2014.

Hassassian, Manuel. "Historical Dynamics Shaping Palestinian National Identity." *Palestine-Israel Journal* 8 (2001): 50–60.

Hastings, Adrian. "Christianity and Nationhood: Congruity and Antipathy." *Journal of Religious History* 25 (2001): 247–60.

Hastings, Adrian. *The Construction of Nationhood: Ethnicity, Religion and Nationalism*. Cambridge University Press, 1997.

Hauerwas, Stanley, and Samuel Wells. "The Gift of the Church and the Gifts God Gives It." In *The Blackwell Companion to Christian Ethics*, edited by Stanley Hauerwas and Samuel Wells, 13–27. Blackwell, 2004.

Haws, Charles. "Suffering, Hope and Forgiveness: The Ubuntu Theology of Desmond Tutu." *Scottish Journal of Theology* 62 (2009): 477–89.

Haynes, Stephen. "Christian Holocaust Theology: A Critical Reassessment." *Journal of the American Academy of Religion* 62 (1994): 553–85.

Haynes, Stephen. *Jews and the Christian Imagination: Reluctant Witnesses*. Basingstoke, UK: Macmillan, 1995.

Haynes, Stephen. *Prospects for Post-Holocaust Theology*. Scholars, 1991.

Hebblethwaite, Peter. "Let My People Go: The Exodus and Liberation Theology." *Religion, State and Society* 21(1993): 105–14.

Hennelly, Alfred. "The Challenge of Juan Luis Segundo." *Theological Studies* 38 (1977): 125–35.

Hirschfeld, Yizhar. *The Judean Desert Monasteries in the Byzantine Period.* Yale University Press, 1992.

Hittinger, Russel. "Justice." In *The Blackwell Encyclopedia of Modern Christian Thought*, edited by Alister E. McGrath, 291–93. Blackwell, 1993.

Horenczyk, Gabriel, and Salim Munayer. "Acculturation Orientations Toward Two Majority Groups: The Case of Palestinian Arab Christian Adolescents in Israel." *Journal of Cross-Cultural Psychology* 38 (2007): 76–86.

Hourani, Albert. *Arabic Thought in the Liberal Age, 1798–1939.* Cambridge University Press, 1962.

Hummel, Thomas. "Between Eastern and Western Christendom: The Anglican Presence in Jerusalem." In O'Mahony, *The Christian Communities of Jerusalem and the Holy Land*, 148–70. University of Wales Press, 2003.

Huyssen, Andreas. *Present Pasts: Urban Palimpsests and the Politics of Memory.* Stanford University Press, 2003.

Irenaeus. *Against Heresies.* Translated by Dominic Unger. Paulist, 1992.

Irshay, Oded. "The Christian Appropriation of Jerusalem in the Fourth Century: The Case of the Bordeaux Pilgrim." *Jewish Quarterly Review* 99 (2009): 465–86.

Isaac, Munther. "Challenging the Empire: Theology of Justice in Palestine." In *Christian Theology in the Palestinian Context*, edited by Rafiq Khoury and Rainer Zimmer-Winkel, 253–64. AphorismA, 2019.

Isaac, Munther. *From Land to Lands, from Eden to the Renewed Earth.* Langham, 2015.

Isaac, Jules. *Jésus et Israël.* Translated by Sally Gran. Holt, Rinehart and Winston, 1971.

Israeli Central Bureau of Statistics. "Christmas 2021—Christians in Israel." December 2021. https://www.cbs.gov.il.

Jacobs, Andrew S. *Remains of the Jews: The Holy Land and Christian Empire in Late Antiquity.* Stanford, CA: Stanford University Press, 2004.

Jacoby, Russell. "A New Intellectual History." *American Historical Review* 97 (1992): 405–24.

Jeanrond, Werner. "From Resistance to Liberation Theology: German Theologians and the Non/Resistance to the National Socialist Regime." In *Resistance Against the Third Reich*, 1933–1990, edited by Michael Geyer and John Boyer, 295–311. University of Chicago Press, 1994.

Jeffery, Laura, and Matei Candea. "The Politics of Victimhood." *History and Anthropology* 17 (2006): 287–96.

Jenkins, Philip. "The Christian Revolution." In *The Next Christendom: The Coming of Global Christianity*, edited by Philip Jenkins, 1–14. Oxford University Press, 2002.

Jeschke, Marlin. "Three Responses to Gary Anderson / 'Israel and the Land': Does the Promise Still Hold?" *Christian Century* 13 (2009): 27.

Judt, Tony. *Postwar: A History of Europe Since 1945.* Penguin, 2005.

Kähler, Martin. *The So-Called Historical Jesus and the Historic Biblical Christ.* Translated by C. Braaten. Fortress, 1964.

Kairos Document (Palestine). 2009. https://www.kairospalestine.ps/index.php/about-kairos/kairos-palestine-document.

Kairos Document (South Africa). 1985. https://kairossouthernafrica.wordpress.com/2011/05/08/the-south-africa-kairos-document-1985.

"Kairos Document—A Moment of Truth: A Word of Faith, Hope and Love from the Heart of Palestinian Suffering." 2009. https://jai-pal.org/files/Kairos%20Palestine_En.pdf.

Kalu, Orji. "James Cone's Legacy in Africa: Confession as a Political Praxis in the Kairos Document." *Verbum et Ecclesia* 27 (2006): 576–92.

Käsemann, Ernst. "The Problem of the Historical Jesus." In *Essays on New Testament Themes*, 15–47. SCM, 1964.

Katanacho, Yohanna. *The Land of Christ: A Palestinian Cry*. Pickwick, 2013.

Kedourie, Elie. *Nationalism*. Blackwell, 1993.

Kessler, Edward. *An Introduction to Jewish-Christian Relations*. Cambridge University Press, 2010.

Kgatla, Selaelo. "Forced Removals and Migration: A Theology of Resistance and Liberation in South Africa." *Missionalia* 41 (2013): 120–32.

Khader, Jamal. "Biblical Hermeneutics in the Kairos Palestine Document." In Raheb, *Biblical Text in the Context of Occupation*, 267–80.

Khader, Jamal. "The Role of the Palestinian Church in the Palestinian Problem in the Aftermath of the June 1967 War: Repercussions of the War on Christian-Muslim Relations." *Al-Liqa' Journal* 28 (2007): 38–45.

Khader, Jamal. "Towards a New Theological Understanding vis-à-vis Palestine in the Twenty-First Century." In *The Invention of History: A Century of Interplay Between Theology and Politics in Palestine*, edited by Mitri Raheb, 211–14. Diyar, 2012.

Khoury, Geries. "Christian-Muslim Dialogue in the Holy Land." In *Christian Theology in the Palestinian Context*, edited by Rafiq Khoury and Rainer Zimmer-Winkel, 183–230. AphorismA, 2019.

Khoury, Geries. *The Intifada of Heaven and Earth*. Nazareth: Al-Hakim, 1989.

Khoury, Geries. "Olive Tree Theology: Rooted in the Palestinian Soul." *Al-Liqa' Journal* 26 (2006): 58–108.

Khoury, Rafiq. "Christian-Muslim Relations: Past, Present and Future." In *Holy Land, Hollow Jubilee: God, Justice and the Palestinians*, edited by Naim Ateek and Michael Prior, 216–32. Melisende, 1999.

Khoury, Rafiq. "The Conflict of Narratives from Memory to Prophecy." In *The Invention of History: A Century of Interplay Between Theology and Politics in Palestine*, edited by Mitri Raheb, 259–68. Bethlehem: Diyar, 2012.

Khoury, Rafiq. "The Effects of Christian Zionism on Palestinian Christians." In *Challenging Christian Zionism: Theology, Politics and the Israel-Palestine*

Conflict, edited by Naim Ateek, Ceder Duaybis, and Maurin Tobin, 145–53. Melisende, 2005.

Khoury, Rafiq. "Palestinian Context and Contextual Theology." *Al Liqa' Journal* 40 (2013): 24–70.

Khoury, Rafiq. "Palestinian Contextual Theology: A General Survey." In *Christian Theology in the Palestinian Context*, ed. Rafiq Khoury and Rainer Zimmer-Winkel, 18. AphorismA, 2019.

Khoury, Rafiq. "Religious Discourse Between Christians and Muslims." *Al Liqa' Journal* 16 (2001): 1–28.

Khoury, Rafiq. "The Role of the Arab Christian in the Arab National Movements." *Al-Liqa' Journal* 35 (2010): 28–37.

Khoury, Rafiq. "The Role of Religious Thought in Building Trust Between the Arab and Muslim World and the West." *Al-Liqa' Journal* 39 (2012): 58–73.

Khoury, Rafiq. "Theology in Palestine: Meaning and Structure." *Al-Liqa' Journal* 29 (2007): 6–20.

Khoury, Rafiq, and Rainer Zimmer-Winkel. *Christian Theology in the Palestinian Context*. AphorismA, 2019.

Kildani, Hanna. *Modern Christianity in the Holy Land*. Bloomington: Authorhouse, 2010.

Kimmerling, Baruch, and Dahlia Moore. "Collective Identity as Agency, and Structuration of Society: The Israeli Example." *International Review of Sociology* 7 (1997): 25–49.

Kort, Wesley. *Bound to Differ: Dynamics of Theological Discourses*. Pennsylvania State University Press, 1992.

Kraft, Charles. *Christianity in Culture: A Study in Biblical Theologizing in Cross-Cultural Perspective*. Orbis, 1979.

Kramer, Lloyd. "Martin Jay and the Dialectical of Intellectual History." In *The Modernist Imagination: Intellectual History and Critical Theory*, edited by Peter Gordon et al., xi–xxxix. Berghahn Books, 2009.

Kuruvilla, Samuel. *Radical Christianity in the Holy Land: A Comparative Study of Liberation and Contextual Theology in Palestine-Israel*. Devon: University of Exeter, 2009.

Kuruvilla, Samuel. "Theologies of Liberation in Latin America and Palestine-Israel in Comparative Perspective: Contextual Differences and Practical Similarities." *Holy Land Studies* 9 (2010): 51–69.

Kurz, Anat. *Fatah and the Politics of Violence: The Institutionalization of a Popular Struggle*. Sussex Academic Press, 2005.

Lacapra, Dominick. "Rethinking Intellectual History and Reading Texts." *History and Theory* 19 (1980): 245–76.

Laird, Lance. "Meeting Jesus Again in the First Place: Palestinian Christians and the Bible." *Interpretation* 55 (2001): 401–10.

Lalloo, Kiran. "The Church and State in Apartheid South Africa." *Contemporary Politics* 4 (1998): 39–55.

Lategan, Bernard. "History and Reality in the Interpretation of Biblical Texts." In *Konstruktion von Wirklichkeit: Beiträge aus geschichtstheoretischer, philosophischer und theologischer Perspektive*, edited by Jens Schröter and Antje Eddelbüttel, 135–52. de Gruyter, 2013.

Le Poidevin, Robin. "Multiple Incarnation and Distributed Persons." In *The Metaphysics of the Incarnation*, edited by Anna Marmodoro and Jonathan Hill, 228–41. Oxford University Press, 2011.

Lessing, Gotthold. *Über den Beweis des Geistes und der Kraft, Lessing's Theological Writing*. Translated by Henry Chadwick. Stanford University Press, 1956.

Levi, Primo. *The Drowned and the Saved*. Translated by Raymond Rosenthal. Random House, 1989.

Levine, Amy-Jill. "Roundtable Discussion: Anti-Judaism and Postcolonial Biblical Interpretation." *Journal of Feminist Studies in Religion* 20 (2004): 91–132.

Levy-Rubin, Milka. "Arabization Versus Islamization." In *Sharing the Sacred: Religion Contacts and Conflicts in the Holy Land*, edited by Arieh Kofsky and Guy Stroumsa, 149–61. Yad Izhak Ben-Zvi, 1998.

Levy-Rubin, Milka. *Non-Muslims in the Early Islamic Empire: From Surrender to Coexistence*. Cambridge University Press, 2011.

Limor, Ora. "Jewish and Christian Pilgrims to Jerusalem in Late Antiquity." In *Jerusalem II: Jerusalem in Roman-Byzantine Times*, edited by Katharina Heyden and Maria Lissek, 311–24. Mohr Siebeck, 2021.

Linder, Amnon. "The Christian Communities in the City." In *The History of Jerusalem: The Early Muslim Period 638–1099*, edited by Yehoshua Praver, 97–132. Yad Izhak Ben-Zvi, 1987.

Littell, Franklin. *The Crucifixion of the Jews: The Failure of Christians to Understand the Jewish Experience*. Harper & Row, 1975.

Lodberg, Peter. "Palestinian Theology Between Construction and Identification: A Comparative Analysis of the Theology of Naim Stifan Ateek and Mitri Raheb." In Raheb, *Biblical Text in the Context of Occupation*, 81–88.

Louth, Andrew. "Christology in the East from the Council of Chalcedon to John Damascene." In *The Oxford Handbook of Christology*, edited by Troy Stefano, 139–53. Oxford University Press, 2015.

Luz, Nimrod. "Aspects of Islamization of Space and Society in Mamluk Jerusalem and Its Hinterland." *Mamluk Studies Review* 6 (2002): 133–54.

Mabuza, Wesley. "Kairos Revisited: Investigating the Relevance of the Kairos Document for Church-State Relations Within a Democratic South Africa." PhD diss., University of Pretoria, 2009.

Mackin, Robert. "Liberation Theology and Social Movements." In *Handbook of Social Movements Across Latin America*, edited by Paul Almeida and Allen Cordero Ulate, 101–16. Springer, 2015.

Makrides, Vasilios. "Why Does the Orthodox Church Lack Systematic Social Teaching?" *Skepsis: A Journal of Philosophy and Interdisciplinary Research* 23 (2013): 281–312.

Mana, Adi, Shifra Sagy, Anan Srour, and Serene Mjally-Knani. "On Both Sides of the Fence: Perceptions of Collective Narratives and Identity Strategies Among Palestinians in Israel and in the West Bank." *Mind & Society* 14 (2015): 57–83.

Mangina, Joseph. *Karl Barth: Theologian of Christian Witness*. Routledge, 2004.

Mansour, Johnny. "International Political Changes and Their Influence on Christian Arabs in the Middle East." In *Al-Liqa' Journal* 24 (2005): 91–105.

Marchadour, Alain, and David Neuhaus. *The Land, the Bible and History: Toward the Land That I Will Show You*. Fordham University Press, 2007.

Margalit, Avishai. *The Ethics of Memory*. Harvard University Press, 2004.

Markschies, Christoph. "Jesus Christ as a Man Before God: Two Interpretive Models for Isaiah 53 in the Patristic Literature and Their Development." In *The Suffering Servant: Isaiah 53 in Jewish and Christian Sources*, edited by Bernd Janowski and Peter Stuhlmacher, 225–324. Eerdmans, 2004.

Markus, Robert. "How on Earth Could Places Become Holy? Origins of the Christian Idea of Holy Places." *Journal of Early Christian Studies* 2 (1994): 257–71.

Marsh, Clive. "Quests of the Historical Jesus in New Historicist Perspective." *Biblical Interpretation* 5 (1997): 403–37.

Marsh, Leonard. "Palestinian Christianity—A Study in Religion and Politics." *International Journal for the Study of the Christian Church* 5 (2005): 147–66.

Marsh, Leonard. "Palestinian Christians: Theology and Politics in the Holy Land." In *Christianity in the Middle East: Studies in Modern History, Theology, and Politics*. Ed. Anthony O'Mahony, 205–18. Melisende, 2008.

Martin, Wallace. "The Hermeneutic Circle and the Art of Interpretation." *Comparative Literature* 24 (1972): 97–117.

Masalha, Nur, and Lisa Isherwood. *Theologies of Liberation in Palestine-Israel: Indigenous, Contextual, and Postcolonial Perspectives*. Lutterworth Press, 2014.

Masters, Bruce. *Christians and Jews in the Ottoman Arab World*. Cambridge University Press, 2001.

Matheny, Paul. *Contextual Theology: The Drama of Our Times*. Pickwick, 2011.

May, Melanie. *Jerusalem Testament: Palestinian Christians Speak, 1988–2008*. Eerdmans, 2010.

McGovern, Arthur. "Dependency Theory, Marxist Analysis, and Liberation Theology." In *The Future of Liberation Theology: Essays in Honor of Gustavo Gutiérrez*, edited by Marc H. Ellis and Otto Maduro, 272–86. Orbis, 1989.

McGovern, Arthur. *Liberation Theology and Its Critics: Toward an Assessment*. Wipf and Stock, 1989.

Medebielle, Pierre. *The Diocese of the Latin Patriarchate*. Jerusalem, 1963.

Merkley, Paul Charles. *Christian Attitudes Towards the State of Israel, 1948–2000*. McGill-Queen's University Press, 2001.

Metz, Johann-Baptist. "Christians and Jews After Auschwitz." In *The Baptist Emergent Church: The Future of Christianity in a Postbourgeois World*. Translated by Peter Mann, 17–33. Crossroad, 1981.

Mi'ari, Mahmoud. "Development of Political Identity of Palestinians in Israel." *Majallat al-Ólum al-Ijtimaéyya* 14 (1986): 215–33.

Mi'ari, Mahmoud. "Political Behavior of University Students in Palestine." *Dirasat: 'Olum Insaniyya* 23 (1996): 278–98.

Mi'ari, Mahmoud. "Traditionalism and Political Identity of Arabs in Israel." *Journal of Asian and African Studies* 22 (1987): 33–44.

Mi'ari, Mahmoud. "Transformation of Collective Identity in Palestine." *Journal of Asian and African Studies* 44 (2009): 579–98.

Michalson, Gordon. "Faith and History." In *The Blackwell Encyclopedia of Modern Christian Thought*, edited by Alister E. McGrath, 210–12. Blackwell, 1993.

Michalson, Gordon. "Faith and History: The Shape of the Problem." *Modern Theology* 1 (1985): 277–90.

Mol, Hans. *Identity and the Sacred: A Sketch for a New Social-Scientific Theory of Religion*. Basil Blackwell, 1976.

Moltmann, Jürgen. "The Crucified God." *Theology Today* 31 (1974): 6–18.

Moltmann, Jürgen. "European Political Theology." In *The Cambridge Companion to Christian Political Theology*, edited by Craig Hovey and Elizabeth Phillip, 3–22. Cambridge University Press, 2015.

Moltmann, Jürgen. *The Experiment Hope*. Augsburg, 1977.

Moltmann, Jürgen. "Hope and History." *Theology Today* 25 (1968): 369–86.

Moltmann, Jürgen. *Theology of Hope: On the Ground and the Implications of a Christian Eschatology*. Translated by James Leitch. SCM, 1967.

Moltmann, Jürgen. *The Way of Jesus Christ: Christology in Messianic Dimensions*. Translated by Margaret Kohl. SCM, 1990.

Morton, Andrew. "Duncan Forrester: A Public Theologian." In *Public Theology for the Twenty-First Century*, edited by William Storrar and Andrew Morton, 25–36. T&T Clark, 2004.

Moxnes, Halvor. *Jesus and the Rise of Nationalism: A New Quest for the Nineteenth Century Historical Jesus*. I. B. Tauris, 2012.

Moyaert, Marianne, and Didier Pollefeyt. "Israel and the Church: Fulfillment Beyond Supersessionism." In *Never Revoked: "Nostra Aetate" as Ongoing Challenge for Jewish-Christian Dialogue*, edited by Marianne Moyaert and Didier Pollefeyt, 159–83. Eerdmans, 2010.

Moyser, George. "Religion and Politics." In *The Routledge Companion to the Study of Religion*, edited by John R. Hinnells, 423–38. Routledge, 2005.

Muir, Diana. "A Land Without a People for a People Without a Land." *Middle East Quarterly* 15 (2008): 55–62.

Muller-Kessler, Christa. "Christian Palestinian Aramaic and Its Significance to the Western Aramaic Dialect Group." *Journal of the American Oriental Society* 19 (1999): 631–36.

Neuhaus, David. "Between Quiescence and Arousal: The Political Functions of Religion—A Case Study of the Arab Minority in Israel; 1948–1990." Ph.D. diss., Hebrew University of Jerusalem, 1991.

Neuhaus, David. *Je vous écris de la Terre Sainte*. Bayard Presse, 2017.

Nineham, Dennis. "Eye-witness Testimony and the Gospel Tradition. III." *Journal of Theological Studies* 11 (1960): 253–64.

Nora, Pierre. *Conflicts and Divisions*. Vol. 1, *Realms of Memory: Rethinking the French Past*. Translated by Arthur Goldhammer. Columbia University Press, 1996.

Norman, Edward. *Christianity and the World Order*. Oxford University Press, 1979.

Novak, David. *Talking with Christians: Musings of a Jewish Theologian*. Eerdmans, 2005.

Nyiawung, Mbengu. "The Prophetic Witness of the Church as an Appropriate Mode of Public Discourse in African Societies." *HTS Theological Studies* 66 (2010): 1–8.

O'Brien, Peter. "Mission, Witness, and the Coming of the Spirit." *Bulletin for Biblical Research* 9 (1999): 203–14.

O'Donovan, Oliver. "Political Theology, Tradition and Modernity." In Rowland, *Cambridge Companion to Liberation Theology*, 265–77.

O'Mahony, Anthony. *The Christian Communities of Jerusalem and the Holy Land*. University of Wales Press, 2003.

O'Mahony, Anthony. "The Christian Communities of Jerusalem and the Holy Land: A Historical and Political Survey." In O'Mahony, *Christian Communities of Jerusalem and the Holy Land*, 1–37.

O'Mahony, Anthony. "The Latin of the East: Jerusalem and the Palestinian Christians." In O'Mahony, *Christian Communities of Jerusalem and the Holy Land*, 90–114.

Omer, Atalia. "The Cry of the Forgotten Stones: The Promise and Limits of a Palestinian Liberation Theology as a Method for Peacebuilding." *Journal of Religious Ethics* 43 (2015): 369–407.

Omer, Atalia. "'It's Nothing Personal': The Globalization of Justice, the Transferability of Protest, and the Case of the Palestine Solidarity Movement." *Studies in Ethnicity and Nationalism* 9 (2009): 497–518.

Oosthuizen, M. J. "Scripture and Context: The Use of Liberation Theology in the Hermeneutics of Liberation Theology." *Scriptura* 25 (1988): 7–22.

Otto, Randall. "God and History in Jürgen Moltmann." *Journal of the Evangelical Theological Society* 35 (1992): 375–88.

Ottuh, John. "Biblical Research in Africa: Historical Jesus Quest in Inculturation Perspective." *Academic Journal of Interdisciplinary Studies* 2 (2015): 183–98.

Pablitzsch, Johannes. "Latins in Byzantium and Orthodox Christians." In *A Companion to Byzantium and the West, 900–1204*, edited by Nicolas Drocourt and Sebastian Kolditz, 391–415. Brill, 2022.

Pablitzsch, Johannes and Daniel Baraz. "Christian Communities in the Latin Kingdom of Jerusalem." In *Christians and Christianity in the Holy Land: From the Origins to the Latin Kingdoms*, edited by Ora Limor and Guy Stroumsa, 205–35. Yad Izhak Ben-Zvi, 2006.

Pannenberg, Wolfhart. "Constructive and Critical Functions of Christian Eschatology." *Harvard Theological Review* 77 (1984): 119–39.

Papastathis, Konstantinos. "Missionary Politics in Late Ottoman Palestine: The Stance of the Orthodox Patriarchate of Jerusalem." *Social Sciences and Missions* 32 (2019): 342–60.

Parratt, John, ed. *An Introduction to Third World Theologies*. Cambridge University Press, 2004.

Patierno, Nicole. "Palestinian Liberation Theology: Creative Resistance to Occupation." *Islam and Christian-Muslim Relations* 26 (2015): 443–64.

Patrich, Joseph. *Sabas, Leader of Palestinian Monasticism: A Comparative Study in Eastern Monasticism, Fourth to Seventh Centuries*. Dumbarton Oaks, 1995.

Pawlikowski, John. "Land as an Issue in Christian-Jewish Dialogue." *CrossCurrents* 59 (2009): 197–209.

Pawlikowski, John. "Reflections on Covenant and Mission Forty Years After *Nostra Aetate*." *CrossCurrents* 56 (2006): 70–94.

Perrone, Lorenzo. "'The Mystery of Judaea' (Jerome, *Ep.* 46): The Holy City of Jerusalem Between History and Symbol in Early Christian Thought." In *Jerusalem: Its Sanctity and Centrality to Judaism, Christianity, and Islam*, edited by Lee Levine, 221–39. Continuum, 1991.

Perrone, Lorenzo. "'Rejoice Sion, Mother of All Churches': Christianity in the Holy Land During the Byzantine Era." In *Christians and Christianity in the Holy Land: From the Origins to the Latin Kingdoms*, edited by Ora Limor and Guy Stroumsa, 141–74. Yad Izhak Ben-Zvi, 2006.

Peters, John. "An Afterword: Torchlight Red on Sweaty Faces." In Frosh and Pinchevski, *Media Witnessing*, 42–48.

Phan, Peter. "Method in Liberation Theology." *Theological Studies* 61 (2000): 40–63.

Phiri, Isabel. "Southern Africa." In *An Introduction to Third World Theologies*, edited by John Parratt, 137–62. Cambridge University Press, 2004.

Prawer, Joshua. "Political History of Crusader and Ayyubid Jerusalem." In *The History of Jerusalem: Crusaders and Ayyubids (1099–1250)*, edited by Joshua Prawer and Haggai Ben-Shammai, 1–67. Yad Izhak Ben-Zvi, 1991.

Raheb, Mitri. *The Arab Christians and the Matter of the Nation: The Variables of the Context and the Periods*. Diyar, 2013.

Raheb, Mitri, ed. *The Biblical Text in the Context of Occupation: Towards a New Hermeneutics of Liberation*. Diyar, 2012.

Raheb, Mitri. "The Church in the Middle East and the Existing Political Authority Based on Its Historical Experience." *Al-Liqa' Journal* 1 (2013): 27.

Raheb, Mitri. "Displacement Theopolitics: A Century of Interplay Between Theology and Politics in Palestine." In *The Invention of History: A Century of Interplay Between Theology and Politics in Palestine*, edited by Mitri Raheb, 11–27. Diyar, 2011.

Raheb, Mitri. *Faith in the Face of Empire: The Bible Through Palestinian Eyes*. Orbis, 2014.

Raheb, Mitri. *I Am a Palestinian Christian*. Fortress, 1994.

Raheb, Mitri. *Sailing Through Troubled Waters: Christianity in the Middle East*. Diyar, 2013.

Raheb, Mitri. "Towards a New Hermeneutics of Liberation: A Palestinian Christian Perspective." In Raheb, *Biblical Text in the Context of Occupation*, 11–28.

Rahner, Karl. "Toward a Fundamental Theological Interpretation of Vatican II." *Theological Studies* 40 (1979): 716–27.

Ratzinger, Joseph. *Many Religions—One Covenant: Israel, the Church, and the World*. Ignatius, 1999.

Raz-Krakotzkin, Amnon. "The Return to the History of Redemption (Or, What Is the 'History' to Which the 'Return' in the Phrase 'The Jewish Return to History' Refers?)." In *Zionism and the Return to History: A Reappraisal*, edited by Shmuel Eisenstadt and Moshe Lissak, 249–79. Yad Izhak Ben-Zvi, 1990.

Reid, Barbara. "The Charism of the Exegetes: Unleashing the Power of the Word." In *Retrieving Charisms for the Twenty-First Century*, edited by Doris Donnelly, 65–84. Liturgical, 1999.

Reif, Stefan. Preface to *Jesus the Jew*, by Géza Vermes. SCM, 2001.

Reisigl, Martin, and Ruth Wodak. "The Discourse Historical Approach." In *Methods of Critical Discourse Analysis*, edited by Ruth Wodak and Michael Meyer, 87–121. Sage, 2001.

Rekhes, Eli. *The Arab Village in Israel: A Renewed Political-National Center*. Markaz Dayan, 1985.

Rekhes, Eli. "The Arabs of Israel After 1967: The Worsening of the Orientation Problem." *Skirot* 45 (1976): 9–56.

Rekhes, Eli. "The Islamic Movement in Israel and Its Relation to Political Islam in the Palestinian Territories." In *The Jewish Arab Split in Israel*, edited by Rut Gavizon and Dafnah Haḳer, 271–96. Israel Democracy Institute, 2000.

Richter, Julius. *A History of Protestant Missions in the Near East*. AMS, 1910.

Ricoeur, Paul. *Freud and Philosophy: An Essay on Interpretation*. Translated by Denis Savage. Yale University Press, 1970.

Robnett, Belinda. "External Political Change, Collective Identities, and Participation in Social Movement Organizations." In *Social Movements: Identity,*

Culture, and the State, edited by David Meyer, Nancy Whittier and Belinda Robnett, 266–87. Oxford University Press, 2002.

Robson, Laura. *Colonialism and Christianity in Mandate Palestine*. University of Texas Press, 2011.

Robson, Laura. "Palestinian Liberation Theology, Muslim-Christian Relations, and the Arab-Israeli Conflict." *Islam and Christian-Muslim Relations* 21 (2010): 39–50.

Robson, Laura. "Recent Perspectives on Christianity in the Modern Arab World." *History Compass* 9 (2011): 312–25.

Rose, Richard. "Communities of Eastern Christians in Crusader Jerusalem." In *The History of Jerusalem: Crusaders and Ayyubids (1099–1250)*, edited by Joshua Prawer and Haggai Ben-Shammai, 176–93. Yad Izhak Ben-Zvi, 1991.

Rossing, Daniel. "Microcosm and Multiple Minorities: The Christian Communities in Israel." *Israel Yearbook & Almanac* 53 (1999): 28–43.

Rousso, Sotiris. "The Greek Orthodox Patriarchate and Community of Jerusalem: Church, State, and Identity." In O'Mahony, *Christian Communities of Jerusalem and the Holy Land*, 39–55. University of Wales Press, 2003.

Rowe, Paul. "The Middle Eastern Christian as Agent." *International Journal of Middle East Studies* 42 (2010): 472–74.

Rowland, Christopher, ed. *The Cambridge Companion to Liberation Theology*. 2nd ed. Cambridge University Press, 2007.

Rowland, Christopher. "Introduction: The Theology of Liberation." In Rowland, *Cambridge Companion to Liberation Theology*, 1–16.

Rowland, Christopher, and Mark Corner. *Liberating Exegesis: The Challenge of Liberation Theology to Biblical Studies*. Westminister John Knox, 1989.

Rubin, Ze'ev. "The Church of the Holy Sepulcher and the Conflict Between the Sees of Caesarea and Jerusalem." *Jerusalem Cathedra* 2 (1982): 79–105.

Ruether, Rosemary. *Faith and Fratricide: The Theological Roots of Anti-Semitism*. Minneapolis: Seabury, 1974.

Ruether, Rosemary. Foreword to Naim Ateek, *Justice, and Only Justice: A Palestinian Theology of Liberation*, xi–xiv. Orbis. 1989.

Ruether, Rosemary, and Herman Ruether. *The Wrath of Jonah: The Crisis of Religious Nationalism in the Israeli-Palestinian Conflict*. Harper & Row, 1989.

Runesson, Andres. "Particularistic Judaism and Universalistic Christianity? Some Critical Remarks on Terminology and Theology." *Studia Theologica—Nordic Journal of Theology* 54 (2000): 55–75.

Sabbah, Michel. *Fourth Pastoral Letter: Reading the Bible Today in the Land of the Bible*. Jerusalem, 1993.

Sabbah, Michel. Preface to *Christian Theology in the Palestinian Context*, edited by Rafiq Khoury and Rainer Zimmer-Winkel, 7–9. AphorismA, 2019.

Sabbah, Michel. *The Second Pastoral Letter: Pray for Peace in Jerusalem*. Jerusalem, 1990.

Sabella, Bernard. "Comparing Palestinian Christians on Society and Politics: Context and Religion in Israel and Palestine." Paper presented at the meeting of the Middle East Studies Association, San Francisco, 2001.

Sabra, George. "Two Ways of Being a Christian in the Muslim Context of the Middle East." *Islam and Christian-Muslim Relations* 17 (2006): 43–53.

Said, Edward. *Culture and Imperialism*. Vintage Books, 1993.

Said, Edward. "The Jewish Jesus and the Israel-Palestine Conflict Palestinian Liberation Theology, Anti-Judaism, and Jewish-Christian Relations." In *The Bible, Zionism, and Palestine: The Bible's Role in Conflict and Liberation in Israel-Palestine*, edited by Michael Sandford, 135–44. Relegere Academic, 2016.

Said, Edward. *The Palestinian Problem*. Times Books, 1979.

Said, Edward. *The Question of Palestine*. Vintage Books, 1979.

Sandford, Michael. "Is Jesus Palestinian? Palestinian Christian Perspectives on Judaism, Ethnicity and the New Testament." *Holy Land Studies* 13 (2014): 123–38.

Sassoon, David. "The Israel Legal System." *American Journal of Comparative Law* 16 (1968): 405–15.

Sayigh, Yezid. *Armed Struggle and the Search for State: The Palestinian National Movement, 1949–1993*. Clarendon Press & Institute for Palestine Studies, 1997.

Schiffrin, Deborah, and Young Kee Lee. "God's Mission in Suffering and Martyrdom." In *Suffering, Persecution and Martyrdom: Theological Reflections*, edited by Christof Sauer and Richard Howell, 215–30. Bonn: ACADSA, VKW, 2010.

Schiffrin, Deborah, Deborah Tannen, and Heidi E. Hamilton. Introduction to *The Handbook of Discourse Analysis*, edited by Deborah Tannen, Heidi E. Hamilton, and Deborah Schiffrin, 1–10. Blackwell, 2001.

Schoffeleers, Matthew. "Black and African Theology in Southern Africa: A Controversy Re-Examined." *Journal of Religion in Africa* 18 (1988): 99–124.

Schreiter, Robert. *New Catholicity: Theology Between the Global and the Local*. Orbis, 2004.

Schwartz, Barry. "The Social Context of Commemoration: A Study in Collective Memory." *Social Forces* 61 (1982): 374–402.

Schweitzer, Albert. *The Quest of the Historical Jesus: A Critical Study of Its Progress from Reimarus to Wrede*. Translated by W. Montgomery. A&C Black, 1910.

Schwobel, Christoph. "Theology." In *The Cambridge Companion to Karl Barth*, edited by John Webster, 17–36. Cambridge University Press, 2000.

Segundo, Juan Luis. *Liberation of Theology*. Translated by John Drury. Orbis, 1976.

Seul, Smith. "'Ours Is the Way of God': Religion, Identity, and Intergroup Conflict." *Journal of Peace Research* 36 (1999): 553–69.

Shalit, Yoram. *The European Powers' Plans Regarding Jerusalem Towards the Middle of the Nineteenth Century*. Klaus-Schwarz-Verlag, 2004.

Shemesh, Moshe. "The PLO Road to Oslo: 1988 as a Turning Point in the History of the Palestinian National Movement." *Iyunim* 9 (1999): 186–245.

Sherman, Franklin, ed. *Bridges: Documents of the Christian-Jewish Dialogue* (Paulist, 2011).

Shorter, Aylward. *Toward a Theology of Inculturation*. Orbis, 1988.

Shoshan, Boaz. "The Islamic Conquest: Continuity and Change." In *Jerusalem II: Jerusalem in Roman-Byzantine Times*, edited by Katharina Heyden and Maria Lissek, 459–74. Mohr Siebeck, 2021.

Siker, Jeffry. "Historicizing a Racialized Jesus: Case Studies in the 'Black Christ,' the 'Mestizo Christ,' and White Critique." *Biblical Interpretation* 15 (2007): 26–53.

Smith, Anthony. *Chosen People*. Oxford University Press, 2003.

Smith, Anthony. *Myths and Memories of the Nation*. Oxford University Press, 1999.

Smith, Harold. "Supersession and Continuance: The Orthodox Church's Perspective on Supersessionism." *Journal of Ecumenical Studies* 49 (2014): 247–73.

Smooha, Sammy. "The Arab Minority in Israel: Radicalization or Politicization?" *Studies in Contemporary Jewry* 5 (1989): 59–88.

Sobrino, Jon. *Jesus the Liberator: A Historical Theological Reading of Jesus of Nazareth*. Translated by Paul Burns and Francis McDonagh. Orbis, 1993.

Sobrino, Jon. *The True Church and the Church of the Poor*. Orbis, 1985.

Soper, Christopher. *Religion and Nationalism in Global Perspective*. Cambridge University Press, 2018.

Soulen, Kendall. *The God of Israel and Christian Theology*. Fortress, 1996.

Soulen, Kendall. "Post-Supersessionism." In *A Dictionary of Jewish-Christian Relations*, edited by Edward Kessler and Neil Wenborn, 350–51. Cambridge University Press, 2005.

Southgate, Beverley. *History, What and Why? Ancient, Modern, and Postmodern Perspectives*. Routledge, 1996.

Spears, Russell. "Group Identities: The Social Identity Perspective." In *Handbook of Identity Theory and Research*, edited by Seth Schwartz, Koen Luyckx, Vivian Vignoles, 201–24. Springer, 2011.

Stackhouse, Max. "Civil Religion, Political Theology and Public Theology: What's the Difference?" *Political Theology* 5 (2004): 275–93.

Stålsett, Sturla. *Discovering Jesus in Our Place: Contextual Christologies in a Globalized World*. ISPCK, 2003.

Stevens, Jennifer. *The Historical Jesus and the Literary Imagination 1860–1920*. Liverpool University Press, 2010.

Stone, Bryan. *Evangelism After Christendom: The Theology and Practice of Christian Witness*. Brazos, 2007.

Stone, Michael E., Roberta R. Ervine, and Nira Stone, eds. *The Armenians in Jerusalem and the Holy Land*. Peeters, 2002.

Suderman, Andrew. "'Who'll Be a Witness for My Lord?': Witnessing as an Ecclesiological and Missiological Paradigm." *Missionalia* 44 (2016): 68–84.

Sugirtharajah, Rasiah. *The Bible and the Third World: Precolonial, Colonial and Postcolonial Encounters*. Cambridge University Press, 2001.

Synod of the Protestant Church of the Rhineland and of Some Key Theologians. "Towards Renovation of the Relationship of Christians and Jews." Translated by Franklin Littell. *Journal of Ecumenical Studies* 17 (1980).

Tajfel, Henri, and John Turner. "The Social Identity Theory of Intergroup Behavior." In *Psychology of Intergroup Relation*, edited by Stephen Worchel and William Austin, 7–24. Nelson-Hall, 1986.

Tapie, Matthew. "Christ, Torah, and the Faithfulness of God: The Concept of Supersessionism in 'The Gifts and the Calling.'" *Studies in Christian-Jewish Relations* 12 (2017): 1–18.

Taraki, Lisa. "The Islamic Resistance Movement in the Palestinian Uprising." *Middle East Report* 156 (1989): 30–32.

Taylor, Vetra, and Nancy Whittier. "Collective Identity in Social Movement Communities: Lesbian Feminist Mobilization." In *Waves of Protest: Social Movements Since the Sixties*, edited by Jo Freeman and Victoria Johnson, 169–94. Rowman & Littlefield, 1992.

ter Haar Romeny, Bas. "From Religious Association to Ethnic Community: A Research Project on Identity Formation Among the Syrian Orthodox Under Muslim Rule." *Islam and Christian-Muslim Relations* 16 (2005): 377–99.

Tertullian. *An Answer to the Jews*. Translated by S. Thelwall. In *Ante-Nicene Fathers*, edited by Alexander Roberts, James Donaldson, and A. Cleveland Coxe. Christian Literature, 1885.

Thomas, Gunter. "Witness as a Cultural Form of Communication." In Frosh and Pinchevski, *Media Witnessing*, 89–111.

Thompson, William. *The Jesus Debate: A Survey and Synthesis*. Paulist, 1985.

Tillich, Paul. *Systematic Theology*. University of Chicago Press, 1951.

Tombs, David. "The Hermeneutic of Liberation." In *Approaches to New Testament Study*, edited by Stanley E. Porter and David Tombs, 310–55. Sheffield Academic, 1995.

Torres, Sergio, and Virginia Fabella. *The Emergent Gospel: Theology from the Underside of History*. Orbis, 1978.

Tracy, David. "Defending the Public Character of Theology." *Christian Century* 11 (1981): 350–56.

Tsimhoni, Daphne. *Christian Communities in Jerusalem and the West Bank Since 1948: An Historical, Social and Political Study*. Praeger, 1993.

Tsimhoni, Daphne. "The Latin Patriarchate of Jerusalem, from the Middle of the Nineteenth Century to the Present Day—Institutional and Social Aspects." *The New East* 24 (1992): 113–38.

Tsimhoni, Daphne. "The Problem of the National Identity of the Christian Arabs in Jerusalem and the West Bank." *Studies in the History of Israel* 3 (1993): 469–96.

Tsimhoni, Daphne. "The Status of the Arab Christians Under the British Mandate in Palestine." *Middle Eastern Studies* 20 (1984): 166–92.

Tutu, Desmond. *Hope and Suffering*. Eerdmans, 1984.

van Aarde, Timothy. "Black Theology in South Africa: A Theology of Human Dignity and Black Identity." *HTS Theological Studies* 72 (2006): 1–9.

van Buren, Paul. *A Christian Theology of the People of Israel*. Seabury, 1983.

van Buren, Paul. *Discerning the Way: A Theology of the Jewish-Christian Reality*. Seabury, 1980.

van der Bent, Ans Joachim. *Historical Dictionary of Ecumenical Christianity*. Scarecrow, 1994.

van Dijk, Teun. "The Study of Discourse." In *Discourse as Structure and Process*, edited by Teun Van Dijk, 1–34. Sage, 1997.

Vanhoozer, Kevin. "Scripture and Tradition." In *The Cambridge Companion to Postmodern Theology*, edited by Kevin Vanhoozer, 149–51. Cambridge University Press, 2010.

Vellem, Vuyani. "Prophetic Theology in Black Theology, with Special Reference to the Kairos Document." *HTS Theological Studies* 66 (2010): 1–6.

Villeneuve, André. "Israel's Eschatological Destiny in the Catholic Interpretation of the Prophets." *Josephinum Journal of Theology* 23 (2016): 1–16.

Vivian, Bradford. *Commonplace Witnessing: Rhetorical Invention, Historical Remembrance, and Public Culture*. Oxford University Press, 2007.

Vlach, Michael. "The Church as a Replacement of Israel: An Analysis of Supersessionism." Ph.D. diss., Southeastern Baptist Theological Seminary, 2004.

Vlach, Michael. "Rejection Then Hope: The Church's Doctrine of Israel in the Patristic Era." *Master's Seminary Journal* 19 (2008): 51–70.

Vlach, Michael. "Various Forms of Replacement Theology." *Master's Seminary Journal* 20 (2009): 57–69.

von Wahlde, Urban. "The Witnesses to Jesus in John 5:31–40 and Belief in the Fourth Gospel." *Catholic Biblical Quarterly* 43 (1981): 385–404.

Wagner, Donald. "Three Responses to Gary Anderson / 'Israel and the Land': Does the Promise Still Hold?" *Christian Century* 13 (2009): 28–29.

Wagner, Donald, and Walter Davis. *Zionism and the Quest for Justice in the Holy Land*. Lutterworth, 2014.

Walker, Peter. *Holy City, Holy Places?* Clarendon, 1990.

Walker, Peter. *Jesus and the Holy City: New Testament Perspectives on Jerusalem*. Eerdmans, 1996.

Walls, Andrew. *Missionary Movement in Christian History: Studies in the Transmission of Faith*. Orbis, 1996.

Walshe, Peter. "South Africa: Prophetic Christianity and the Liberation Movement." *Journal of Modern African Studies* 29 (1991): 27–60.

Wansbrough, Ann. "The Relationship Between Theology and Reality." In *Reliving Our Faith Today*, edited by Antone Hope and Yong Ting Jin, 105–24. Hong Kong: World Christian Federation, Asia-Pacific Region, 1992.

Weber, Joseph. "Dogmatic Christology and the Historical-Critical Method: Some Reflections on Their Interrelationship." *Christian Scholar* 47 (1964): 315–26.

West, Gerald. "The Bible and the Poor: A New Way of Doing Theology." In Rowland, *Cambridge Companion to Liberation Theology*, 159–82.

Wicker, Brian. *Witness to Faith? Martyrdom in Christian and Islam*. Ashgate, 2006.

Wilken, Robert. *The Land Called Holy: Palestine in Christian History and Thought*. Yale University Press, 1992.

Williamson, Clark. *Has God Rejected His People? Anti-Judaism in the Christian Church*. Wipf and Stock, 1982.

Winter, Jay. "The Moral Witness and the Two World Wars." *Ethnologie française* 37 (2007): 467–74.

Wirth, Louis. "The Problem of Minority Groups." In *The Science of Man in the World Crisis*, edited by Ralph Linton, 347–72. Columbia University Press, 1945.

Witherington, Ben, III. *The Jesus Quest: The Third Search for the Jew of Nazareth*. IVP Academic, 1995.

Wodak, Ruth. "Critical Discourse Analysis, Discourse-Historical Approach." In *The International Encyclopedia of Language and Social Interaction*, edited by Karen Tracy, 1–14. Wiley Blackwell, 2015.

Wolter, Michael. "Which Jesus Is the Real Jesus?" In *The Quest for the Real Jesus*, edited by Jan van der Watt, 1–18. Brill, 2013.

Wood, John. "'Blessed Is the Nation'? Christianity and National Identity in Twentieth Century Europe." In *Christianity and National Identity in Twentieth Century Europe: Conflict, Community, and the Social Order*, edited by John Wood, 11–34. Vandenhoeck & Ruprecht, 2016.

Wright, N. T. *Jesus and the Victory of God*. Fortress, 1996.

York, Tripp. "Early Church Martyrdom: Witnessing For or Against the Empire." In *Witness of the Body: The Past, Present, and Future of Christian Martyrdom*, edited by Michael L. Budde and Karen Scott, 20–42. Eerdmans, 2011.

Younan, Munib. *Witnessing for Peace: In Jerusalem and the World*. Fortress, 2003.

Young, Robert. *Postcolonialism: An Historical Introduction*. John Wiley & Sons, 2016.

Index

www.ingramcontent.com/pod-product-compliance
Lightning Source LLC
Chambersburg PA
CBHW030207280925
33250CB00003B/8

* 9 7 8 1 4 8 1 3 2 3 7 1 0 *